Perspectives on Complementation

Perspectives on Complementation

Structure, Variation and Boundaries

Edited by

Mikko Höglund
Stockholm University, Sweden

Paul Rickman, Juhani Rudanko and Jukka Havu
University of Tampere, Finland

First published 2015 by
PALGRAVE MACMILLAN

Palgrave Macmillan in the UK is an imprint of Macmillan Publishers Limited, registered in England, company number 785998, of Houndsmills, Basingstoke, Hampshire, RG21 6XS.

Palgrave Macmillan in the US is a division of St Martin's Press LLC, 175 Fifth Avenue, New York, NY 10010.

Palgrave is the global academic imprint of the above companies and has companies and representatives throughout the world.

Palgrave® and Macmillan® are registered trademarks in the United States, the United Kingdom, Europe and other countries.

ISBN 978–1–137–45005–0

This book is printed on paper suitable for recycling and made from fully managed and sustained forest sources. Logging, pulping and manufacturing processes are expected to conform to the environmental regulations of the country of origin.

A catalogue record for this book is available from the British Library.

A catalog record for this book is available from the Library of Congress.

Typeset by MPS Limited, Chennai, India.

List of Figures

QC	question clitic
SG	singular
SUP	supine
TRANS	translative

Introduction[1]

Mikko Höglund
University of Tampere

Complementation has been the object of many a study during the past four or five decades and there is still much that is unexplored. Even the definition of 'complementation' and what a 'complement' is varies depending on the framework one is working with. For example, Quirk et al. (1985: 65) define complementation as 'the function of a part of a phrase or clause which follows a word, and completes the specification of a meaning relationship which that word implies'. Biber et al. (1999: 658) state that '[c]omplement clauses are a type of dependent clause used to complete the meaning relationship of an associated verb or adjective in a higher clause'. Within the Cognitive Grammar framework Langacker (1987: 309) sees complements in terms of autonomous (*A*) and dependent (*D*) predications. When there is an *A/D* asymmetry, the relation is either a complement relation or a head/modifier relation. He states that '[w]hen *D* is the profile determinant [in an *A/D* asymmetry situation] [...], we speak of complements (rather than heads and modifiers)'. What is common to all interpretations of 'complementation' is the idea that the complement completes the linguistic manifestation of some abstract unit of meaning.

The present volume brings together 11 chapters representing some of the latest work in complementation studies. The contributors range from the more experienced generation of scholars to upcoming young researchers on the subject. The book is divided into three parts – Structure, Variation and Boundaries – and the chapters represent these different perspectives on complementation. Naturally, the division is not to be understood exclusively, since there is a considerable amount of overlap. The first part, Structure, includes chapters that take a more theoretical approach to matters of complementation. The chapters in the second part, Variation, investigate the variation in complementation patterns and try to find reasons behind it. Complements are closely related to adjuncts and sometimes the boundaries are not clear, and the third part, Boundaries, comprises chapters that discuss these outer limits of complementation. In the following, a brief outline of the chapters is provided, followed by editors' thanks and final comments.

The first part of the volume, Structure, begins with a chapter by **Michaelis**, who discusses complementation on a general level utilizing a construction grammar framework, and more specifically Sign-Based Construction Grammar (SBCG), which is a highly formal manifestation of construction grammar. In her chapter, after a comprehensive introduction, Michaelis provides a synopsis of SBCG, which gives the reader the basic tenets of the theory. She then proceeds to argue against an Aktionsart-driven model of argument structure promoted by Rappaport Hovav and Levin (1998), and provides evidence suggesting that the constructional mechanism in which verbs combine with constructions is a better descriptive tool than the Aktionsart model since it can account for instances which the Aktionsart model cannot explain.

Rostila's chapter discusses two opposing views that have been and are prominent in the ongoing debate over matters of complementation. On one hand, the complement-taking predicate can be viewed as being in charge of selecting its complement (the more traditional approach), but on the other hand, a more recent constructionist approach claims that the situation might be the opposite: the complement selects its head. Rostila provides evidence from German and Swedish prepositional object complement constructions, suggesting that the binary division might not be plausible, and that there might be a diachronic cycle from one selection type to another.

The third and final chapter of the first part of the volume provides a cross-linguistic perspective to different aspects of the *tough* construction (TC). **Havu and Höglund** discuss the TC in three languages – English, Spanish and Finnish – and compare the complementation patterns. In all three languages a TC-type construction is attested, which conveys the TC meaning, but in all three languages the form of the complement is slightly different. In addition to the form of the complement, the chapter discusses which semantic types of adjectives can occur in the TC, what the status of the topical element in the TC is, and whether the complement clause can be omitted altogether, and if so, what the conditions are under which this can be done.

Cuyckens and D'hoedt begin the second part of the volume, Variation, with their discussion of the verb *admit*. They state that *admit* is highly variable regarding its complementation, as it can take three types of non-finite complements and two types of finite ones. The goal of the chapter is to explore what determines the choice of the complement type. For this purpose Cuyckens and D'hoedt employ a logistic regression model, which they use to analyse corpus material from the Late Modern English period as well as from present-day English. Using the statistical model, they examine which factors affect the choice of the complement and whether there is variation over time.

Rohdenburg's chapter discusses the Complexity Principle in relation to Horn's (1978) Embedded Negation Constraint. According to the Complexity Principle, complex environments favour more explicit syntactic structures, and the Embedded Negation Constraint can be seen as a special instance of the Complexity Principle as it states that negated complements prefer more explicit structures. Rohdenburg puts the Embedded Negation Constraint to the test by conducting 14 corpus studies, in which he observes pairs of embedded clause types, of which one is considered to be more explicit than the other. For instance, he notes that the *help* + direct object construction favours the *to*-infinitive over the bare infinitive when the complement clause is negated. This holds true for both BrE and AmE, and is also in line with the Embedded Negation Constraint. Rohdenburg's results from the studies confirm and strengthen the predictions made by the Complexity Principle and the Embedded Negation Constraint.

Rudanko's chapter investigates the syntax and semantics of the transitive *into -ing* pattern, as in *I frightened you into running away*. The study incorporates traditional notions about complementation and enriches them with more recent ideas from construction grammar. It is argued that the transitive *into -ing* pattern should be analysed with the help of two subevents, verbal and constructional, and this is illustrated with examples from corpora. Rudanko also refers to Davies (2012), where it is observed that in AmE the pattern emerged in the first half of the nineteenth century, and Rudanko's own corpus study in the chapter demonstrates that in BrE the pattern emerged even earlier, in the eighteenth century.

Rickman presents a study that investigates the verbs *spend* and *waste*, and the variation in the form of their complements. The two verbs allow both the bare *-ing* complement and also the *in -ing* type. Rickman studies this variation with evidence from four standard corpora: the CLMETEV, COHA, the BNC and COCA. The study presents diachronic and synchronic accounts of the variation, and it also discusses the possible different senses of the two complement types, and the effect of idiomaticity on the choice of the complement.

The final chapter of the second part of the book discusses the Finnish verb *epäillä*, which can be interpreted in two ways: it can mean either 'to doubt' or 'to suppose'. In her chapter **Salminen** discusses *epäillä* and the diachronic development of these two interpretations in light of different complement options. She presents data that suggests that while the negation-inclining interpretation may be the more fundamental and perhaps the original one, the affirmation-inclining reading has gained more ground and is the more common option in Modern Finnish. However, the interpretation ultimately depends on the complementation of the verb, of which there are four different types discussed.

The first chapter of the third part, Boundaries, is authored by **Fanego**, who explores the complement–adjunct continuum with a discussion of the development of ACC-*ing* gerundives. She examines the pattern and its rise in light of recent proposals (Van de Velde et al. 2013 and others) that suggest that there can be, and probably usually are, several reasons and multiple sources that contribute to the rise of a certain linguistic phenomenon. Fanego thus argues that the ACC-*ing* gerundive construction is the result of speakers employing their knowledge of several related structures, and that these multiple sources lead to the rise of the ACC-*ing* construction.

In his chapter, **Broccias** explores the boundaries of complementation within the Cognitive Grammar framework. He discusses the different patterns that occur with the perceptual verb *watch*, and argues that not only should the traditional patterns NP + bare infinitive and NP + *-ing* be considered complements of *watch* but also patterns that involve the conjunction *as*. Broccias demonstrates how the VO*as* (*watched Sally as she fetched*) and V*as* patterns (*watched as she fetched*) are equivalent to the 'traditional' patterns, and puts forward the view that they should be on an equal footing with complements in the more conventional sense.

The third part is concluded by **Duffley and Dion-Girardeau**, who present a study in which the notion of control, usually associated with complementation, is discussed in relation to free adjuncts. With corpus evidence, they investigate the relationship between subject control and non-subject control in free adjuncts in English and in French. The adjuncts under investigation are of the present participle and infinitival types. They compare the frequencies of subject control and non-subject control in different environments such as when the matrix clause is in the passive and the matrix clause has an expletive subject. It is observed that, as expected, free adjuncts are not as integrated in the matrix clause as complements, and that the adjuncts in general accept a wider range of controller types than complements.

To conclude the introduction, the editors would like to thank all the contributors. The present volume shows that even though complementation is a much studied area in linguistics, there is still much more to do. New, larger corpora are increasingly available, and frameworks and new methods are continuously being developed. This opens up new avenues for linguistic research, including complementation studies.

Note

1. The editing process of the present volume was partially funded by the Emil Aaltonen Foundation.

References

Biber, D., S. Johansson, G. Leech, S. Conrad and E. Finegan (1999) *Longman Grammar of Spoken and Written English* (Harlow: Longman).

Davies, M. (2012) 'Some Methodological Issues Related to Corpus-Based Investigations of Recent Syntactic Changes in English' in T. Nevalainen and E. Traugott (eds) *The Oxford Handbook of the History of English* (Oxford: Oxford University Press), pp. 157–74.

Horn, L. R. (1978) 'Some Aspects of Negation' in J. H. Greenberg (ed.) *Universals of Human Language*. Vol. 4 (Stanford: Stanford University Press), pp. 127–210.

Langacker, R. W. (1987) *Foundations of Cognitive Grammar*. Vol. 1: *Theoretical Prerequisites* (Stanford: Stanford University Press).

Quirk, R., S. Greenbaum, G. Leech and J. Svartvik (1985) *A Comprehensive Grammar of the English Language* (London: Longman).

Rappaport Hovav, M. and B. Levin (1998) 'Building Verb Meanings' in M. Butt and W. Geuder (eds) *The Projection of Arguments* (Stanford: CSLI Publications), pp. 97–134.

Van de Velde, F., H. De Smet and L. Ghesquière (2013) 'Introduction: On Multiple Source Constructions in Language Change' Special issue of *Studies in Language*, 37 (3): 473–89.

Part I
Structure

1
Constructions License Verb Frames

Laura A. Michaelis
University of Colorado Boulder

1.1 Introduction[1]

Where does a verb's frame come from? The obvious answer is the verb itself, and this is the answer that syntacticians have traditionally provided, whether they describe predicator–argument relations as syntactic sisterhood relations or as lexical properties (the predicator's combinatoric potential, or valence). Thus, Haegeman, in her introduction to Government and Binding theory, states, "the thematic structure of a predicate, encoded in the theta grid, will determine the minimal components of the sentence" (Haegeman 1994: 55). Similarly, Bresnan, in her introduction to Lexical Functional Grammar (LFG), states, "[o]n the semantic side, argument structure represents the core participants and events (states, processes) designated by a single predicator. [...] On the syntactic side, argument structure represents the minimal information needed to characterize the syntactic dependents of an argument-taking head" (Bresnan 2001: 304). In lexicalist theories like LFG, whenever the arguments of a verb can have more than one set of syntactic realizations, each distinct realization pattern corresponds to a different mapping from semantic roles to grammatical functions, as expressed in a unique lexical entry, and lexical entries, or classes of lexical entries, are related by lexical rules (Neidle 1994).

The drive to streamline lexical entries by removing predictable properties has led theorists to develop more general, putatively universal, mapping principles, as well as principles for deriving the semantic roles themselves, typically from the positions that they occupy in a decomposed representation of the verb's event-structure properties. In this approach, as Van Valin and LaPolla (1997: 154) describe it, "[t]here is no need to specify the thematic relations that a verb takes; they follow without stipulation from the logical structure, since they follow by definition from its structure." Thus few syntacticians currently assume gestalt-like, semantically based verb classes of the type that figure in frame-semantic analysis, for example verbs denoting acts of theft, requesting or attaching (Ruppenhofer et al. 2002). But however they are construed, verbs and verb classes continue to be regarded as the only source of syntactically relevant meaning (Pinker 1989, Van Valin and LaPolla 1997, Levin and Rappaport Hovav 2005). Syntactically relevant meaning is generally identified with aspectual meaning and verb classes with aspectual classes. Syntactic theorists typically represent verb meanings through a form of decompositional analysis, inspired by Dowty (1979) and Jackendoff (1990), that picks out components of causation, change and/or stasis from the scene denoted by a verb (Croft 2012: Ch. 2). For example, in a discussion of Italian auxiliary selection, Levin and Rappaport Hovav (2005: 12ff.) argue that accounts based on the change-of-state entailment are more predictive of *essere* selection than those that make use of gestalt-like semantic classes like "verbs of bodily process." At the same time, frame membership has been shown to predict certain verbal syntactic affordances, including null complementation (Ruppenhofer and Michaelis 2014).

While there are differing approaches to lexical–semantic representation, there is little dissent concerning the directionality of the syntax–semantics interface: the verb selects its frame but frames do not select verbs. It is difficult, however, to square this seeming truism with the observation, made by Goldberg (1995, 2006), Kaschak and Glenberg (2000, 2002), Partee and Borschev (2007) and Michaelis and Ruppenhofer (2001), among others, that verbs can appear in unexpected frames, which nonetheless make sense in context. For example, as shown in (1–3), single-argument activity verbs like *melt* and *sparkle*, which have nothing intrinsically to do with location, can appear in the "locative inversion" pattern, resulting in what Bresnan (1994: 91) calls an "overlay" of the locative–theme frame:

(1) In Maria's sticky hand melted a chocolate-chip ice-cream cone. (Birner and Ward 1998: 193)
(2) And in this lacey leafage fluttered a number of grey birds with black and white stripes and long tails. (Levin and Rappaport Hovav 1995: 226)
(3) Down at the harbor there is a teal-green clubhouse for socializing and parties. Beside it sparkles the community pool. (*Vanity Fair*, 8/01)

In (1–3), the verb appears to describe what an entity is doing while in its location (melting, fluttering, sparkling) rather than a location state per se. Looking at a similar class of examples in Russian, Partee and Borschev (2007: 158) observe, "[o]ne could say that THING and LOC are roles of the verb [*be*], but it is undoubtedly better to consider them roles of the participants of the situation (or state) of existing or of being located." They go on to point out that the situation of existing involves not only a location state but also a particular perspective on that state, which they describe with a visual analogy:

In an existential sentence, the LOC is chosen as the perspectival center; [the sentence asserts] of the LOC that it has THING in it. [...] An existential sentence is analogous to the way a security camera is fixed on a scene and records whatever is in that location. (Partee and Borschev 2007: 156)

The security-camera metaphor aptly captures the stylistic effect of the locative–inversion pattern, but if we take it seriously we have to acknowledge that word meaning and syntactic meaning are far more similar than traditional models of syntax would care to admit. Like a word, a syntactic pattern may be conventionally associated with a highly elaborated semantic frame, including a perspectival one. This is the view taken in construction-based syntax, as described by Goldberg (1995, 2002, 2006) and others. According to this view, argument-structure patterns are form–meaning pairings that denote situation types like those denoted by verbs (e.g., an event of transfer, a locational state). As a corollary, a verb's meaning and combinatory potential (or *valence*) can change to fit the meaning of a given construction (Goldberg 1995, 2002, 2006, Michaelis and Ruppenhofer 2001, Michaelis 2004). Argument-structure constructions in this model are conceived as constraints on classes of verb entries, which are in turn understood as feature-structure descriptions that specify values for the features that determine morphophonemic form, frame-semantic meaning, valence and syntactic category. The construction-based model of argument structure described in the works cited above is based on reconciling the verb's feature specifications with those of the construction, rather than the licensing of arguments by verbs. This reconciliation operation requires an overlap between the verb's semantic representation and that of the construction. Combining verb meaning and construction meaning requires interpreters to create a semantic link between the event denoted by the verb and that denoted by the construction. The possible "linkage" relations, as described by Goldberg (1995: Ch. 2), include *instance, means* and *manner*. A result of this integration mechanism is *valence augmentation*: the set of arguments licensed by the construction may properly include that licensed by the verb with which the construction is combined. Examples of valence augmentation are given in (4–5):

(4) Most likely they were fellow visitors, just **panting** up to the sky-high altar out of curiosity. (L. Davis, *Last Act in Palmyra*, p. 28)

(5) When a visitor passes through the village, young lamas stop picking up trash to mug for the camera. A gruff "police monk" **barks** them back to work. (*Newsweek* 10/13/97)

In (4), *pant*, a verb that otherwise licenses only a single argument, appears with two: it denotes the *manner* of the directed-motion event denoted by the construction. In (5), *bark*, another otherwise monovalent activity verb, has two additional arguments, a direct object and an oblique expression that indicates direction; in this context, the verb denotes the *means* by which a (metaphorically construed) caused-motion event, denoted by the construction, occurs. Rather than presuming a nonce lexical entry for *pant* in which it means "move toward a goal while panting' and for *bark* in which it means 'move something from one place to another by barking," a constructionist presumes that the verbs in (4–5) mean what they always mean; arguments not licensed by the verb are licensed by the construction with which the verb combines. The constructional model of verbal syntactic variability is therefore more parsimonious than a lexicalist one: it uses a small number of argument-structure constructions and assumes that these constructions can alter verb meanings whenever there is a clash between a verb's meaning (and its valence) and a construction's meaning (and its valence). Because it allows novel verb types to be constructed online, the constructional model limits the number of lexical entries needed for each verb.

The problem is, however, that the patterns we use for creating phrases are not supposed to denote anything: they combine symbols rather than being symbols themselves. Only words bear conventionally assigned meanings. In the prevailing view of meaning composition, syntactic rules do no more than determine what symbol sequences function as units for syntactic purposes (Kay and Michaelis 2012). So while syntactic rules assemble words and their dependent elements into phrases, and the phrases denote complex concepts like predicates and propositions, the rules cannot add conceptual content to that contributed by the words; nor can they alter the combinatoric properties of the words. On this view, which Jackendoff (1997: 48) describes as the "doctrine of syntactically transparent composition," "[a]ll elements of content in the meaning of a sentence are found in the lexical conceptual structures [...] of the lexical items composing the sentence." If the rules of syntactic combination do not add conceptual content to that contributed by the words, they should not be able to alter the combinatory potential of words. Thus, whatever the source of the "extra" arguments found in examples like (4) and (5), it cannot reasonably be a syntactic rule.

In order to preserve a compositional model of sentence meaning, one might choose to view valence augmentation and other construal-based semantic effects on verbs as the products of lexical derivations that build up complex event structures from simpler ones. A model of this nature is proposed by Rappaport Hovav and Levin (1998) (henceforth, RHL; see also Levin 2000 and Levin and Rappaport Hovav 2005). Under this model, semantic verb classes are epiphenomenal, because it is the sum of a verb's meaning components, rather than the verb's semantic-class membership, that actually explains syntactic behaviors like auxiliary selection. Unlike the construction-based model outlined above, the RHL model is based on lexical projection; as they put it: "Many aspects of the syntactic structure of a sentence—in particular, the syntactic realization of arguments—are projected from the lexical properties of the verbs" (RHL: 97). Each of a verb's syntactic frames is associated with a distinct verb meaning, although every verb has one basic class membership. An implication of this model is that most verbs are polysemous, and many verbs are highly so. Since RHL assume (in accordance with Pinker 1989 and others) that the only syntactically relevant component of verb meaning is aspectual meaning, the more aspectual representations a verb has the more syntactic variation it will display, and vice versa. To represent verb meaning and semantic operations on verb meaning, RHL propose (a) a set of Aktionsart-based schemas and (b) an operation that augments one such schema up to another one. Both the schemas and the augmentation operation are independently motivated; they appear, for example, in the transition network used by Moens and Steedman (1988) to model aspectual type-shifts triggered by verb morphology. An example of one such shift is given in (6):

(6) Mary was winning the race (when she was tripped by Zola).

In (6) we see that the progressive construction, which seeks a durative event as its daughter, can combine with a verb denoting a momentaneous event (*win*) and in so doing create a construal in which winning is preceded by a preparatory process. In terms of the Moens and Steedman analysis, the progressive operator applies to the process phase of a culminated process (i.e., an accomplishment verb) that is derived from a culmination (i.e., an achievement verb) via augmentation (i.e., the addition of an activity representation or "run-up process"). In the RHL model, verb meanings are represented by the set of event-structure templates given in Table 1.1. In these representations, variables represent participants licensed by the event-structure template, predicates in small caps (e.g., ACT) represent subevents and capitalized italic terms in angled brackets represent idiosyncratic meaning components contributed by whatever verb happens to combine with the template.

The valence of the verb may be lower than, higher than or equal to the number of argument slots in the template. Argument roles licensed by event-structure templates are referred to as *structure participants* while those

Table 1.1 Event-structure templates (based on Rappaport Hovav and Levin 1998)

Aktionsart class	Semantic representation
State	[x <*STATE*>] e.g., *shine*
Activity	[x ACT <*MANNER*>] e.g., *skip*
Achievement	[BECOME [x <*STATE*>]] e.g., *sink*
Accomplishment (external cause)	[[x ACT <*MANNER*>] CAUSE [BECOME y <*STATE*>]] e.g., *build*
Accomplishment (internal cause)	[x CAUSE [BECOME y <*STATE*>]] e.g., *break*

licensed only by the verb are referred to as *constant participants*. Thus, for example, activity verbs like *chew* or *sweep* are structurally intransitive: the second argument is a lexically licensed (constant) participant that does not fuse with any role of the activity event-structure template. RHL propose two argument realization conditions on verb-template unification:

(7) **Argument realization condition 1**: Each structure participant must be realized by an XP.

(8) **Argument realization condition 2**: Each XP must correspond to a subevent.

According to the condition given in (7), which will be the focus of our attention in section 1.3.2, the second argument of an activity verb need not be realized, as it is a constant rather than a structural argument, while the second argument of an accomplishment verb, a structural argument, must be realized: **They hammered flat*. Variations in the syntactic frame of a verb are viewed as resulting from semantic operations that transform one semantic representation into a more fully expanded semantic representation. Two such operations are given in (9–10):

(9) $[[x \text{ ACT} <MANNER>] \rightarrow [x \text{ ACT} <MANNER>] \text{ CAUSE } [\text{BECOME } y <STATE>]]$

(10) $[x <STATE>] \rightarrow [\text{BECOME } [x <STATE>]]$

The operation shown in (9) transforms an activity verb, as in (11), into an (externally caused) change-of-state verb, as in (12), via the addition of a CAUSE operator linking the activity representation to an achievement representation:

(11) Shira skipped.

(12) Shira skipped down the corridor.

(Note that in the representation of self-propelled motion, as in (12), the variables x and y will be equated.) The operation shown in (10) transforms a state verb, as in (13), into an achievement verb, as in (14), by adding the operator BECOME to the input state:

(13) She sat on the couch (as she spoke).

(14) She sat on the couch (after she came into the house).

While (13) describes the maintenance of a body posture, (14) describes movement into a new body posture.

The RHL model preserves the strict version of compositionality alluded to above, in which conceptual content comes from the lexicon. In this model, a verb's syntactic frame, or combinatoric potential, comes from its semantic representation, rather than the inverse. We need not presume that syntactic rules, like the rule that pairs a verb like *skip* with a directional PP like *down the corridor*, "add meaning" to verbs. Instead, syntactic rules are syntactic in the traditional sense: they represent the constituents that are created when a lexical head (e.g., a verb) combines with the arguments and adjuncts that it semantically selects. In addition to ensuring that syntactic rules do no semantic work, the RHL model factors syntactic information out of lexical entries, allowing a set of putatively universal morphosyntactic realization rules to link participant roles to grammatical functions. Thus, RHL's model of the syntax–semantics interface achieves a strict separation of syntax and semantics. This is a desirable goal, since form and meaning are demonstrably two different levels of organization; for one thing, most lexical entailments (e.g., evaluative components of words like *excuse* (vs. *justification*) and *credit* (vs. *blame*) are simply "invisible to syntax" (Jackendoff 1997: 34).

In this chapter, however, I will discuss five classes of phenomena that suggest that verbs have the arguments that they do not because their event-structure representations are subject to semantic operations but because they combine with grammatical constructions that have gestalt-like meanings similar to those of traditional frame-semantic classes. This in turn suggests that semantic gestalts like "locative state," "creation event" and "directed motion event" cannot be replaced by an inventory of meaning components and rules for combining them. To capture the effects at issue, I will propose a formal model of argument-structure constructions based on Sign-Based Construction Grammar (SBCG), a formalized version of Construction Grammar (Fillmore et al. 1988, Goldberg 1995, Michaelis and Lambrecht 1996, Kay and Fillmore 1999) developed by Sag (2010, 2012) and others (see Michaelis 2009 and other papers in Boas and Sag 2012). The linguistic phenomena that I will discuss are as follows:

- *Aspectual underspecification.* A verb's syntactic behavior cannot always be traced to its Aktionsart classification(s).
- *Null complementation.* The circumstances under which a given argument of a given verb may be phonetically unrealized are not accurately described by augmentative operations on event structure of the type described by RHL.
- *Weird sisterhood.* Many verb frames specify sisterhood relations that are not predicted by the general-purpose constituency rules that combine heads and complements and heads and specifiers.
- *Quantification of argument NPs.* Stating constraints on quantifier scope in certain argument structures and explaining "operator-free" nominal type coercion requires recourse to semantic frames, including quantifier frames.
- *Effects of syntactic context.* Certain verbs take certain complements only when negated, indicating that the complementation possibility in question is not a semantic property of the verb, but rather a constructional property.

This chapter will be structured as follows. In section 1.2, I will provide a synopsis of SBCG. In section 1.3, I will discuss the five classes of phenomena described above. Section 1.4 will offer concluding remarks.

1.2   Sign-Based Construction Grammar

SBCG uses the formal architecture of Head-Driven Phrase Structure Grammar (HPSG; Pollard and Sag 1987, 1994, Ginzburg and Sag 2000) to model the range of idiomatic patterns targeted by the Berkeley Construction Grammar framework (BCG; Fillmore et al. 1988, Goldberg 1995, Kay and Fillmore 1999, Kay 2002, Michaelis and Lambrecht 1996). The goal of SBCG is to enhance the formal precision of BCG while also expanding the range of linguistic phenomena covered by HPSG. The fusion of the two frameworks is made possible by their shared foundational assumptions. Both assume that grammar, rather than representing a series of modules through which linguistic information is passed in the course of a derivation, is a network of linguistic patterns defined by constraints on form, meaning and use. Both BCG and HPSG are declarative, nonmodular models of grammar. That is, both assume interpretations to be directly associated with rules of syntax, rather than being 'read off' syntactic representation once they are passed to an interpretive component of the grammar.

In SBCG, the basic object of grammatical description is the sign. A language is taken to be an infinite set of signs, and a grammar is taken to be a description of the recursive embedding of signs that constitutes the target language. While the term *sign* is understood in something close to its Saussurean sense, as a pairing of form and meaning, signs in SBCG are used to model not only words and lexemes but also phrases. Signs are types of linguistic objects and are organized by means of a type hierarchy (for example, the sign type *word* is a subtype of the sign type *lexical-sign*, as is the sign type *lexeme*). Formally, a sign is a feature structure that specifies values for the features listed in (15–19):

(15) SYN(TAX) describes the grammatical behavior of a sign. Its values are the features CAT(EGORY) and VAL(ENCE). The values of CAT are complex syntactic categories, represented as typed feature structures, e.g., *noun, verb, preposition*. The VAL feature represents the objects with which a given sign can combine. The VAL value of pronouns, proper nouns and most common nouns is an empty list. The VAL value of a verb is its combinatoric potential; for example, the VAL value of a transitive verb is <NP, NP>.

(16) ARGUMENT STRUCTURE (ARG-ST) is a ranked list of the participant roles assigned by a predicator, along with any lexically assigned case properties of those participant roles. Unlike VAL, ARG-ST is a feature only of lexical entries (not of phrases).

(17) SEM(ANTICS) describes the meaning of a sign; its values are the features INDEX and FRAMES. INDEX is the extension of a sign. The FRAMES feature is used to enumerate the predications that together specify the meaning of a sign. Among the frames that will be relevant to us here are *quantifier frames*. For example, the meaning of the indefinite article *a* in English is represented by means of an existential-quantifier frame.

(18) FORM is used to specify the morphological properties of a given sign; the value of FORM is a list of morphological entities. PHON(OLOGY) describes the phonological phrase corresponding to a given sign.

(19) CONTEXT (CTXT) is used to specify features of context that are relevant to the interpretation and use of a given sign. The values of CTXT include *topic* and *focus*.

Constructions in SBCG are descriptions of the possible signs and sign combinations in the target language. SBCG recognizes two kinds of constructions: *lexical-class constructions*, which describe properties common to sets of words and lexemes (e.g., the class of transitive verbs), and *combinatoric constructions*, which describe classes of *constructs* (Sag 2010, 2012, Michaelis 2012). A construct can be viewed as a local tree licensed by a rule of the grammar. However, the SBCG description language does not include trees; SBCG contains no linguistic constraints that make reference to global properties of trees (e.g., c-command and subjacency). Instead, the combinatory constructions that describe possible constructs of the language are simply feature structures that contain a MOTHER (MTR) feature and a DAUGHTERS (DTRS) feature. An example of a combinatoric construction in English is the subject–predicate construction.

Like the phrase-structure rules of context-free grammar, combinatoric constructions build phrases like simple clauses and VPs, but they also do some work that phrase-structure rules do not: they build words (e.g., the third-person singular form of the lexeme *laugh*) and lexemes (e.g., the causative lexeme corresponding to the inchoative lexeme *boil*). Constructions of the former type are called *inflectional constructions* and constructions of the latter type are called *derivational constructions*.

Accordingly, the grammar is viewed as consisting of a lexicon—a finite set of lexical descriptions (descriptions of feature structures whose type is either *lexeme* or *word*) and a set of constructions. Figure 1.1 gives an example of a lexeme description.

Figure 1.1 is a lexical entry describing the English lexeme *drink*. The semantic properties of this lexeme are represented by a series of frames (e.g., the frame abbreviated as *drink-fr*). Frames are used to capture the requirement that the drinker be animate and that the consumed item be a liquid. The combinatoric properties of this lexeme are represented in its valence set,

$$\begin{bmatrix} lexeme \\ \text{FORM } drink \\ \text{SYN|VAL} \ \left\langle \text{NP}\begin{bmatrix} overt \\ \text{INST } i \end{bmatrix}, \ \text{NP}\begin{bmatrix} (ini) \\ \text{INST } x \end{bmatrix} \right\rangle \\ \text{SEM|FRAMES} \ \left\langle \begin{bmatrix} drink\text{-}fr \\ \text{DRINKER } i \\ \text{DRAFT } x \end{bmatrix}, \begin{bmatrix} animate\text{-}fr \\ \text{INST } i \end{bmatrix}, \begin{bmatrix} liquid\text{-}fr \\ \text{INST } x \end{bmatrix} \right\rangle \end{bmatrix}$$

Figure 1.1   A lexeme description

which includes two noun phrases—the first of which is coindexed with the "drinker" participant in the drink semantic frame and the second of which is coindexed with the "draft" participant in the drink frame. In addition, each valence member (or valent) is tagged with a feature that represents its instantiation properties: the first valent (the subject NP) is obligatorily instantiated, while the second is optionally null instantiated. As indicated, the second valence member, when null instantiated, has an indefinite or, equivalently, existential interpretation. For example, sentence (20) means something like "She drank some liquid substance from a plastic mug" (Fillmore 1986):

(20) She **drank** from a plastic mug.

Figure 1.2 shows an inflectional construct licensed by the preterite construction, an inflectional construction that yields past-tense word forms of a verb lexeme (in this case, the lexeme *laugh*).

As an inflectional construct, this construct has a word as mother and a lexeme as daughter. The two occurrences of the tag [1] indicate that the SYN values of mother and daughter are identical. The past-tense meaning contributed by the construction is represented by the frame labeled *past-fr* in the mother's frame set. The single argument of this frame is the frame expressed by the verb lexeme (i.e., the laugh-frame), as indicated by the two occurrences of the tag [2] in the MTR.

Figure 1.3 shows a derivational construct of a type that will recur in our discussion of the quantification of argument NPs in section 1.3.4 below.

As in all derivational constructs, both the mother and daughter signs are lexemes. This particular construct is licensed by an English construction that we may refer to as the *Bare Noun Pumping* construction. Bare Noun Pumping yields determinerless plural NPs capable of occupying grammatical-function positions, as in (21–22):

(21) **Bagels** are boiled.
(22) We served **bagels**.

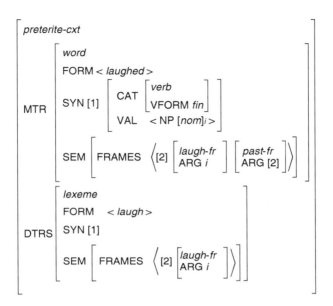

Figure 1.2 An inflectional construct

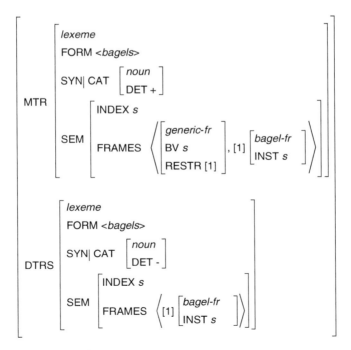

Figure 1.3 A derivational construct

Bare nominal expressions can serve as arguments insofar as they receive quantified interpretations. In (21), for example, the bare plural noun *bagels* is interpreted as expressing universal quantification over individuals of the type *bagel*, while in (22) it is interpreted as expressing an existentially quantified aggregate (in terms of Chierchia 2003). This means the bare nominal construction must supply a quantifier that would otherwise be supplied by a determiner. In fact, it appears that there must be two derivational constructions for bare plurals in English: one that provides for generic quantification of undetermined noun phrases and another that provides for existential quantification of undetermined noun phrases. The nominal construct in Figure 1.3 is licensed by the former construction; generic quantification is represented by the *generic* frame in the construction's MTR. The variable bound by the quantifier is represented as an argument of the quantifier frame (BV), as is the restriction on the range of the quantifier (RESTR). The letter *s* used to represent the bound variable is intended to capture its ontological type (aggregate or, equivalently, sum individual).

What we have seen of the SBCG formalism in this section is, I hope, sufficient to convey the scope of the model: constructions are used not only to represent the composition of phrases but also lexical classes (lexical-class constructions), the realization of morphological categories (inflectional constructions) and lexeme–lexeme relationships (derivational constructions). The SBCG approach to verbal argument structure departs from that of BCG, in which argument-structure constructions were uniformly one-level. In BCG, argument-structure constructions were treated as schematic verb entries with which verbs unified in order to ensure grammatical expression of their semantic roles. In cases of valency mismatch like (4–5) above, the construction supplies whatever arguments the verb lacks. In SBCG, by contrast, only the two-level derivational constructions, and not lexical-class constructions, perform valence augmentation. The SBCG alternative, as described by Sag (2012: 115–16), involves a two-step analysis. First an intransitive verb lexeme (e.g., *pant*) is licensed with the singleton ARG-ST list characteristic of all strictly intransitive verbs. Second, another lexeme, whose ARG-ST list contains a directional expression (e.g., *pant up to the sky-high altar*) is built from this lexeme via a derivational construction whose MTR sign is a directed-motion lexeme. This constructed lexeme has a longer ARG-ST list than does its daughter lexeme. Derivational constructions capture the effect of lexical rules without requiring conservation of verbal thematic structure (Michaelis and Ruppenhofer 2001: Ch. 1).

Common to all construction-based approaches is the idea that a verb's array of arguments, and the manner of each argument's realization, is determined by the argument-structure construction with which the verb combines. In this fundamental respect, construction-based models differ from lexicalist approaches like that of RHL, in which a verb's argument-licensing properties are determined by its Aktionsart representation and the morphosyntactic expression of its arguments by realization rules. The evidence to be reviewed in the following section will suggest that verb frames are not built up via operations on semantic structure but rather licensed by templates that constrain the syntax, semantics and discourse status of the arguments in quite detailed ways.

1.3 Evidence against an Aktionsart-driven model of argument structure

In this section, I will discuss five lines of evidence which converge to suggest that a verb's argument structure is determined by the construction with which it combines rather than by its Aktionsart structure, derived or otherwise. The evidence comes from aspectual underspecification (1.3.1), null complementation (1.3.2), the special-case nature of rules governing syntactic sisterhood relationships (1.3.3), quantification of argument NPs (1.3.4) and effects of syntactic context (in particular, negation) on a verb's combinatoric potential (1.3.5).

1.3.1 Aspectual underspecification

Recall that, according to RHL, a verb's valence is a reflex of its Aktionsart class, and valence variability occurs when a verb has multiple Aktionsart classes, related to one another by semantic transformations. There are, however, numerous argument-structure patterns that appear neutral with regard to Aktionsart. The English transitive pattern is one such example. As an illustration, consider instances in which the verb *walk* appears as a transitive, with a direct object denoting the surface covered. Such predications may be telic, as in (23), or atelic, as in (24):

(23) Accomplishment: This would be bad except the dearth of things to see meant we'd **walked the floor** in 70 minutes.

(24) Activity: He **walked the floor** for half an hour puzzling over his enigma.

The evidence for telicity in each case comes from the temporal adverbials used: the *in*-headed frame adverbial combines only with telic predications, as in (23), while the *for*-headed durational adverbial combines only with atelic predications, as in (24). The problem is that both examples would count as instances of template augmentation, in particular augmentation of an activity representation up to that of an accomplishment: [[x ACT <*MANNER*>] CAUSE [BECOME y <*STATE*>]]. There is no other obvious means by which the otherwise intransitive *walk* would receive a direct object denoting a surface. The verb *walk*, as a self-motion verb, selects for an oblique second argument denoting a path or direction, but, as a self-motion verb, it does not intrinsically denote coverage of a surface, as it does in

(23–24). While it seems reasonable to conclude that (23) is an instance of template augmentation (activity → accomplishment), example (24) remains unaccounted for. If it is an accomplishment, it should be telic, but the presence of the durational adverbial headed by *for* in (24) demonstrates that this predication is in fact atelic. We must conclude that the transitive pattern illustrated in (23–24) is underspecified with regard to telicity. While one might be tempted to associate the locative-object (or, equivalently, applicative) pattern with accomplishment Aktionsart, insofar as the pattern implies "affectedness," "coverage" or "saturation" of the location denoted by the object NP, it appears that applicative verbs have both telic (accomplishment) and atelic (activity) construals. Whatever the meaning of the applicative pattern, it cannot be exclusively Aktionsart-based. In a construction-based model of valence augmentation, however, the meanings of argument-structure patterns are unconnected to Aktionsart representations. Aspectual underspecification is therefore expected.

1.3.2 Null complementation

The RHL model makes three predictions about null complementation (Ruppenhofer and Michaelis 2014, Goldberg 2001, 2005). These are given in (25–27):

(25) As nonstructural arguments, the second arguments of bivalent state, achievement and activity verbs should always be omissible.

(26) Nonstructural participants are subject only to a recoverability condition based on prototypicality (RHL: 115); therefore all null complements should have existential (indefinite) interpretations.

(27) As structural arguments, patient arguments of accomplishment verbs should never be omissible.

Each of these predictions proves false. First, as shown in (28–30), it is not the case that all bivalent state, achievement and activity verbs allow omission of their second arguments:

(28) **State:** She resembles *(Aunt Molly).

(29) **Achievement:** I found *(my watch).

(30) **Activity:** We discussed *(the issue).

Second, as shown in (31–34), null-instantiated second arguments of verbs in these Aktionsart classes do not necessarily have an existential interpretation; such arguments often have anaphoric interpretations:

(31) **State:** My feelings are similar (to yours).

(32) **State:** I remember (that).

(33) **Achievement:** I won (the race).

(34) **Activity:** I prepared (for that event) for weeks.

Third, as observed by Goldberg (2005), patient arguments of accomplishment verbs are in fact omissible, despite the fact that these are *ipso facto* structural arguments in the RHL model: verbs of emission/ingestion like *spit*, *swallow* allow omission of their patient arguments (as in, for example, *He spat onto the sidewalk*) and, as shown in (35–37), almost any verb, including an accomplishment verb, allows existential null complementation of its second argument in an iterated-event context:

(35) Owls only kill (things) at night.
(36) China produces (things) and the US imports (things).
(37) She has never failed to impress (people).

Additional problematic aspects of the RHL model of null complementation are as follows. First, null-instantiated complements of *nonverbal* predicators, illustrated by (38–40), simply remain unexplained, because such predicators presumably lack Aktionsart structure:

(38) **Noun:** Make me a copy (of that).
(39) **Preposition:** She walked over (here).
(40) **Adjective:** I'm taller (than you).

Second, as observed by Ruppenhofer (2012), null-complementation affordances of verbs are affected by context; when a motion verb is interpreted as denoting a path shape rather than actual movement, it does not generally allow omission of its landmark argument:

(41) Actual motion: Where did she cross (the road)?
(42) Fictive motion: Where does Highway 42 cross *(Highway 287)?

Although fictive- and actual-motion verbs do differ aspectually (the former being stative and the latter dynamic), the null-complementation split in (41–42) is the reverse of the one predicted by the RHL model, which treats the second arguments of state verbs, but not accomplishment verbs, as omissible.

The flip side of valence reduction is valence augmentation, and this phenomenon also presents problems for an Aktionsart-driven model of argument structure. Recall from Table 1.1 that, in the RHL model, accomplishment verbs like *break* have the Aktionsart representation x CAUSE [BECOME y <STATE>]. Recall too principle (8): Each XP must correspond to a subevent. Given these two conditions, we have no easy way to account for the well-formedness of (43–44):

(43) She crumbled the crackers into the soup.
(44) The snow broke the branches off the tree.

The above examples should be ungrammatical, because in each a directional expression (*into the soup* or *off the tree*) denotes a resultant state distinct from that entailed by the verb's Aktionsart representation (the resultant states of being crumbled and broken, respectively). These PPs therefore are XPs that do not correspond to a subevent, in violation of (8). The facts in (43–44) are, however, captured by a construction-based model: the verb denotes the means by which a causation-of-motion event, denoted by the construction, occurs. For example, in (43), crumbling is construed as the means by which the crackers are moved from one location (the agent) to another (the soup).

The constructional account of argument structure treats verb-valence variability as the product of constructional affordances, and not as effects of a verb's semantic representation, whether basic or altered via semantic transformation. The constructional account does not, for example, assume a class of "structurally intransitive" verbs. Instead, it posits an array of derivational constructions that build verb lexemes of a particular type: those which allow a particular argument to be unexpressed (for details, see Michaelis 2012: 53–4). These constructions, which include the existential perfect construction, license verb lexemes that have the instantiation properties of the lexeme *drink* in Figure 1.1. Recall that the "draft" argument of *drink* is subject to (indefinite) null instantiation. Through these derivational constructions, the grammar licenses, for example, a verb lexeme *kill* that has a (potentially) null-instantiated "victim argument." This *kill* lexeme is then a potential daughter lexeme for a null-instantiation construction. Null-instantiation constructions are derivational constructions that effectively remove arguments from a verb's valence list, while ensuring that the quantifier frame of the null-instantiated argument remains in the MTR verb's ARG-ST list. According to Michaelis (2012), the MTR lexeme's semantic frames include the quantifier frame missing from the valence set of the daughter, as well as a frame that indicates whether the null-instantiated argument is construed anaphorically, as in (31–34), or existentially, as in (35–37). An example of a null-instantiation construction is that which licenses existentially interpreted null-instantiated theme arguments of emission verbs, for example, *spit*, *sneeze* (Goldberg 2005). Evidence for this construction comes from coercion phenomena involving verbs of vision:

(45) She frowned into the mirror.
(46) She glanced over her shoulder.

Neither *frown* nor *glance* semantically selects for a directional argument; it is only via combination with the construction that licenses an existentially construed null-instantiated theme argument that these verbs may be augmented up to causation-of-motion verbs. Such augmentation involves a metaphorical construal of vision in which an "eye beam" moves from one location, the perceiver, to another, the percept (Slobin 2008). What might seem paradoxical—that a "subtraction" construction here adds an argument (a directional expression) to a verb of vision—makes sense on the constructional account: the construction that licenses verbs of emission that have an unexpressed theme argument denotes an event of transfer. That is, the SEM value of the MTR contains a trivalent transfer frame. In addition to capturing such coercion effects, null-complementation constructions enable us to account for override effects involving null-complementation restrictions on verbs. While, as observed above, accomplishment verbs do not select for null-instantiated theme arguments when construed episodically, they do when construed iteratively, as shown in (35–37). We can therefore conclude, following Goldberg (2005), that aspectual constructions like the existential perfect construction carry constraints on argument instantiation, allowing indefinite null complementation in examples like (37). Such cases demonstrate that constructions can alter the combinatoric properties of the verbs with which they combine.

1.3.3 Weird sisterhood

A number of argument-structure patterns involve verbal complementation patterns that are not licensed by the general-purpose head-complement or specifier-head phrase-building rule schemas. Many of these patterns have specialized communicative functions. These phenomena suggest that highly detailed constructions, rather than non-category-specific phrase-structure rules, pair predicates and their complements. In this section, we will look at three cases of weird sisterhood found in English: Nominal Extraposition, *Just Because* and Hypotactic Apposition. The data discussed in this section are taken from two corpora of English telephone conversations available through the Linguistic Data Consortium (www.ldc.upenn.edu): the Switchboard corpus (sw) or the Fisher corpus (fe).

1.3.3.1 *Nominal Extraposition*

In Nominal Extraposition, an exclamatory adjective, for example, *amazing*, licenses an NP complement:

(47) I know it's just it's unbelievable the different things that are happening in America today. (sw03982B)

(48) I'll date myself a little bit but it it's remarkable the number of those things they need. (sw02392B)

(49) I know. I love that game. It's amazing the words they come up with. (fe_03_08039A)

The pattern exemplified in (47–49) is idiosyncratic in two respects. First, adjectives are not case assigners and should not therefore license nonoblique NP complements. Second, this NP complement is interpreted as denoting a scalar degree (Michaelis and Lambrecht 1996). In (49), for example, the NP *the words they come up with* stands in for a scalar expression like "the number of words they come up with" or "the quality of the words they come up with." The fact that the complement of *amazing* in (49) has a scalar interpretation follows from the fact that (49) is an exclamation, but the pairing of an exclamatory adjective with an NP sister that denotes a degree, metonymically or otherwise, requires a construction that provides for this syntax and this meaning.

1.3.3.2   Just Because

In the *Just Because* construction, a negated epistemic verb, typically *mean*, licenses a finite clause subject introduced by the subordinating conjunction *just because* (Bender and Kathol 2001):

(50) Just because they use primitive means of doing things does not mean that they can't expand. (fe_03_06870A)

(51) Just because they say it doesn't mean that's the only way to look at it. (fe_03_00135A)

Clausal subjects are ordinarily introduced by *that*, not a subordinating conjunction like *because*, so we cannot use the general-purpose constituency rule that pairs a specifier with a head to account for the pattern in (50–51). Instead, as Bender and Kathol argue, the grammar of English must contain an argument-structure construction that allows the verb *mean*, when negated, to license a clausal subject introduced by *just because*.

1.3.3.3   Hypotactic Apposition

When English speakers use a cataphoric demonstrative pronoun to announce forthcoming propositional content, they may do so by means of either the paratactic construction in (52) or the subordinating construction in (53–54), the latter of which Brenier and Michaelis (2005) refer to as Hypotactic Apposition:

(52) That's what I've been telling you: you need to call.

(53) That's the problem is that they just hate us so much and I never re- I never really realized. (fe_03_01019A)

(54) That's the main thing is that I can't tell whether the thing is going to fit. (sw03729A)

In Hypotactic Apposition, the copula licenses two arguments that it would not license ordinarily: a clause containing a cataphoric pronoun and a clausal complement that is coreferential with the cataphoric pronoun contained in its clausal sister. This is not the licensing behavior of equational *be*, as found, for example, in *The problem is that they just hate us so much*; it is the licensing behavior of the Hypotactic Apposition construction.

1.3.4   Argument quantification

In quantifier-scope hierarchies, the quantifiers of topical and/or subject referents outscope those of nontopical and nonsubject referents (Ioup

1975, Kuno 1991). While these hierarchies capture robust cross-linguistic interpretive tendencies, they do not explain scope constraints in certain argument-structure patterns. The two argument-realization patterns that we will consider here are discussed in detail by Basilico (1998). They are the *creation* pattern, exemplified by (55), and the *transformation* pattern, exemplified by (56):

(55) **Creation:** She made a paperweight from a rock.
(56) **Transformation:** She made a rock into a paperweight.

The creation–transformation alternation hinges on whether the "raw material" role (in this case, the rock) is played by a source argument, *from a rock*, as in (55), or a theme argument, *a rock*, as in (56). In the latter (transformation) case, the "product" role is played by an oblique goal argument. In the creation pattern, both the theme argument and the source argument can take narrow scope, as shown in (57–58), respectively:

(57) **Narrow scope theme argument: A mighty oak** grew from every acorn.
(58) **Narrow scope source argument:** Every oak grew from **a tiny acorn.**

In the transformation pattern, however, the theme argument must take wide scope, as in (59):

(59) **Every acorn** grew into a beautiful oak.

Evidence for this quantifier-scope constraint comes from semantic anomalies like (60), where the # symbol indicates that the sentence is well formed but has a bizarre interpretation:

(60) **Wide scope theme argument:** #An acorn grew into every oak.

In (60), the theme argument necessarily has wide scope: this sentence can only be interpreted as asserting "There exists a single acorn from which all of the oaks grew." This scoping creates a nonsensical reading: we know that one acorn cannot produce many oaks. There are two plausible ways to explain why (60) has the anomalous reading it does. The first explanation is based on the quantifier-scope hierarchy: the sensible interpretation of (60), in which there is a one-to-one mapping between oaks and acorns, requires the quantifier of an oblique argument (the universal quantifier of *into every oak*) to have wide scope relative to the quantifier of the subject argument (the existential quantifier of *an acorn*). Since this scoping violates the quantifier-scope hierarchy, (60) has only the nonsensical reading. The second explanation involves topicality: subject NPs are grammaticalized clause-level topics (Mithun 1991, Lambrecht 1994: Ch. 4), and as such tend to have specific referents. Because the sensible reading of (60) requires that the subject NP *an acorn* receive a nonspecific reading, in which it denotes any acorn rather than a unique acorn, (60) is anomalous. As shown by (61), however, both explanations fail to generalize:

(61) An oak grew out of every acorn.

In (61), an instance of the transformation pattern, the subject is a theme argument, just as it is in (60). Further, this subject NP is both nonspecific and scoped by an oblique argument (*every acorn*). And yet (61) has a sensible interpretation, in which there is a one-to-one mapping between oaks and acorns, while (60) does not. This suggests that what gives (60) the nonsensical reading it has is a constraint specific to the transformation pattern. I propose that the transformation pattern constrains its locative argument in a way that the creation pattern does not. The creation pattern allows its locative argument (i.e., the source argument) to be either topic or focus. This is shown in (62–63), respectively, where the points of prosodic prominence are indicated by small caps:

(62) **Topical source argument:** An OAK grew out of it.
(63) **Focal source argument:** That oak grew out of an ACORN.

The transformation pattern, by contrast, is pragmatically constrained. Its locative argument (i.e., its goal argument) is necessarily interpreted as focal. This is shown by the ungrammaticality of (64), in which the goal argument is topical (as indicated by its pronominal expression), as compared to (65), in which the goal argument is focal (as indicated by its prosodic prominence):

(64) **Topical goal argument:** *A tiny acorn grew into it.
(65) **Topical theme argument:** The tiny acorn grew into an OAK.

Unlike the goal argument, the theme argument of the transformation pattern must be assigned a topic role, as indicated by the ungrammaticality of both the intransitive (66) and the transitive (67):

(66) *A tiny ACORN grew into that old oak.
(67) *I made a ROCK into a paperweight.

As a topic, the theme argument of the transformation pattern cannot readily be interpreted as nonspecific; this follows from Lambrecht's Topic Acceptability Hierarchy (Lambrecht 1994: 165–71). Because it must be interpreted as denoting a specific entity, an existentially quantified theme argument in the transformation pattern cannot take narrow scope relative to a universally quantified goal argument. This leads to the nonsensical reading in (60), in which *an acorn* denotes a single acorn. To represent such constraints we must characterize the arguments licensed by verbs in terms of their pragmatic roles, for example, topic and focus. As shown in Table 1.1, event-structure templates of the type proposed by RHL contain unbound variables in place of arguments. While the semantic role of an argument can be inferred from its position in decompositional structure, its pragmatic role cannot. SBCG constructions provide a simple way to describe contextual features of argument roles of verbs. The lexical-class constructions of SBCG have ARG-ST sets whose members are sign descriptions. The signs described are coindexed with arguments of frames within the construction's SEM value. These frame arguments can in turn be coindexed with arguments of the construction's CTXT attribute. The (intransitive) transformation pattern, which licenses verbal lexemes like *grow* as in (59), is represented by the lexical class construction shown in Figure 1.4.

Another interpretive phenomenon that suggests that verb classes constrain the quantification of their arguments is one that I will call *operator-free nominal coercion*. Nominal coercion is reinterpretation of a nominal in order to resolve conflict between the type required by an operator and the type of the nominal argument supplied (Jackendoff 1997: Ch. 3). For example, the English partitive article *some* induces the interpreter to construe the noun *pillow* as denoting a mass rather than a bounded entity in **some pillow*. However, an operator-based model of nominal coercion only goes so far; it does not explain the interpretive effects evident in (68–69):

(68) **Apple** dries easily.
(69) You have **apple** on your shirt.

Neither *dry* nor *have* selects a mass-type second argument, so what can account for the portion or type reading of *apple* in these contexts? As

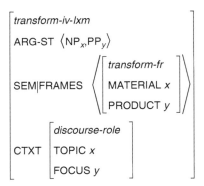

Figure 1.4 The intransitive transformation lexical-class construction

discussed in section 1.3.2 above, arguments of verbs, whether phonetically instantiated or not, have to be quantified. This requirement is represented in SBCG by associating a quantifier frame with each of the verb's ARG-ST elements in the lexical-class construction that represents that verb's lexical class. Lexical classes are broad, and include transitive verb lexemes, intransitive verb lexemes, and so on (Sag 2012: 100ff.). In English, the primary means by which a common noun gets a quantified interpretation is through combination with a determiner. The only other way is through the Bare Noun Pumping Construction shown in Figure 1.3. As discussed there, this construction yields existentially and generically quantified interpretations of undetermined nouns. What triggers the use of this pumping construction? Simply put, it is the requirement that the nominal arguments of a predicator be quantified. Aktionsart representations do not contain quantifiers, but lexical-class constructions do. As we saw earlier in this section, lexical-class constructions contain FRAMES among their semantic attributes. These frames include quantifier frames.

1.3.5 Effects of syntactic context

In a lexically driven model of verbal argument selection, it is assumed that a verb will select the same repertoire of complements irrespective of the syntactic context in which it appears. This is because syntactic context does not affect lexical-class membership, whether the lexical class in question is syntactic (the class of extraposition verbs that includes *seem* and *appear*) or semantic (the class of transfer verbs). Against this background, the following facts seem genuinely puzzling:

(70) [If I don't answer] it's *(not) that I don't want to.
(71) I *(can't) believe how much weight I've gained!

The main clause in (70) illustrates a construction referred to by Delahunty (2001) as the inferential sentence type or sentence-focus cleft. Inferential sentences assert that some state of affairs (the one following the copula) is responsible for a state of affairs under discussion. An attested example of an inferential sentence is shown in (72), where the inferential sentence is boldfaced:

(72) And it never fails if they have a cat [laughter]. It's gonna sit on my lap and I get hives and my throat swells up when I get near a cat. **And it's not that I don't like 'em.** I'm just allergic to them and it never fails when I go in the home. (fe_03_06266A)

What makes the attested inferential sentence in (72) well formed while the starred version in (70) is not? The simple answer is: the presence of negation in the attested example. English inferential clefts either serve to reject, or presuppose rejection of, a potential explanation for the state of affairs under discussion. In the case of (72) the speaker rejects "dislike of cats" as the cause of her avoidance of cats. A speaker who uses an inferential sentence might follow up by asserting an actual cause, and this cause is typically presented as less extreme, on some pragmatic scale, than the previously rejected one. In (72), the purported actual cause is the speaker's allergies: *I'm just allergic to them*. Assertion of the actual cause might itself take the form of an inferential cleft, resulting in the sequence *It's not that S; it's just that S*. Thus, both the negative morpheme and the adverbial minimizer *just* are closely associated with inferential sentences. However, it would make little sense to say that the copula *be* selects the complements *it* and *that S* just in case it is accompanied by *not* or *just*. The adverbial-modification facts make sense only under a construction-based account that attributes very specific use conditions to the inferential cleft sentence type.

Something similar can be said in the case of (71). In (71), we see that the verb *believe* takes a WH-interrogative complement only in case it is negated. Again, this fact would be inexplicable in a lexical model of complement selection, in which verbs take the complements they do by virtue of their lexical classes. There is no lexical class of "negated verbs." Instead, the negation requirement in (71) appears to be a constructional effect. Michaelis and Lambrecht (1996) call the construction in question the Abstract Exclamative Construction (AEC), and claim that all exclamatory sentences encode the discourse-pragmatic "ingredients" of the AEC in some form. Exclamatory sentences, according to their analysis, express that the degree of some scalar property (e.g., weight), as achieved by some topical referent (e.g., the speaker), is sufficiently extreme to cause expectation violation. Expectation violation may be expressed by an adjective like *amazing* or *remarkable*, an interjection like *God* or a negated verb of belief. The scalar degree is typically encoded by the WH-phrase of a WH-interrogative (e.g., *how much weight I've gained*). Thus, the verb *believe* has the complement it does in (71) because, in the context of an exclamatory utterance, it is functioning to encode expectation violation. The moral of the story is yet again that constructions— whether concrete, like the inferential sentence type, or abstract, like the AEC—determine the combinatoric potentials of verbs.

1.4 Conclusion

The evidence that we have reviewed here suggests that verbal argument structure is not derived from or 'read off' semantic representation. On the alternate approach described here, verbs license the arguments that they do because they combine with constructions that (a) determine what semantic and syntactic elements will accompany the verb, (b) provide quantifiers for each argument, (c) determine which argument will be topic and which focus and (d) add to the array of semantic and pragmatic frames that the verb has independently. These constructions include both derivational constructions like the null instantiation construction and lexical-class constructions like the intransitive transformation construction. On this approach, semantic roles exist only in *theta frames* (e.g., causation of result and caused motion); there is no semantic-role hierarchy of the type used to assign grammatical functions in most current accounts of argument structure, including RHL. As Fillmore and Kay (1995) point out, the semantic-role hierarchy, despite its widespread currency, is a poor candidate for a linguistic generalization because it features combinations of semantic roles that no verb would ever license. Theta frames, by contrast, express only those semantic-role sets that play a role in verb-valence descriptions. But no speaker ever encounters a naked theta frame: the generalizations about semantic-role combinations that speakers learn and use are theta frames *as expressed by morphosyntactic patterns*, and these morphosyntactic patterns, as we have seen, contain a good deal of idiomatic information about meaning, use and form. In sum, the study of verbal complement licensing, like Bybee's studies of the inflectional morphology (Bybee 2001), could be said to demonstrate that linguistic generalizations are simply not that general.

Note

1. I am grateful to Paul Kay and Adele Goldberg for providing discussion, inspiration and insights that have enriched and clarified the material presented here, although neither necessarily endorses my claims or analyses. This chapter is dedicated to the memory of my friend and mentor Charles J. Fillmore.

References

Basilico, D. (1998) 'Object Position and Predication Forms'. *Natural Language and Linguistic Theory*, 16 (3): 491–539.

Bates, E. and J. C. Goodman (1997) 'On the Inseparability of Grammar and the Lexicon: Evidence from Acquisition, Aphasia and Real-Time Processing'. *Language and Cognitive Processes*, 12 (5/6): 507–84.

Bender, E. and A. Kathol (2001) 'Constructional Effects of *Just Because ... doesn't Mean ...*', paper presented at the Twenty-Seventh Annual Meeting of the Berkeley Linguistics Society, Berkeley, Calif.

Birner, B. J. and G. Ward (1998) *Information Status and Noncanonical Word Order in English* (Amsterdam/Philadelphia: John Benjamins).

Boas, H. and I. A. Sag (eds) (2012) *Sign-Based Construction Grammar* (Stanford: CSLI Publications).

Brenier, J. M. and L. A. Michaelis (2005) 'Optimization via Syntactic Amalgam: Syntax–Prosody Mismatch and Copula Doubling'. *Corpus Linguistics and Linguistic Theory*, 1(1): 45–88.

Bresnan, J. (1994) 'Locative Inversion and the Architecture of Universal Grammar'. *Language*, 70 (1): 72–131.

Bresnan, J. (2001) *Lexical-Functional Syntax* (Oxford: Blackwell).

Bybee, J. (2001) *Phonology and Language Use* (Cambridge: Cambridge University Press).

Chierchia, G. (2003) 'Language, Thought and Reality after Chomsky' unpublished MS, University of Milan-Bicocca.

Croft, W. (2012) *Verbs: Aspect and Causal Structure* (Oxford: Oxford University Press).

Delahunty, G. (2001) 'Discourse Functions of Inferential Sentences'. *Linguistics*, 39 (3): 517–45.

Dowty, D. (1979) *Word Meaning and Montague Grammar: the Semantics of Verbs and Times in Generative Semantics and in Montague's PTQ* (Dordrecht: Kluwer Academic Publishers).

Fillmore, C. J. (1986) 'Pragmatically Controlled Zero Anaphora' in V. Nikiforidou, M. Van Clay, M. Niepokuj, and D. Feder (eds) *The Twelfth Annual Meeting of the Berkeley Linguistics Society* (Berkeley: BLS, Inc.), pp. 95–107.

Fillmore, C. J. and P. Kay (1995) 'Construction Grammar', unpublished MS, University of California, Berkeley.

Fillmore, C. J., P. Kay and M. C. O'Connor (1988) 'Regularity and Idiomaticity in Grammatical Constructions: the Case of *Let Alone*'. *Language*, 64 (3): 501–38.

Ginzburg, J. and I. A. Sag (2000) *Interrogative Investigations: the Form, Meaning and Use of English Interrogatives* (Stanford, Calif.: CSLI Publications).

Goldberg, A. (1995) *Constructions: a Construction Grammar Approach to Argument Structure* (Chicago: University of Chicago Press).

Goldberg, A. (2001) 'Patient Arguments of Causative verbs Can be Omitted: the Role of Information Structure in Argument Distribution'. *Language Sciences*, 23 (4/5): 503–24.

Goldberg, A. (2002) 'Surface Generalizations: an Alternative to Alternations'. *Cognitive Linguistics*, 13 (4): 327–56.

Goldberg, A. (2005) 'Constructions, Lexical Semantics and the Correspondence Principle: Accounting for Generalizations and Subregularities in the Realization of Arguments' in N. Erteschik-Shir and T. Rapoport (eds) *The Syntax of Aspect* (Oxford: Oxford University Press), pp. 212–36.

Goldberg, A. (2006) *Constructions at Work: the Nature of Generalization in Language* (Oxford: Oxford University Press).

Haegeman, L. (1994) *Introduction to Government and Binding Theory*, 2nd edn (Oxford: Blackwell).

Ioup, G. (1975) 'Some Universals for Quantifier Scope' in J. Kimball (ed.) *Syntax and Semantics*, Vol. 4 (New York: Academic Press), pp. 37–58.

Jackendoff, R. (1990) *Semantic Structures* (Cambridge, Mass.: MIT Press).

Jackendoff, R. (1997) *The Architecture of the Language Faculty* (Cambridge, Mass.: MIT Press).

Kaschak, M. and A. Glenberg (2000) 'Constructing Meaning: the Role of Affordances and Grammatical Constructions in Language Comprehension'. *Journal of Memory and Language*, 43 (3): 508–29.

Kaschak, M. and A. Glenberg (2002) 'Grounding Language in Action'. *Psychonomic Bulletin and Review*, 9 (3): 558–65.

Kay, P. (2002) 'English Subjectless Tag Sentences'. *Language*, 78 (3): 453–81.

Kay, P. and C. J. Fillmore (1999) 'Grammatical Constructions and Linguistic Generalizations: the 'what's X doing Y' Construction'. *Language*, 75 (1): 1–33.

Kay, P. and L. A. Michaelis (2012) 'Constructional Meaning and Compositionality' in C. Maienborn, K. von Heusinger and P. Portner (eds) *Semantics: an International Handbook of Natural Language Meaning*, Vol. 3 (Berlin: de Gruyter), pp. 2271–96.

Kuno, S. (1991) 'Remarks on Quantifier Scope' in H. Nakajima (ed.) *Current English Linguistics in Japan* (Berlin: Mouton de Gruyter), pp. 261–87.

Lambrecht, K. (1994) *Information Structure and Sentence Form* (Cambridge: Cambridge University Press).

Levin, B. (2000) 'Aspect, Lexical Semantic Representation and Argument Expression' in L. J. Conathan, J. Good, D. Kavitskaya, A. B. Wulff and A. Yu (eds) *The Proceedings of the Twenty-Sixth Annual Meeting of the Berkeley Linguistics Society* (Berkeley: BLS, Inc.), pp. 413–29.

Levin, B. and M. Rappaport Hovav (1995) *Unaccusativity: at the Syntax–Lexical Semantics Interface* (Cambridge, Mass.: MIT Press).

Levin, B. and M. Rappaport Hovav (2005) *Argument Realization* (Cambridge: Cambridge University Press).

Michaelis, L. A. (2004) 'Type Shifting in Construction Grammar: an Integrated Approach to Aspectual Coercion'. *Cognitive Linguistics*, 15 (1): 1–67.

Michaelis, L. A. (2009) 'Sign-Based Construction Grammar' in B. Heine and H. Narrog (eds) *The Oxford Handbook of Linguistic Analysis* (Oxford: Oxford University Press), pp. 155–76.

Michaelis, L. A. (2012) 'Making the Case for Construction Grammar' in H. Boas and I. A. Sag (eds) *Sign-Based Construction Grammar* (Stanford: CSLI Publications), pp. 29–60.

Michaelis, L. A. and K. Lambrecht (1996) 'Toward a Construction-Based Model of Language Function: the Case of Nominal Extraposition'. *Language*, 72 (2): 215–47.

Michaelis, L. A. and J. Ruppenhofer (2001) *Beyond Alternations: a Construction-Based Approach to the Applicative Pattern in German* (Stanford: CSLI Publications).

Mithun, M. (1991) 'The Role of Motivation in the Emergence of Grammatical Categories: the Grammaticization of Subjects' in E. C. Traugott and B. Heine (eds) *Approaches to Grammaticalization*, Vol. 2 (Amsterdam: John Benjamins), pp. 159–84.

Moens, M. and M. Steedman (1988) 'Temporal Ontology and Temporal Reference'. *Computational Linguistics*, 14 (2): 15–28.

Neidle, C. (1994) 'Lexical Functional Grammar'. *Encyclopedia of Language and Linguistics*, Vol. 5 (New York: Pergamon Press), pp. 2147–53.

Partee, B. and V. Borschev (2007) 'Existential Sentences, BE and the Genitive of Negation in Russian' in K. von Heisenger and I. Comorovski (eds) *Existence: Semantics and Syntax* (Berlin: Springer Verlag), pp. 147–90.

Pinker, S. (1989) *Learnability and Cognition* (Cambridge, Mass.: MIT Press).

Pollard, C. and I. A. Sag (1987) *Information-Based Syntax and Semantics*, Vol. 1: *Fundamentals* (Stanford: CSLI Publications).

Pollard, C. and I. A. Sag (1994) *Head-Driven Phrase Structure Grammar* (Chicago: University of Chicago Press).

Rappaport Hovav, M. and B. Levin (1998) 'Building Verb Meanings' in M. Butt and W. Geuder (eds) *The Projection of Arguments* (Stanford: CSLI Publications), pp. 97–134.

Ruppenhofer, J. (2012) 'Fictive Motion: Construction or Construal?' in Z. Antic, M. Babel, C. Chang, J. Hong, M. Houser, F.-C. Liu, M. Toosarvandani and Y. Yao (eds) *The Proceedings of the Thirty-Second Annual Meeting of the Berkeley Linguistics Society: Parasession on Theoretical Approaches to Argument Structure* (Berkeley: BLS, Inc.).

Ruppenhofer, J., C. F. Baker and C. J. Fillmore (2002) 'Collocational Information in the FrameNet Database' in A. Braasch and C. Povlsen (eds) *Proceedings of the Tenth Euralex International Congress*, Vol. I (Copenhagen, Denmark), pp. 359–69.

Ruppenhofer, J. and L. A Michaelis (2014) 'Frames and the Interpretation of Omitted Arguments in English' in S. Katz Bourns and L. Myers (eds) *Linguistic Perspectives on Structure and Context: Studies in Honor of Knud Lambrecht* (Amsterdam: Benjamins), pp. 57–86.

Sag, I. A. (2010) 'English Filler-Gap Constructions'. *Language*, 86 (3): 486–545.

Sag, I. A. (2012) 'Sign-Based Construction Grammar: an Informal Synopsis' in H. C. Boas and I. A. Sag (eds) *Sign-Based Construction Grammar* (Stanford: CSLI Publications), pp. 69–202.

Slobin, D. I. (2008) 'Relations between Paths of Motion and Paths of Vision: a Crosslinguistic and Developmental Exploration' in V. M. Gathercole (ed.) *Routes to Language: Studies in Honor of Melissa Bowerman* (Mahwah, NJ: Lawrence Erlbaum Associates), pp. 197–221.

Van Valin, R. D. and R. J. LaPolla (1997) *Syntax* (Cambridge: Cambridge University Press).

2
Inside Out: Productive German Prepositional Objects as an Example of Complements Selecting Heads[1]

Jouni Rostila
University of Helsinki

2.1 Introduction

Projectionist theories like Chomskyan generative grammar and different versions of valency theory assume that heads determine the elements needed to build them into phrases. Most notably the verb – the most central head category because of its role in building sentences – is assumed to select certain complements in order to form a complete phrase. Thus for instance the verb *dart* needs a directional complement, for example *into the lift*. In largely the same way it also requires the presence of a phrase denoting a darting entity, its subject, but views differ as to whether this is to be seen as a complement among others. Valency theory in its classic form puts the subject largely on a par with other complements (cf. e.g. Helbig and Schenkel 1982: 26, Welke 1988: 92), while Chomskyan generative grammar invests it with a special status, that of the so-called external argument (Williams 1980, Chomsky 1986: 116). Regardless of such details, the subject shares the crucial property of being selected by the head with other complements, and thus can be seen at least as a special kind of complement.

Among projectionist approaches, there are also differences as to whether heads only determine their complements semantically (cf. s-selection; Chomsky 1986: 86) or also with reference to their syntactic category (cf. Odijk 1997 for discussion).[2] Pesetsky (1982: 199) and Napoli (1989: 9, 32) propose that so-called l(exical)-selection is also needed, that is, the selection of a certain case or preposition within the complement by a lexical head.[3] Setting details aside, the essential common denominator of projectionist approaches is the determination of complement properties by heads at least in terms of assigning the corresponding arguments a semantic role. For two reasons, this could be called the traditional take on complementation. First, this view historically precedes the approach advocated by some Construction Grammarians, to be outlined next; second, the head-centred view can be seen as more basic, since it chooses a tangible element of language, a lexical head, or word, as its point of departure in understanding more complex phenomena.

Goldberg's (1995, 2006) Construction Grammar (CxG) approach turns this view inside out: verbs are embedded into templates called **argument structure constructions** (henceforth **a-constructions**) that could be viewed as **complement constellations**. For example, the English ditransitive construction can be seen as a group of four (non-ordered) 'slots' or variable positions: one for an AGENT subject, a second for a RECIPIENT indirect object, a third for a PATIENT/THEME direct object, and a fourth for a verb compatible with the meaning of the construction, which roughly corresponds to that of the verb *give* (cf. Goldberg 1995: 48–52). The conditions placed by the construction on its slot fillers constrain both the meaning and form of the fillers (ideally, semantic conditions suffice to constrain the form as well), so that a-constructions can be seen as capturing all the essential properties of verb complements. Since such templates represent closed-class or grammatical elements that require lexical fillers for their variable positions in order to be used at all (Rostila 2006b: section 6), it seems natural to assume that they choose a verb to complete them. A more concrete indication that a-constructions select verbs can be seen in the circumstance that a-constructions incorporate information regarding the relation in which the meaning of the embedded verb ought to stand to constructional meaning – the so-called R relation.[4] Thus, a-constructions display information about verbs to be embedded in them, but notably not vice versa.[5]

Placing an a-construction at the centre of the sentence has its advantages,[6] most notably the possibility to describe creative verb uses such as those in (1) without having to assume less conventionalized and therefore implausible verb senses (cf. Goldberg 1995: 9).[7]

(1) a. Dan talked himself blue in the face. (Goldberg 1995: 9)
    b. ... he and his family were bombed out of their home. (Nichol, p. 28)[8]
    c. Fire would rip through the aircraft until it reached the bomb bay. (Nichol, p. 120)
    d. ... three Mosquitoes peeled away on a spoof raid. (Nichol, p. 117)
    e. Dick's flight engineer tried to feather the engines ... (Nichol, pp. 121–2)
    f. ... he staggered back into the main body of the plane ... (Nichol, p. 74)

As I have shown in my previous work (Rostila 2005, 2007, 2014, in press) and will demonstrate below, a-constructions may even prove useful for the description of phenomena traditionally thought to be verb-centred: among German **prepositional object** (PO) structures[9] (e.g. *auf jemanden/ etwas warten*, 'wait for someone/something'; lit. 'on someone/something wait'), where the choice of preposition is traditionally thought to be lexically governed by the predicate head (Breindl 1989: 39; cf. also Lerot 1982: 273),[10] there are productive cases that can be adequately described with the aid of a-constructions in a rule-like fashion. Nevertheless, proponents of the construction-centred approach may be taking it too far: in their concentration on a-constructions they seem to be losing sight of the fact that there are also verb-centred structures, more specifically lexically determined complement relations in language. Indications of such a distortion of view can be seen for example in Croft's (2001: 247–54) arguments against directionality in subcategorization and government relations. Another example can be seen in Goldberg and Jackendoff (2004: n. 7), where Goldberg maintains that verbs are always embedded in a-constructions. This would mean that they never select their complements.[11]

In section 2.2, I will show that there are strong reasons for regarding many German prepositions of prepositional objects – a phenomenon hitherto considered lexically determined – as manifestations of a-constructions. Some similar cases in Swedish and English are also considered. In addition, I will demonstrate that there are, nevertheless, also head-centred patterns in verb complementation to be found, and among PO structures in particular. The section is rounded up by a sketch of the properties of a-constructions in the guise of PO prepositions. Finally, in section 2.3 I will present a scenario for a cyclic change in languages from predominantly verb-centred complementation to the predominance of a-constructions and vice versa that might to some degree explain why it is understandable that extreme views concerning the nature of complement relations should gain a foothold in linguistics.

2.2   Prepositions of prepositional objects: idiosyncrasies and productive patterns

As pointed out above, the choice of preposition in German PO structures is traditionally thought to be lexically determined by a verb or another predicative head. This view is corroborated by cases like (2), where it is very hard to detect a semantic regularity in the choice of P and the morphological case governed by it.[12]

(2) a. Er **zweifelte an** seinen Fähigkeiten.[13]
he doubted at his.DAT skills
'He doubted his skills.'

b. Er **nahm an** dem Wettbewerb **teil**.
he took at the.DAT competition part
'He took part in the competition.'

c. Er hat **an** Autorität **gewonnen**.
he has at authority.DAT gained
'He has gained in authority.'

d. Er **besteht auf** dieser Lösung.
he insists on this.DAT solution
'He insists on this solution.'

e. Wir **verfügen** nicht **über** die nötigen Mittel.
   we possess not over the.ACC requisite means
   'We do not have the requisite funding at our disposal.'
f. Sie hat **sich in** ihr Schicksal **gefügt.**
   she has herself in her.ACC fate joined
   'She has accepted her fate.'

That is, the same P + case combination seems to be selected by heads with widely differing meanings (cf. 2a–c). Moreover, parallel cases – semantically similar heads selecting the same P + case combination – are often hard to come by: for instance, the cases in (2d–f) appear as isolates in the PO complement lists of Duden (1984). The examples in (3) suggest that similar conditions hold for PO prepositions in English:

(3) a. They **decided on** a different course of action.
    b. I'm **working on** it.
    c. She was **intent on** pursuing a career in business.[14]
    d. Your body **draws on** its reserves of fat during the times when you are fasting.[15]
    e. He **took part/participated in** the competition.
    f. He was **interested in** the case.
    g. He **took to** the idea immediately.
    h. He was **oblivious to** the noise.

Cases like (4) in turn show another type of head-specific argument marking, one that historically precedes PO prepositions in Germanic languages (cf. Korhonen 2006): lexical cases,[16] illustrated here on the basis of two German verbs governing the genitive case:[17]

(4) a. Sie haben [...] beobachtet, wie in der Ukraine des Kriegsendes gedacht wurde.[18]
       they have [...] observed how in the Ukraine the.GEN war end reminisced was
       'They observed [...] how people in Ukraine reminisced about the end of the war.'
    b. Steven Spielberg [hat] sich erneut eines historischen Themas angenommen.[19]
       Steven Spielberg has himself again a.GEN historical topic on taken
       'Steven Spielberg has again taken on a historical topic.'

The existence of such lexically determined argument-marking patterns in languages necessitates assuming complement selection by verbs alongside a-constructions (cf. also Müller and Wechsler, forthcoming: section 7.4) – in other words, alongside verb selection by complement constellations.

Nevertheless, selection by complement constellations might be dominant in many languages, since it is, in a certain sense, rule-based. In Rostila (2007), I argue for the view that the linking of verb arguments in German is essentially based on a-constructions: in order to be linked, verbs are usually embedded into a-constructions on the basis of their semantic compatibility with such templates.[20] Hence, this operation displays semantic regularities. On the other hand, cases like (2), where an individual head determines its argument-marking pattern, represent a peripheral, idiosyncratic, and hence less grammaticalized option. In other words, central verb complementation patterns might (even cross-linguistically) boil down to complements – more precisely, complement constellations – selecting heads, but there is no denying the need to also recognize cases of verbs selecting their complements; this option is, however, essentially lexical-idiosyncratic in nature. Nevertheless, this option might even be the predominant one in some languages, as will be proposed in section 2.3.

Notwithstanding the above observations, it is to be emphasized that regularities also exist among structures like (2). A look at lists of such structures that can be found for instance in Duden (1984) may even give the impression that regularity instead of idiosyncrasy is the rule: it is fairly easy to see semantic similarities between heads choosing the same preposition. This may be due in part to the difficulty of reliable semantic comparisons, and in part to complex diachronic relationships between the cases: many head + P combinations may have been formed on the basis of more than one model. Still, fairly clear regularities can also be recognized, that is, cases following the logic of 'verb displaying meaning component X selects preposition Y'. In Rostila (2007, 2014, in press), I argue that in such cases, verbs do not select similar complements because of their semantic similarity, but are actually embedded into a-constructions semantically compatible with them. Thus, the constructions themselves carry the semantics common to such parallel patterns.[21] In the following, I present my main arguments for this view.

In order to prove that certain PO prepositions actually represent a-constructions, it is necessary to show that a certain PO preposition makes an independent semantic contribution and is productive, that is, it can be freely combined with semantically compatible predicate heads. Cases like the following, where certain PO prepositions in German occur with several semantically similar predicate heads, and the POs denote semantically similar entities, suggest both of these conclusions. For instance, the PO preposition *auf* occurs widely with prospective heads, while the POs can be considered to denote future events:[22]

(5) a. Er **wartet/hofft auf** einen Börsensturz.
    he waits/hopes on a.ACC stock market crash
    'He waits/hopes/is waiting/hoping for a stock market crash.'

b. Er **bereitet sich auf** einen Börsensturz **vor/macht sich auf** einen Börsensturz **gefasst.**
   he prepares himself on a.ACC stock market crash/makes himself on a.ACC stock market crash prepared
   'He prepares/is preparing for/takes/is taking precautions against a stock market crash.'

c. Wir sind schon sehr **gespannt auf** eure Zeichnungen.[23]
   we are already very excited on your.ACC drawings.
   'We are already very excited about your drawings.'

d. Denksport macht [einen] **neugierig auf** mehr.[24]
   thoughtsports make [one] curious on more.ACC
   'Mental sports make [one] curious about more.'

e. Wenn dies eine **Aussicht auf** Entsatz sein sollte, [...]
   if this a perspective on relief.ACC be should, [...]
   'If this was supposed to be a chance for relief, [...]'
   (Schröter, p. 203)

f. **Einigen sich** Demokraten und Republikaner nicht **auf** eine Anhebung, [...][25]
   Agree themselves democrats and republicans not on a.ACC raise
   'If Democrats and Republicans do not agree on a raise, [...]'

Similarly, *über* often accompanies heads denoting activities involving mental processes, and the PO expresses the topic of a mental activity:

(6) über etw. sprechen/schreiben/berichten/diskutieren/erzählen/ nachdenken/informieren
    over something.ACC speak/write/report/discuss/tell/reflect/inform

Since the predicate heads occurring with a certain PO preposition are semantically similar, it would seem natural to conclude that they are combined with the PO preposition in question on the basis of their semantics – and that such combination can take place provided that a head displays such semantics. In other words, the data would seem to testify to productivity. On the other hand, since the PO preposition remains constant while all else varies across parallel cases such as those illustrated in (5) and (6), the PO preposition might be taken to be the locus of the common semantics that likewise remains constant. However, data like this do not constitute conclusive evidence for either conclusion. Each of the predicate heads might still lexically determine the PO preposition, and the common semantics of the parallel cases might only stem from the meaning of the predicate heads, not from the PO preposition. Alternatively, the fact that the same P is chosen in each group might be due to the usual case of semantically similar heads selecting semantically similar complements (cf. e.g. verbs of duration selecting complements denoting duration: *The meeting lasted/took an hour*).[26]

The nature of the PO preposition as an independent sign productively combined with predicate heads[27] only surfaces transparently in cases of the type (1) – that is, in cases where the verb cannot be considered to contribute certain meaning components that nevertheless are present. Similar cases among PO structures can be seen in (7b–e), where the verb itself hardly displays prospective semantics, but the future-oriented meaning component is imposed on it by the PO preposition.[28] The example pair (7a, b) is the most illustrative, since it shows that prospectivity in the meaning of *sich freuen* 'delight' results from the choice of the preposition.

(7) a. Ich **freue mich über** das Ende des Semesters.
     I delight myself over the.ACC end of term
     'I am delighted/glad about the end of term.'
   b. Ich **freue mich auf** das Ende des Semesters.
     I delight myself on the.ACC end of term
     'I look forward to the end of term.'
   c. Das Start-up-Unternehmen [...] ist ebenfalls **auf** Wachstum
     programmiert.[29]
     the start-up firm [...] is also on growth.ACC programmed
     'The start-up firm is also intent on growth.'
   d. Resch [...] hatte [...] seine Nerven dar-**auf trainiert**, [...]
     Resch [...] had [...] his nerves it-on trained
     'Resch had trained his nerves for it, [...]'
     (Olivier, p. 483)
   e. Das haben sie in den 50er Jahren **auf** modern **gemacht.**[30]
     that have they in the 50 years on modern made
     'They modernized that in the fifties.'

Similarly, (8a) illustrates a case where the PO preposition *über* coerces *arbeiten* into an 'intellectual activity' reading. (8b–e), on the other hand, testify to the PO preposition *um* imposing over verbs as diverse as *schreien* 'cry (out)', *schießen* 'shoot', *zittern* 'tremble' and *anrufen* 'telephone' semantics normally associated with *bitten* + *um* 'ask for', that is, the meaning component 'acquisition or maintenance of possession'.

(8) a. Er **arbeitet über** Brecht.
     he works/is working over Brecht.ACC
     'He works on Brecht.'
     (Lerot 1982: 273)
   b. [...] falls er es doch schaffen sollte,
     um sein erbärmliches Leben zu **schreien** [...]
     about/around his.ACC pitiful life to cry
     '[...] in case he should manage to cry for his pitiful life [...]'
     (Kunkel, p. 533)

c. Neuner **schießt sich um** einen Podestplatz.[31]
Neuner shoots herself about/around a.ACC podium appearance
'Neuner shoots herself out of a place on the podium.'

d. Er **zitterte um** sein Vermögen.
he trembled about/around his.ACC wealth
'He trembled at the thought of losing his wealth.'
(cf. DUWB, s.v. *zittern*)

e. Im vorliegenden Fall war der EuGH in drei Fällen von einem spanischen Gericht
um Klärung **angerufen** worden.[32]
about/around clarification.ACC telephoned become
'In this case, the European Court of Justice had been called by a Spanish court three times in order to obtain clarification.'

Leaving perhaps the most productive pattern for last, the PO preposition *an* seems to be able to impose an incremental semantics on any transitive verb denoting an activity where intermediate stages are discernible:

(9) a. Er **baute an** einem Haus.
he built at a.DAT house
'He was building a house.'

b. Er **trank an** einem Bier.
he drank at a.DAT beer
'He was drinking a beer.'

c. Er **schrieb an** einem Buch.
he wrote at a.DAT book
'He was writing a book.'

In other words, the meaning of this PO preposition seems to resemble the aspectual contribution of the English progressive.[33]

Data such as (8) and (9) provide conclusive evidence that PO prepositions actually carry independent meanings and can be productively combined with predicate heads. This is because there is no overlapping predicate head semantics to obscure the independent contribution of the PO preposition. As regards productivity, data like this show that the patterns in question are strong – or productive – enough to even assume verbs not fully semantically compatible with them.[34] However, it is necessary to point out at this juncture that with the possible exception of *an* as in (9), all the PO prepositions for which I advocate an a-construction analysis are less than 100 per cent productive with respect to heads that ought to be compatible with them – for instance, the German noun *Plan* does not combine with *auf*, but *für* (cf. DUWB, s.v. *Plan*), despite its prospective semantics. Because of this, they might be considered patterns of coining instead of constructions (cf. Kay 2005). See Rostila (in press) for a refutation of this view based on the concept of pre-emption (Goldberg 1995: 30) and a view of constructions associating their productivity with the degree of grammaticalization they have attained.[35]

Cases like the following also testify to the productivity and independent meaningfulness of certain PO prepositions, and therefore support the consideration of them as manifestations of a-constructions. What seems to be at stake here is that the availability of the prospective *auf* pattern exerts a certain attraction on heads usually displaying another (probably lexically determined) complementation pattern, or not having any conventionalized complementation pattern at all:

(10) a. Derzeit **bewirbt** er **sich auf** Jobs.[36]
       at the moment applies he himself on jobs
       At the moment, he is applying for jobs.'
    b. EM-Gastgeber Ukraine: **Favorit aufs** Ausscheiden[37]
       EC host Ukraine: favourite on.ACC dropping out
       'E(uropean) C(hampionships) host Ukraine: favourite for dropping out'
    c. Guttenberg sieht **Chance auf** Staatshilfe für Arcandor schwinden.[38]
       Guttenberg sees chance on state subventions.ACC for Arcandor disappear
       'Guttenberg sees the chances of Arcandor getting state subventions disappear.'
    d. Auch wenn Minogues Songs hauptsächlich von der Liebe handeln, tragen sie nicht
       das **Versprechen auf** romantische Zweisamkeit in sich.[39]
       the promise on romantic togetherness.ACC
       'Even though Minogue's songs are mostly about love, they do not express the promise of romantic togetherness.'
    e. Eine **Garantie auf** einen solchen [Studien]Platz zu haben, ist enorm wichtig.[40]
       A guarantee on a.ACC such [study] place to have is enormously important
       'It is enormously important to have a guarantee that one can have such a place of study.'
    f. das in der US-Verfassung festgeschriebene **Recht auf** das Tragen von Waffen[41]
       the in the US constitution stated right on the.ACC carrying of arms
       'the right to carry arms enshrined in the US constitution'

In contrast to the cases illustrated in (7), all the heads combining here with *auf* are themselves prospective, and the resulting semantic compatibility might be the reason why they make use of the *auf* pattern. The cases (10a–d) speak most clearly for the attraction of the *auf* pattern for prospective heads, since the heads in question either usually select another preposition, or do not exhibit a prepositional complementation pattern at all: according to DUWB, *sich bewerben* selects *um*, while only *Favorit* + *für* is mentioned in this dictionary (notably in exactly the sense illustrated in (10b). *Chance* and *Versprechen*, on the other hand, are not listed in DUWB as selecting a preposition at all. As regards (10e, f), the nouns in question are listed in DUWB as selecting *auf*; my proposal is that this is precisely due to the availability and semantic compatibility of the prospective *auf* pattern.

Rather striking manifestations of the status of productive PO prepositions as a-constructions, and hence as signs in their own right, can be seen in cases like the following, where, under certain textual conditions (those of greetings and titles), PO prepositions are able to appear even without a verb in the sense they express as verb complements:

(11) a. Auf Wiedersehen!
          on seeing-again.ACC
      b. Tom Schimmeck über Kreuzzüge gestern und heute[42]
          Tom Schimmeck over crusades.ACC yesterday and today
          'Tom Schimmeck on crusades past and present'

My proposal is that (11a), a common German farewell expression, actually represents a fossilized case of the independent use of the prospective *auf* construction, while (11b) results from the independent use of the *über* construction denoting intellectual activity. Both cases show that PO prepositions can act as independent signs, as can be expected of a-constructions because of their independent meaningfulness.

Productive PO prepositions like those illustrated above for German probably exist in all Germanic languages. For instance, there is an *at* pattern in English expressing the skill of X in a certain activity, see (12a). On the other hand, the cases in (12b) suggest that English might exhibit a prospective *for* pattern similar to German prospective *auf*:

(12) a. He is good/bad/lousy/talented at languages/skilful at tennis. (Cf. Napoli 1989: 32)
      b. He waits/hopes/prepares/longs/strives for a stock market crash.

Finding further such cases in English and describing them as a-constructions might be a fruitful avenue of study.[43] Instead of delving further into this field, I will demonstrate that a-constructions in the guise of PO prepositions also exist in Swedish and might display interesting degrees of generalization compared to their German counterparts. First, the cases in (13) show a pattern based on the PO preposition *på* 'on' that seems to have attained a considerable degree of generalization. On the basis of the cases (13a–e), where *på* occurs in conjunction with prospective predicates, one is tempted to conclude that Swedish exhibits a prospective a-construction quite similar to that proposed above for German. This is all the more so since *på* is the Swedish cognate of German *auf*.

(13) a. Han **väntar på** tåget.
     he waits on train.DEF
     'He is waiting for the train.'
  b. Vi **hoppas på** bättre tider. (SOB, s.v. *hoppas*)
     we hope on better times
     'We hope for better times.'
  c. Vi hade **inställt oss på** en trevlig utflykt. (SOB, s.v. *inställa sig*)
     we had prepared ourselves on a nice trip
     'We had been expecting a nice trip.'
  d. Vi har **förberett oss på** det här.[44]
     we have prepared ourselves on this
     'We have prepared for this.'
  e. De var mycket **nyfikna på** hennes nye pojkvän. (SOB, s.v. *nyfiken*)
     they were very curious on her new boyfriend
     'They were very curious about her new boyfriend.'
  f. **Titta/lyssna på** det här!
     look/listen on this
     'Look at/listen to this!'
  g. Jag **tror/tvivlar på** det.
     I believe/doubt on it
     'I believe in/doubt it.'

However, further cases such as those in (13f, g) suggest that this is too hasty a conclusion. The Swedish *på* pattern seems to extend much further than the German *auf* pattern, covering the direction of attention in general. Notably, the corresponding German verbs do not occur in the *auf* pattern – *ansehen* 'look (at)' and *anhören* 'listen (to)' both take a direct (accusative) object (cf. DUWB). Thus, there seem to be grounds for concluding that Swedish displays a more general, or schematic, a-construction compared to the German prospective *auf* pattern.

The cases in (14), on the other hand, suggest that Swedish also possesses an *i* 'in' pattern interestingly restricted in its productivity. According to my informants, the pattern only extends to the predicates in (14):

(14) strunta/skita/ge fan i något
     ignore/shit/give devil in something
     'to ignore something/not give a damn about something'

The semantics of this pattern can be loosely characterized as '(aggressively) ignoring proposition Y'. The relevant question here is whether this type of *i* is to be regarded as a pattern yet. Notably, all three predicates express indifference by themselves, so that at least on the basis of the coercion criterion applied above, this type of Swedish PO preposition *i* cannot be considered productive. However, this only serves to make *i* all the more interesting: it might actually be a pattern in the making. Its possible extension to further predicates could be a useful subject of studies conducted on the basis of corpora of present-day Swedish, since such investigations might reveal how originally lexically determined PO preposition patterns acquire the status of a-constructions. To my knowledge, this has hitherto only been hypothesized (cf. Rostila 2005, 2007, 2014, in press). Such an undertaking might even shed light on how a-constructions in general emerge historically – a question that has largely been neglected in CxG studies (but cf. Israel 1996).

I will close this section by outlining the properties of a-constructions in the guise of PO prepositions on the basis of the German prospective *auf* pattern. Like constructions of this type in general, this construction displays two arguments: a subject, or first argument carrying a role that can be informally defined as FUTURE-ORIENTED ENTITY, and an object, or second argument with the role FUTURE EVENT. Notably, the semantic roles expressed by constructions of this type are at an intermediate level of generalization compared to the head-specific participant roles of individual verbs and familiar semantic roles such as AGENT, PATIENT, RECIPIENT, and so on – hence their somewhat clumsy labels. This is in keeping with the low degree of grammaticalization, or generalization, attained by such constructions compared to a-constructions denoting more central relations in human experience like the transitive and ditransitive constructions.[45] In addition to such intermediate-level semantic roles, the arguments of PO constructions carry perspectival roles (Welke 1988, 1994, 2002, Rostila 2007) that essentially amount to profiling differences (cf. Goldberg 1995: 26, 49). Such constellations of roles – two semantic roles chained together, each paired with a perspectival role – are symbolized by the PO preposition alone, the nominative case of their first argument belonging to another construction (cf. Rostila, in press: section 2.3 for details). Hence, the label 'complement constellation' introduced above does not optimally apply to a-constructions based on PO prepositions: such constructions capture the semantics of two complements, but only the form of one.

2.3   From the dominance of complement constellations to head-specific complementation – and back?

To put my overall proposal in Rostila (2007) slightly differently, present-day German is, in a sense, driven by a-constructions, or complement constellations: in order to be linked, verbs are mostly embedded in a-constructions, among them a-constructions in the guise of productive PO prepositions. Such productive patterns have in turn probably emerged diachronically from verb-specific complementation patterns in a grammaticalization process closely resembling the acquisition of a-constructions (Rostila, in press; cf. Tomasello 2003 and Goldberg 2006 for the acquisition process). On the other hand, Nørgård-Sørensen (2010) observes that verbs were flexibly used in various meaningful syntactic patterns in Old Russian, whereas present-day Russian is dominated by verb-centred patterns. Taken together, these findings could mean that a reign of complement constellations may be succeeded by that of complement selection by verbs – or vice versa. If valid, they suggest that languages might vacillate between the two options of a-construction based and verb-centred complementation (cf. Rostila 2014: 112–13 for factors bringing this about).[46] Needless to say, empirical diachronic studies of a broad range of languages are needed before such a cyclic change can be considered a fact. In any case, the empirical verification of the scenario seems a goal worth pursuing, since its existence would suggest that languages might typologically cover a continuum from complement selection by heads to head selection by complement constellations.[47] This in turn might partially explain how widely differing views or uncertainty about the direction of complementation relations comes about: not for the first time in linguistics, discrete categories of description clash with a real-life continuum.

Notes

1. This chapter presents arguments previously published in German in Rostila (2007, 2014) from a new perspective, that of complementation. For the sake of coherence, it is also necessary to recapitulate arguments from Rostila (in press). Minor revisions mostly aiming at greater clarity appear throughout, however, and some new findings are presented. The main *raison d'être* of the chapter is to present a complementation perspective on the results of Rostila (2007, 2014), and to make research reported in German accessible to a wider audience.
2. Cf. Chomsky (1995: 312) for the implementation of these types of selection within the Checking operation of Minimalism.
3. There seems to be considerable confusion regarding this concept: its relation to abstract case is anything but clear, it is sometimes applied to prepositions for which s-selection would be the right tool, and the need for this type of selection often seems to be overlooked. See Rostila (2007: 204–14) for discussion.
4. Cf. Goldberg (1995: 60–6), Stefanowitsch (2008: 247) and Rostila (2007: 179–80, in press: section 2.3) for discussion.
5. Fillmore's case frames were obvious precursors to a-constructions, but in contrast to a-constructions, they were selected by verbs, cf. Fillmore (1968: 29) and Welke (2009: 83). See also Ziem (2014) for the role of case frames as a basis for various present-day CxG concepts.
6. It also has its problems, cf. Müller (2006) and Müller and Wechsler (2014). However, it seems to me that most of the problems pointed out by Müller and Wechsler are due to a rigid computational linguistic approach to language and would not appear nearly as serious on a psychologically more valid view. Moreover, some of the problems might be solved by reconsidering the CxG

description of for example the passive, but this is not a suitable context for such an undertaking. Notably, there is also a lexicalist solution for cases like (1) within CxG, Boas' (e.g. 2003, 2011) mini-constructions. See Rostila (in press: section 3.1) for some arguments why this approach might need back-up from Goldberg-style a-constructions capturing broader generalizations.

7. Many of the verb uses in (1), e.g. the use of *feather* as a verb in a certain technical sense, may actually already be conventionalized. This does not refute the constructional analysis, though: precisely the frequent use of heads in a certain construction may lead to the establishment of new readings.

8. See the list of Sources for the origin of examples drawn from literary works.

9. The term 'prepositional object' is sometimes used to refer to the internal argument of a preposition in general, for instance *the island* in the PP *on the island*. In this chapter, I use the term in a more restricted sense common within German linguistics: a prepositional object is an internal argument of a verb or another predicative head marked as such by a certain preposition (cf. e.g. *refrain from/ conscious of/interested in something*).

10. Also Brinton and Traugott (2005: 123) and Lehmann (2002: 12) view prepositions of this type as an essentially lexically determined phenomenon.

11. Also Müller and Wechsler (2014: 41) point out that variants of CxG working with a-constructions neglect head-specific argument-marking patterns in languages. However, they argue in part on the basis of cases that allow for generalizations – e.g. *warten + auf* in German and *wait + for* in English, cf. section 2.2 below – and therefore are amenable to an account in terms of a-constructions.

12. It is important to note that PO prepositions and the cases governed by them – as a rule either accusative or dative – constitute units: once a predicate head selecting a certain PO preposition has been chosen, the choice of both the preposition and the case have been determined as well.

13. For the sake of clarity, and in the interest of readers less familiar with German and Swedish, I have frequently made use of simple constructed or dictionary examples when the argument concerns basic properties of prepositional objects and clearcut grammaticality judgements. More complex authentic examples from the web and literary sources are used when suitably simple cases could be found, or to illustrate phenomena of borderline character that might be worth a more thorough empirical study. In all examples, glossing (especially in terms of grammatical categories) only extends to the parts relevant for the discussion. To avoid unnecessary details, no segmentation of grammatical morphemes is undertaken; thus for instance *an seinen Fähigkeiten* in (2a) is glossed 'at his.DAT skills', although an analysis like *an sein-en Fähigkeiten* 'at his-DAT skills' would be more to the point.

14. http://www.ldoceonline.com/dictionary/intent_1; 17.06.2014.

15. http://www.macmillandictionary.com/dictionary/british/draw-on; 17.06.2014.

16. Within Chomskyan generative grammar, such cases are termed 'inherent cases'. This term is somewhat misleading, since the choice of case is by no means inherent to the NP, but is governed by the verb. The term 'lexical case' seems to give rise to some degree of confusion, too; see Rostila (2007: 204–14) for discussion.

17. Sigurðsson (2003: 241) proposes that the choice of lexical cases in Icelandic is subject to phonological regularities. If valid and extendable to further languages, such a view would suggest that lexical cases are not lexically determined by the heads governing them, after all, but constitute a rule-based phenomenon. However, pending the discovery of truly general rules of this type (possibly also for PO prepositions), I consider lexical determination the more plausible option,

since it is compatible with the existence of certain phonological regularities in this domain: the frequent use of any phonological rules for the choice of cases and Ps is likely to be conventionalized as features of verb entries.

18. http://www.spiegel.de/politik/ausland/russland-gegen-die-ukraine-historiker-ueber-erinnerung-an-weltkrieg-a-974402.html; 15.6.2014.

19. http://www.rhein-zeitung.de/startseite_artikel,-Kritik-Spielberg-zeigt-Freiheitskampf-zur-Zeit-der-Sklaverei-_arid,39560.html#.U6AzfHZUY3w; 17.06.2014.

20. The most central of such patterns is the German transitive construction signified by the case pair nominative–accusative. See Rostila (2007: 330–41) for arguments for the independent meaningfulness of this pattern.

21. In Rostila (2005, 2007, 2014, in press), I argue that the diachronic source of the semantics of such constructions is the meaning of the heads that previously lexically selected a certain PO preposition. This is in contrast to the traditional view that regards the meaning of the corresponding full lexical P, e.g. *agree with Jane* vs *go with Jane*, as the source of the meaning of a PO preposition (cf. Dürscheid 1999: 12, Zifonun et al. 1997: 1368), if an independent meaning can be discerned at all. Such cases probably represent the diachronically younger layer of PO prepositions, while the productive cases presented in this chapter emerge from a process of grammaticalization whose point of departure is precisely such a full lexical P. See Rostila (in press) for the details of this process, as well as arguments for considering the emergence of such meaningful complementation patterns, and that of a-constructions in general, a case of grammaticalization.

22. In Rostila (2014, in press), I argue that this construction is in fact polysemous, its possibly original branch denoting goal orientation rather than prospectivity, and that there are borderline cases between the two branches that might even belong to both of them, cf. e.g. (7e). The same probably goes for most of the productive PO preposition patterns; see Rostila (in press) for some observations on *über*.

23. http://www.pummeldex.de/; 02.03.2006.

24. http://www.faz.net/aktuell/wissen/mensch-gene/training-fuer-senioren-denksport-macht-neugierig-auf-mehr-11633105.html; 11.05.2013.

25. http://www.spiegel.de/wirtschaft/soziales/schuldengrenze-eine-billion-dollar-muenze-aus-platin-soll-usa-retten-a-875814.html; 05.01.2012.

26. In the case of PO prepositions, this would mean that e.g. *warten* selected a lexical item *auf* with a prospective sense. It is important to note that this differs from the lexical selection of a PO preposition by a head, which is purely idiosyncratic in nature, that is, it is not based on semantics. See Rostila (2004, 2006a, in press) for why assuming ordinary lexical entries and meanings for PO prepositions is a dead end, and why the independent semantics of productive PO prepositions has to be accounted for in terms of a-constructions instead.

27. Not only predicate heads can be inserted into a-constructions based on PO prepositions, but whole predicates as well; see Rostila (2006a: 368–70) for details.

28. I have relied on *Duden Universalwörterbuch* (DUWB) in this respect, in general deeming verb senses not listed in it as testifying to coercion.

29. http://www.spiegel.de/auto/aktuell/0,1518,650453,00.html; 22.09.2009.

30. Example heard on 10 June 2014 in Belm, Germany.

31. http://www.spiegel.de/; 16.12.2010.

32. http://www.spiegel.de/reise/aktuell/0,1518,771125,00.html; 28.06.2011.

33. *An* (+ dative) has been noted earlier as an example of a PO preposition with an independent semantics, cf. Breindl (1989: 39), but to my knowledge an a-construction status as the source of the semantic contribution has not been proposed prior to Rostila (2004, 2007).

34. See Rostila (in press: section 2.3) for a detailed semantic analysis of how verbs can be coerced by a-constructions based on PO prepositions; cf. Michaelis (2004) for the relevant concept of coercion.
35. Rostila (in press) also refutes further counterarguments to an account of productive PO prepositions in terms of a-constructions, most notably arguments based on the homonymy of PO prepositions.
36. http://www.spiegel.de/unispiegel/studium/promovieren-doktortitel-kann-die-jobsuche-erschweren-a-843999.html; 31.8.2012.
37. http://www.spiegel.de/sport/fussball/em-2012-gastgeber-ukraine-droht-in-der-gruppenphase-zu-scheitern-a-837698.html; 12.06.2012.
38. http://www.spiegel.de/; 03.06.2009.
39. http://www.spiegel.de/kultur/musik/0,1518,748296,00.html; 01.03.2011.
40. http://www.spiegel.de/karriere/berufsstart/dieter-lenzen-fordert-master-abschluss-fuer-alle-a-834469.html; 22.05.2012.
41. http://www.spiegel.de/politik/ausland/us-vizepraesident-joe-biden-empfiehlt-schrotflinten-a-884415.html; 20.02.2013.
42. http://www.woche.de/titelthema2.htm; 25.09.2001.
43. Cf. e.g. *rely/depend/reckon on*, which bear a strong resemblance to some prospective *auf* cases, e.g. *sich auf etw. verlassen* 'rely on something', *auf etw. rechnen* 'reckon on something'. Also the prepositions *of, for* and *to* that figure prominently in the generative literature at the cost of other English PO prepositions might profit from an analysis as a-constructions. Compared to e.g. *at* expressing skill, the constructions underlying *of, for* and *to* have only grammaticalized to a higher degree (cf. Rostila 2007: 215).
44. http://www.aftonbladet.se/nyheter/article14901642.ab; 18.06.2014.
45. See Goldberg (1995) for these constructions in English, and Rostila (2007) for the German transitive construction. Rostila (in press) argues for a-constructions as products of grammaticalization.
46. Cf. also Hyvärinen (2000: 189) and Rostila (2009: 109) for similar observations.
47. The nature of the verb-specific patterns involved in the cycle is a further question to be considered. In Rostila (2007), I propose that verb-specific argument marking such as idiosyncratic PO prepositions only involves verb-specific, or participant roles. In other words, such structures would be essentially on a par with the verb islands of child language (cf. Tomasello 2003). However, certain principles of the usage-based model (cf. e.g. Croft and Cruse 2004) suggest that properties of a-constructions such as generalizations like AGENT and PATIENT might attach to individual verbs often embedded in them, leading to the emergence of traditional valency information in lexical entries. This might in turn lead to an erosion of a-constructions in a particular language (cf. Rostila 2014: 113).

Sources

DUWB: *Duden Deutsches Universalwörterbuch*, 7th edn. Dudenverlag, Mannheim/Zurich, 2011.
Kunkel, T.: *Endstufe*. Eichborn, Berlin, 2004.
Nichol, J.: *The Red Line: the Gripping Story of the RAF's Bloodiest Raid on Hitler's Germany*. William Collins, London, 2014.
Olivier, S.: *Jedem das Seine*. Nannen-Verlag, Hamburg, 1961.
Schröter, H.: *Stalingrad. Bis zur letzten Patrone*. Cinema-Verlag, Waiblingen, 1961.
SOB: *Svensk ordbok*. Språkdata, University of Gothenburg and Esselte Ordbok, 1990.

References

Boas, H. C. (2003) *A Constructional Approach to Resultatives* (Stanford: CSLI Publications).

Boas, H. C. (2011) 'Coercion and Leaking Argument Structures in Construction Grammar'. *Linguistics*, 49 (6): 1271–303.

Breindl, E. (1989) *Präpositionalobjekte und Präpositionalobjektsätze im Deutschen* (Tübingen: Niemeyer).

Brinton, L. J. and E. Closs Traugott (2005) *Lexicalization and Language Change* (Cambridge: Cambridge University Press).

Chomsky, N. (1986) *Knowledge of Language. Its Nature, Origin, and Use* (New York: Praeger).

Chomsky, N. (1995) *The Minimalist Program* (Cambridge, Mass.: MIT Press).

Croft, W. (2001) *Radical Construction Grammar: Syntactic Theory in Typological Perspective* (Oxford: Oxford University Press).

Croft, W. and D. A. Cruse (2004) *Cognitive Linguistics* (Cambridge: Cambridge University Press).

Duden (1984) *Grammatik der deutschen Gegenwartssprache*, 4th edn (Mannheim/Vienna/Zurich: Dudenverlag).

Dürscheid, C. (1999) *Die verbalen Kasus des Deutschen. Untersuchungen zur Syntax, Semantik und Perspektive* (Berlin/New York: Walter de Gruyter).

Fillmore, C. J. (1968) 'The Case for Case' in E. Bach and R. T. Harms (eds) *Universals in Linguistic Theory* (New York: Holt, Rinehart and Winston), pp. 1–88.

Goldberg, A. E. (1995) *Constructions. A Construction Grammar Approach to Argument Structure* (Chicago/London: University of Chicago Press).

Goldberg, A. E. (2006) *Constructions at Work. The Nature of Generalization in Language* (Oxford: Oxford University Press).

Goldberg, A. E. and R. Jackendoff (2004) 'The English Resultative as a Family of Constructions'. *Language*, 80 (3): 532–68.

Helbig, G. and W. Schenkel (1982) *Wörterbuch zur Valenz und Distribution deutscher Verben* (Leipzig: VEB Bibliographisches Institut).

Hyvärinen, I. (2000) 'Valenz und Konstruktion'. *Neuphilologische Mitteilungen*, CI: 185–207.

Israel, M. (1996) 'The *Way* Constructions Grow' in A. E. Goldberg (ed.) *Conceptual Structure, Discourse and Language* (Stanford: CSLI Publications), pp. 217–30.

Kay, P. (2005) 'Argument Structure Constructions and the Argument–Adjunct Distinction' in M. Fried and H. C. Boas (eds) *Grammatical Constructions: Back to the Roots* (Amsterdam: John Benjamins), pp. 71–98.

Korhonen, J. (2006) 'Valenzwandel am Beispiel des Deutschen' in V. Ágel et al. (eds) *Dependenz und Valenz. Ein internationales Handbuch der zeitgenössischen Forschung* (Berlin/New York: Walter de Gruyter), pp. 1462–74.

Lehmann, C. (2002) 'New Reflections on Grammaticalization and Lexicalization' in I. Wischer and G. Diewald (eds) *New Reflections on Grammaticalization* (Amsterdam/Philadelphia: John Benjamins), pp. 1–18.

Lerot, J. (1982) 'Die verbregierten Präpositionen in Präpositionalobjekten' in W. Abraham (ed.) *Satzglieder im Deutschen: Vorschläge zur syntaktischen, semantischen und pragmatischen Fundierung* (Tübingen: Narr), pp. 261–91.

Michaelis, L. A. (2004) 'Type Shifting in Construction Grammar: an Integrated Approach to Aspectual Coercion'. *Cognitive Linguistics*, 15 (1): 1–67.

Müller, S. (2006) 'Phrasal or Lexical Constructions?' *Language*, 82(4): 850–83.

Müller, S. and S. M. Wechsler (2014) 'Lexical Approaches to Argument Structure'. *Theoretical Linguistics*, 40 (1–2): 1–76.

Napoli, D. J. (1989) *Predication Theory. A Case Study for Indexing Theory* (Cambridge: Cambridge University Press).

Nørgård-Sørensen, J. (2010) 'What Languages Must Convey: the Construction-Based Syntax of Old Russian'. *Acta Linguistica Hafniensia*, 42 (1): 46–59.

Odijk, J. (1997) 'C-Selection and S-Selection'. *Linguistic Inquiry*, 28 (2): 365–71.

Pesetsky, D. (1982) 'Paths and Categories'. PhD dissertation, MIT.

Rostila, J. (2004) 'Towards a Construction Approach to Grammaticalization in Prepositional Objects' in M. Nenonen (ed.) *Papers from the 30th Finnish Conference of Linguistics* (Joensuu: University of Joensuu), pp. 192–200.

Rostila, J. (2005) 'Zur Grammatikalisierung bei Präpositionalobjekten' in T. Leuschner, T. Mortelmans and S. De Groodt (eds) *Grammatikalisierung im Deutschen* (Berlin/New York: Walter de Gruyter), pp. 135–66.

Rostila, J. (2006a) 'Construction Grammar as a Functionalist Generative Grammar' in P. P. Chruszczewski, M. Garcarz and T. P. Górski (eds) *At the Crossroads of Linguistics Sciences* (Cracow: Tertium), pp. 365–76.

Rostila, J. (2006b) 'Storage as a Way to Grammaticalization'. *Constructions*, 1/2006 (available at: http://www.elanguage.net/journals/index.php/constructions/issue/view/16).

Rostila, J. (2007) *Konstruktionsansätze zur Argumentmarkierung im Deutschen*. PhD dissertation, University of Tampere (Tampere: Tampere University Press; available at: http://urn.fi/urn:isbn:978-951-44-7085-1).

Rostila, J. (2009) 'Review of *Constructional Reorganization*'. *SKY Journal of Linguistics*, 22: 293–300.

Rostila, J. (2014) 'Inventarisierung als Grammatikalisierung: produktive Präpositionalobjekte und andere grammatikalisierte Linking-Muster' in A. Lasch and A. Ziem (eds) *Grammatik als Inventar von Konstruktionen: Sprachwissen im Fokus der Konstruktionsgrammatik* (Berlin: Walter de Gruyter), pp. 97–116.

Rostila, J. (in press) 'Argument Structure Constructions among German Prepositional Objects' in H. C. Boas and A. Ziem (eds) *Constructional Approaches to Syntactic Structures in German* (Berlin/New York: de Gruyter).

Sigurðsson, Halldór Ármann (2003) 'Case: Abstract vs. Morphological' in E. Brandner and Heike Zinsmeister (eds) *New Perspectives on Case Theory* (Stanford: CSLI Publications), pp. 223–68.

Stefanowitsch, A. (2008) 'R-Relationen im Sprachvergleich: die Direkte-Rede-Konstruktion im Englischen und Deutschen' in A. Stefanowitsch and K. Fischer (eds) *Konstruktionsgrammatik II: Von der Konstruktion zur Grammatik* (Tübingen: Stauffenburg), pp. 247–61.

Tomasello, M. (2003) *Constructing a Language. A Usage-Based Theory of Language Acquisition* (Cambridge, Mass./London: Harvard University Press).

Welke, K. (1988) *Einführung in die Valenz- und Kasustheorie* (Leipzig: VEB Bibliographisches Institut).

Welke, K. (1994) 'Thematische Relationen. Sind thematische Relationen semantisch, syntaktisch oder/und pragmatisch zu definieren?' *Deutsche Sprache*, 22 (1): 1–18.

Welke, K. (2002) *Deutsche Syntax funktional. Perspektiviertheit syntaktischer Strukturen* (Tübingen: Stauffenburg).

Welke, K. (2009) 'Konstruktionsvererbung, Valenzvererbung und die Reichweite von Konstruktionen'. *Zeitschrift für germanistische Linguistik*, 37(3): 514–43.

Williams, E. (1980) 'Predication'. *Linguistic Inquiry*, 11(1): 203–38.

Ziem, A. (2014) 'Von der Kasusgrammatik zum FrameNet: Frames, Konstruktionen und die Idee eines Konstruktikons' in A. Lasch and A. Ziem (eds) *Grammatik als Inventar von Konstruktionen: Sprachwissen im Fokus der Konstruktionsgrammatik* (Berlin: Walter de Gruyter), pp. 263–90.

Zifonun, G., L. Hoffmann, B. Strecker et al. (1997) *Grammatik der deutschen Sprache* (Berlin/New York: Walter de Gruyter).

3
A Cross-Linguistic Perspective on Complementation in the *Tough* Construction

Jukka Havu and Mikko Höglund
University of Tampere

3.1 Introduction

This chapter presents an overview of the complementation and other features of the so-called *tough* construction (TC) in a cross-linguistic perspective. The TC typically has an adjectival predicate which is complemented by an infinitive clause or a similar form. It is an interesting construction in that its complement clause has a 'gap' in the object position, whose interpretation is found in the matrix clause. Examples of the TC in English, Spanish and Finnish are provided in (1–3):

(1) This book is easy to read.
(2) Este libro es fácil de leer.
(3) a. Tämä   kirja   on   helppo   lukea.
       This.NOM book.NOM be.3SG easy.NOM read.INF
    b. Tä-tä   kirja-a   on   helppo   lukea.
       This-PART book-PART be.3SG easy.NOM read.INF

All three languages belong to different language families representing Germanic and Romance (both Indo-European) and Finnic (Uralic) languages, and this gives the research cross-linguistic depth and relevance.

In a cross-linguistic study, different levels of description have to be taken into consideration: the syntactic, semantic and pragmatic levels (Dik 1978: 13). In other words, we have to consider the form, meaning and function of the entities we are discussing. In this chapter, we are advocating a combined definition of the TC, which covers all three levels. Firstly, syntactically the TC in each language has to have an adjective[1] which is complemented by a verb or a verb phrase. The specific type of the verb complement is left unspecified, since there is some variation in different languages. Additionally, the VP has to have a missing element, usually an object, whose interpretation is found in the matrix clause. Secondly, this syntactic requirement should entail a semantic link between the three concepts – the adjective modifies the process indicated by the verb, and this combination of the adjective and the verb in turn characterizes a nominal entity, the 'missing' object, found in the matrix clause. Lastly, the function of the TC is a direct corollary of the syntax of the 'missing' object: by having the notional object element in the matrix clause, it receives a more prominent pragmatic status.

The present study focuses mainly on English, Spanish and Finnish, but examples from other languages are provided as well. The TC in English has been studied in some great detail in the generative framework (e.g. Chomsky 1964, 1970, Rosenbaum 1967, Ross 1967, Postal 1971, Lasnik and Fiengo 1974, Chae 1992), and more recently by, for instance, Langacker (1999), Fischer et al. (2000), Chung (2001), Vosberg (2011) and Höglund (2014b). Reider (1993) and Bosque (1999) have provided accounts of the TC in Spanish, but we are not aware of any works discussing the TC in Finnish.

In this chapter, the TC in these three languages will be investigated from different perspectives. In section 3.2, an overview of the TC is provided with a discussion of the structure consisting of the *tough* adjective and its complement, and the syntactic position of the structure. In section 3.3, the TC complementation systems and the different types of TC complements occurring in the three languages will be discussed. Section 3.4 investigates the conditions under which the complement in the TC can be omitted altogether, which adjectives usually occur in the TC across languages, and how different adjectives affect the interpretation of the construction. Section 3.5 concludes the chapter. In order to illustrate and substantiate our claims, we present authentic language material from corpora and Internet sources. The corpora used include the CLMETEV, CEAL,[2] BNC, COCA, COHA, CORPES XXI, CREA and Corpus del Español.

3.2 *Tough* construction: an overview

Prototypically the TC consists of a combination of an adjective and an infinitival verb, and this combination predicates something about an entity usually found in the subject position in the matrix clause. Further, the adjective usually denotes the degree of difficulty or pleasantness (Langacker 1999: 352). The most frequent adjectives in the TC in English are *difficult, easy* and *hard* (Höglund 2014b), and the translation equivalents of these are the most common in Spanish and Finnish as well. As can be seen in Table 3.1, occasionally even NPs can occur in the construction when they convey a sense of a degree of difficulty or pleasantness. In Finnish NPs are also possible in the TC, and in Spanish this kind of construction is infrequent and restricted to words like *un placer, una tristeza, un horror,* and so on.

In the TC, the scope of the adjective reaches both the verb in the complement clause and the entity which is being described.

(4) John is difficult to please.

Table 3.1   Division of typical TC adjectives into semantic fields

	Positive	Negative
Difficulty	*easy, simple, a breeze*	*difficult, hard, impossible, tough*
Pleasantness	*pleasant, enjoyable, a joy, a pleasure*	*unpleasant, unenjoyable, disagreeable, a bitch*

Example (4) does not mean that John is difficult (i.e. a difficult person), but that John is difficult in relation to someone trying to please him. An appropriate paraphrase would be 'to please John is difficult'.

The TC is a construction with a number of peculiar features, and because of that it is perhaps somewhat surprising to encounter it across languages and even language families. The most striking feature is that the TC has a passive-like meaning without any passive syntax:

(5) [The letter]$_{PAT}$ was easy to write.

The NP *The letter*, which occurs in the subject position, is the understood object of the verb *write* in the lower clause and has the semantic role of patient. This type of behaviour, that is, a subject with a patient role, is typical of passive constructions, for example, but in passive constructions there is a syntactic signal which indicates that we are dealing with a passive form. In English, the verb is in the past participle form and the auxiliary *be* is inserted:

(6) Someone wrote [the letter]$_{PAT}$ → [The letter]$_{PAT}$ was written.

In the TC the syntax does not differ from active clauses which have the active meaning such as the control construction (7):

(7) [Dave]$_{AGT}$ is eager to please.

From this we can infer that it must be the semantics of the adjectival predicate that renders the passive-like meaning. In the following sections, among other matters, we will investigate whether the passive meaning in different languages is conveyed by the semantics of the adjective alone, or whether there are syntactic clues as well.

Nanni (1980) has proposed a somewhat different analysis of the TC. She argues that the Adj + *to* + infinitive sequence found in the TC is best treated as a complex adjective. In this analysis the sequence is thought to have a lexical status and it would be considered a predicative to the subject nominal. She argues that the sequence behaves syntactically like individual adjectives:

(8) a. John is considered to be [clever].
    b. John is considered to be [easy to please].

(9) a. How [clever] do you think John is?
   b. How [easy to please] do you think John is?

The Adj + *to* + infinitive sequence can even have the attributive function:

(10) a. This is an easy-to-use interface.
   b. John is an easy-to-please person.

It seems that there are grounds for the complex adjective analysis in English, whereas in Spanish, due to a different morphosyntactic structure, similar constructions are not found.

In Finnish, which is a morphologically rich language, a change from predicative to attributive function would result in a compound adjective with a derivational adjectival suffix:

(11) a. Tä-tä   kone-tta   on   helppo käyttää.
      This-PART machine-PART be.3SG easy   use.INF

   b. Tämä   on   helppo-käyttö-inen kone.
      This.NOM be.3SG easy-use-ADJSUF   machine.

In fact, the Finnish example provides cross-linguistic cognitive evidence for Nanni's claim. In the attributive position the concept 'easy to use' is also syntactically a complex adjective, that is, a conceptual whole. However, in Finnish this type of derivation is restricted only to certain verbs that can take the derivational suffix, and it seems that often these are the same verbs that in English more naturally occur as parts of the complex adjective in the attributive position.

(12) a. An easy-to-understand plan.
   b. Helppotajuinen suunnitelma.

(13) a. An easy-to-read book.
   b. Helppolukuinen kirja.

(14) a. An easy-to-explain concept.
   b. ? Helpposelitteinen konsepti.

(15) a. ? An easy-to-write letter.
   b. * Helppokirjoitteinen kirje.

The scope of verbs that in Finnish can take the derivational suffix is quite restricted, and thus the scope of *tough*-related constructions occurring in the attributive position is more limited than in English. It seems that in Finnish only some verbs, perhaps the ones that have been used frequently in the past in this construction, have acquired the derivational morphology. In English there are no morphosyntactic restrictions on the Adj + *to* + infinitive sequence in attributive position, and the only factor delimiting the scope would be convention.

As Givón (1985: 202) argues in his proximity principle, if two concepts are related semantically or functionally, they are probably also close together in the code syntactically. This is exactly the case in the TC. The adjective and the verbal complement together form a unit, a concept that expresses a single proposition. This is seen in the adjacency of the elements, and regarding the attributive function also in the Finnish compound form, and in English in the tendency to use hyphens between the three elements.

3.3   TC and complementation

3.3.1   TC in English

In English, the core of the TC is roughly of the form Adj + *to* + infinitive (*easy to write, difficult to please*). That is, the adjective is complemented by a *to*-infinitive clause. There are also other ways of expressing the same proposition as the TC:

> (16) a. It was easy to write the letter.
> b. To write the letter was easy.
> c. ? The letter wrote easily.

Example (16c) with the adverbial form is rare and only natural in certain contexts, but the first two – extraposition and infinitive subject – are fairly productive, albeit the extraposition construction is by far the more frequent one. Even though these constructions express more or less the same proposition as the TC, all these constructions have a different pragmatic function and they are used in different contexts and for different purposes.

The TC has a *to*-infinitive complement, which is the standard in present-day English. However, there is an alternative complementation pattern that used to occur alongside the *to*-infinitive:

> (17) The letter was easy to be written.

In this construction, the complement is a passive infinitive with the auxiliary *be* and the past participle form of the main verb. The passive infinitive was first observed in the TC in the fifteenth century (Van Der Wurff 1990, Fischer et al. 2000), and it was used up until the late nineteenth century. Höglund (2014b) investigated the use of the TC and the passive variant (TCpass) in British and American English from the early eighteenth century to present-day English. In British English, the two constructions were still used in approximately similar numbers in the early 1700s, but at that time the TC began to spread at the expense of the TCpass. A similar development took place in American English, although it started somewhat later. Figure 3.1 illustrates the development in the two varieties of English.

As shown in Figure 3.1, the decline of the TCpass began around the mid-1700s, and by the turn of the twentieth century the TCpass was very rare. In present-day English only sporadic examples are found in the BNC and COCA. Figure 3.2 illustrates, with data from COHA, the development of the TCpass in American English from 1810 to the present day and confirms the declining trend of the TCpass.

However, in one particular environment in present-day English the TCpass is still used frequently. That is with non-prototypical TC adjectives that can also occur in a Control construction:

(18) a. John is ready to play. (Control)
     b. The game is ready to play. (TC)

In (18a), the subject is the agent, and in (18b) the subject is the patient, that is, the notional object of the infinitival verb. The fact that adjectives

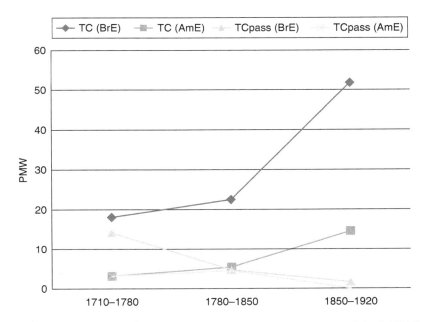

Figure 3.1   Development of the TC and TCpass in BrE (CLMETEV) and AmE (CEAL)

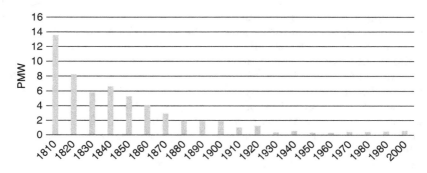

Figure 3.2   Development of the TCpass in American English (COHA)[3]

such as *ready* can occur in both constructions makes sentences like (19) ambiguous:

(19) The chicken is ready to eat.

In these types of environments, the TCpass is still used in present-day English to convey the TC sense if there is the slightest chance of misunderstanding. Höglund (2014a) observed that when *ready* is complemented by a *to*-infinitive, and the TC meaning is meant to be conveyed, both the TC and TCpass are used, and the TCpass is used a little more frequently than the TC. Moreover, the TCpass is the exclusive choice in sentences in which the subject is [+HUMAN].

In summary, historically there are two different complementation patterns in the TC – the active and the passive infinitive. The passive infinitive appeared in the fifteenth century, and after a fairly short-lived run was almost completely ousted by the active infinitive by the twentieth century. In present-day English the passive occurs only sporadically with prototypical TC adjectives. However, the passive infinitive has kept its position as an interchangeable variant with the active with ambiguous adjectives such as *ready* and *fit*, and it is even the preferred option when the subject is human.

3.3.2   TC in Spanish

The *tough* construction in Spanish is of the form *Este libro es fácil de leer* 'this book is easy to read', in which the *tough* adjective is complemented by the preposition *de* and an infinitival form of the verb. Like in English, the Spanish TC is related to other constructions from a cognitive and semantic point of view but is syntactically different from them:

(20) a. Es fácil leer este libro.   'it is easy to read this book'
     b. Leer este libro es fácil.   'to read this book is easy'
     c. Este libro se lee fácilmente. 'this book reads easily'

The aforementioned constructions give roughly the same semantic information as the TC, but they are syntactically quite different from it. In (20a) and (20b), the patient (*libro* 'book') is the direct object of the verb, which in itself constitutes a substantial difference between these sentences and the *tough* construction. In (20c), it is not altogether clear whether it is a case of a reflexive verb or of a pronominal passive. In case of a pronominal passive (where *se* might be considered the marker of an impersonal subject), the patient *este libro* is the direct object of the verb, whereas in the case of a reflexive verb *este libro* is the subject and thus comes conceptually close to the *tough* construction.[4]

Bosque (1999) gives a thorough analysis of the *tough* construction in Spanish. He divides the adjectives that enter this construction into different groups according to their meaning and also gives examples of the construction in the earlier stages of the language. He makes the following classification of the adjectives compatible with the *tough* construction: (a) adjectives denoting possibility, facility or difficulty; (b) adjectives that are not directly related to facility or difficulty but acquire this property in the *tough* construction (e.g. *duro de sobrellevar* 'hard to bear'); (c) adjectives denoting positive or negative sensations (e.g. *este texto es interesante de leer* 'this text is interesting to read'); (d) a heterogeneous group of adjectives, some of them expressing worthiness, estimation, relevance and frequency, but only a few adjectives belong to this group (e.g. *estas cuestiones son importantes de recordar* 'these questions are important to recall').

As in English, there is also a passive infinitive in Spanish: *Este libro es fácil de ser leído* 'This book is easy to be read'. However, this construction, though perfectly grammatical, is not very often used with the exception of cases where the agent is explicitly expressed, like in *El libro es fácil de ser leído por cualquier persona* 'The book is easy to be read by anybody'.

In the Spanish *tough* construction, the infinitival complement is introduced by the preposition *de*. However, the preposition *de* does not have a similar role of a complementizer as *to* has in English. In Romance languages in general (with the exception of Romanian, see below), the infinitive is either linked directly to the preceding element (a noun, an adjective or a verb) without a complementizer, introduced by a semantically empty preposition (in most cases the etymological counterparts of the Latin prepositions *ad* or *de*) or connected with a preposition governed by the conjugated verb. These cases are exemplified by the following pairs of constructions:

(21) a. *Prefiero leer este libro* vs *Prefiero este libro.*
 'I prefer to read this book' vs 'I prefer this book.'
 b. *Aprendo a hablar español* vs *Aprendo español.*
 'I learn to speak Spanish' vs 'I learn Spanish.'
 c. *Sueño con viajar a Chile* vs *Sueño con un viaje a Chile.*
 'I dream of travelling to Chile' vs 'I dream of a trip to Chile.'

Moreover, these constructions are subject to frequent diachronic and regional variation in Spanish as in other Romance languages as well.

The preposition *de* of the Spanish *tough* construction is a semantically empty relational element, but like in other Romance languages, it marks clearly the difference between the *tough* construction (*Este libro es fácil de leer* 'This book is easy to read', where the infinitive is introduced by the preposition *de*) and the related impersonal structure of the type *Es fácil leer este libro* 'It is easy to read this book', where the infinitive is not preceded by a preposition. In French, the corresponding constructions would be *Il est facile de lire ce livre* vs *Ce livre est facile à lire*, and in Italian, *È facile leggere questo libro* vs *Questo libro è facile da leggere*.

An interesting case is Romanian, where the *tough* construction appears in a very different syntactic form. In Romanian, like in most Balkan languages, the infinitive is not widely used.[5] In the *tough* construction, the supine form, introduced by the preposition *de,* is used instead of the infinitive to express the verbal complement, and the qualifying element is an invariable adverbial form of the adjective:

(22) a. Carte-a   aceasta e uşor   de   citit.
      Book-DEF this   is easy(ADV) PREP read.SUP
      'This book is easy to read.'

   b. Cărţi-le   acestea sunt uşor   de   citit.
      Books-DEF these   are   easy(ADV) PREP read.SUP
      'These books are easy to read.'

As we can see, most Romance languages share similar structures for expressing the *tough* construction. The differences concern mainly the use and form of prepositions. The Romanian construction, however, shows that identical semantic information can be rendered by very different syntactic structures even within closely related languages.

3.3.3   TC in Finnish

In English and Spanish the *tough* constructions follow more or less the same pattern. In both languages, the patient of the action expressed by the infinitive is the syntactic subject of the sentence. The third language analysed in this study is Finnish, a language in many ways quite different from the other two. Finnish has a rich inflectional morphology with 15 nominal cases and a rather complicated verbal conjugation (especially the nominal forms of the verb with three infinitives and four participles are a rather intricate subsystem). One of the complexities of the Finnish language is the case of the direct object, and although within the scope of this study it is not possible to give a thorough description of the system; a brief outline of its main syntactic and semantic properties is necessary in order to grasp the *tough* construction in Finnish.

The direct object has two categories, Total Object (TO) and Partial Object (PO). The TO has three morphological realizations: nominative, genitive and accusative (the accusative is used only with personal pronouns and the interrogative pronoun *kuka* 'who'). The case of the PO is systematically partitive. The choice between the TO and PO depends on the properties of the verb. Some verbs systematically take the TO, some the PO, and with some verbs there is variation which depends on aspectual factors. With accomplishment verbs,[6] the alternation of the TO and PO produces an aspectual difference between a perfective (23a) and an imperfective (23b) interpretation:

(23) a. Hän   luk-i   kirja-n. (TO)
         she/he read-PRET.3SG book-GEN
         'S/he read a/the book.'

     b. Hän   luk-i   kirja-a. (PO)
         she/he read-PRET.3SG book-PART
         'S/he was reading a/the book.'

With activity verbs and atelic momentaneous verbs the object case is partitive (24a, atelic) if there is no secondary resultative expression (24b, telic):

(24) a. Hän   työn-si   lastenvaunu-ja. (PO)
         she/he push-PRET.3SG pram-PART.PL
         'S/he was pushing the pram.'

     b. Hän   työn-si   lastenvaunu-t (TO) piha-lle.
         she/he push-PRET.3SG pram-NOM.PL   yard-ALL
         'S/he pushed the pram to the yard.'

With state verbs no alternation is possible. The direct object is either a TO or PO, according to the meaning of the verb (e.g. verbs of emotion normally take the PO, verbs of knowledge and quasi-resultative verbs take the TO).

In negative sentences, the direct object systematically takes the PO (even with verbs that otherwise always take the TO):

(25) a. Lue-n   kirja-n. (TO)
         read-1SG book-GEN
         'I shall read the book.'

     b. E-n   lue   kirja-a. (PO)
         NEG-1SG read.CNG book-PART
         'I don't read/shall not read the book.'

Moreover, when the direct object is in the plural form, the TO (always in the nominative form in the plural) is interpreted like a definite, and the PO like an indefinite expression:

(26) a. Lue-n   kirja-t. (TO)
read-1SG book-NOM.PL
'I shall read the books.'

b. Lue-n   kirjo-ja. (PO)
read-1SG book-PART.PL
'I read/am reading/shall read/shall be reading some books.'

Regarding complementation, the Finnish version of the *tough* construction behaves more or less like the English and Spanish TC. A notable difference in syntax is that Finnish does not have a complementizer between the adjective and the infinitive form. The adjective is directly complemented by an (active) infinitive form which has a passive interpretation and its 'missing' subject is located in the matrix clause. The Finnish passive voice, sometimes called the fourth person, is different from the Germanic passive and there is no passive infinitive form. So regarding complementation the Finnish TC is not very interesting as the complement is invariably the infinitive form. In other respects the Finnish TC behaves somewhat differently from what we have seen above in English and Spanish *tough* constructions. At first sight, the element that occupies the same position as the syntactic subject in English and Spanish constructions seems to behave morphologically like a direct object:

(27) a. Tämä   kirja (TO) on   helppo   lukea.
this.NOM book.NOM be.3SG easy.NOM read.INF
'This book is easy to read.'

b. Tä-tä   kirja-a (PO) on   helppo   lukea.
this-PART book-PART be.3SG easy.NOM read.INF
'This book is easy to read.'

In (27a) the subject is in the nominative case, which can be the case of the TO, but also the case of a typical subject. In this sense (27a) does not tell much about the status of this element, but in (27b) the partitive case reveals that the syntactic subject behaves morphologically like an object. This would also suggest that in (27a) the syntactic subject is actually a TO. Further, the forms seem to be the exact counterparts of the impersonal construction, in which the patient of the action also has the syntactic status of a direct object:

(28) a. On   helppo   lukea   tämä   kirja. (TO)
be.3SG easy.NOM read.INF this.NOM book.NOM
'It is easy to read this book.' (TO; the whole book)

b. On   helppo   lukea   tä-tä   kirja-a (PO)
be.3SG easy.NOM read.INF this-PART book-PART
'It is easy to read this book.' (PO; progressive, reading still ongoing)

However, the Finnish *tough* construction is slightly more complicated. In a typical TC, when the lexical element in the subject position is in the plural, the verb and the adjective agree in number with the subject in the case of a perfective reading (TO) but not in the case of an imperfective reading (PO):[7]

(29) a. Nämä   kirja-t (TO)   o-vat   helppo-ja   lukea.
     this.NOM.PL book-NOM.PL be-3PL easy-PART.PL read.INF
     'These books are easy to read.'

  b. Näitä   kirjo-ja (PO)   on   helppo   lukea.
     this.PART.PL book-PART.PL be.3SG easy.NOM.SG read.INF
     'These books are easy to read.'

As can be seen in (29b), even though the subject is plural, the copula and the adjective are singular when we have an imperfective meaning.

As stated above and demonstrated in (25b), in negated sentences the direct object is always in the partitive case. However, in negated TCs, the element in the subject position, in spite of being the patient of the action expressed by the verb, normally takes the nominative form:

(30) Tämä   kirja   ei   ole   helppo   lukea.
     this.NOM book.NOM NEG.3SG be.CNG easy.NOM read.INF
     'This book is not easy to read.'

However, it is also possible to use the partitive form in these kinds of negated sentences:

(31) Tä-tä   kirja-a   ei   ole   helppo   lukea.
     this-PART book-PART NEG.3SG be.CNG easy.NOM read.INF
     'This book is not easy to read.'

The sentence where the patient is in the partitive form (31) conveys an imperfective meaning, but it is not altogether clear whether it can also have the same meaning as (30) in which the reading is perfective. According to most native informants, a perfective reading is possible in (31) but it is contextually or conversationally determined. However, with verbs that normally do not have the TO/PO variation and invariably take the TO, such as *tietää* 'know', the partitive case in the negated TC is the only option, and the nominative TO is not possible as in (30).

The Finnish aspectual system (and, consequently, the *tough* construction) is quite complicated because of the heterogeneous nature and intricate interaction of its constitutive elements. The *tough* construction in Finnish can be compared with other quite frequent structures, where the subject is rather a topicalized element and cannot be defined morphologically:

(32) Aki-lla   on   auto.
     Aki-ADE be.3SG car.NOM
     'Aki has a car.'

(33) Laps-ia   leikkii   piha-lla.
     child-PART.PL play.3SG yard-ADE
     'Some children play in the yard.'

(34) Sinun   täytyy   mennä koti-in.
     you.GEN must.3SG go.INF home-ILL
     'You must go home.'

(35) Häne-stä tuntuu   paha-lta.
     s/he-ELA feel.3SG bad-ABL
     'S/he feels bad.'

In (32–35) the initial NPs all have different cases. It is thus unclear whether they can be called subjects or whether they are rather just unspecified topicalized phrases.

We have seen that the *tough* construction in Finnish is somewhat different from the corresponding constructions in English and Spanish, mostly because of the variation in the case of the direct object. When the patient of the action is considered from a perfective viewpoint as being totally affected or effectuated, it has the syntactic status of a subject. This is corroborated by the fact that the verb is inflected for singular or plural and, moreover, it does not necessarily take the partitive form in negated sentences (see example 30). On the other hand, when there is an imperfective reading, the patient of the action takes the partitive form. One might argue that the partitive is not a structural case at all and that its use is determined by factors like lexical and grammatical aspect, quantification, negation, and so on (see Mahieu 2007). This would mean that the verbs that systematically take a partitive object, like state verbs expressing emotions (*miellyttää* 'to please', *rakastaa* 'to love', *vihata* 'to hate', etc.), would be incompatible with the traditional syntactic definition of the *tough* construction and that in this sense there is no Finnish counterpart of the English sentence 'John is tough to please'. From a cognitive point of view, however, the following sentence would undoubtedly be interpreted in the same way as the English sentence:

(36) John-ia   on   vaikea miellyttää.
     John-PART be.3SG tough please.INF
     'John is tough to please.'

To sum up what has been said about the Finnish variant of the *tough* construction we can observe that the complexity of its form is due to the rich morphology of the language and in particular to the fact that certain cognitive categories, like the opposition between perfective and imperfective interpretation of a sentence, are often overtly expressed by the case of the direct object. In consequence, it is only when the verb is compatible with a TO case that the typical *tough* construction (the subject of the sentence being the patient of the action) is possible. When the patient of the action is in the PO case (this includes the verbs that admit both object cases TO and PO, albeit with different meanings, and the verbs that are compatible only with the partitive object), the patient of the action cannot be considered to be the subject of the sentence. These constructions can be related to numerous other structures where the subject is not determined morphologically but rather by its semantics and by its topicalized position in the sentence.

The last remark on the Finnish TC pertains to one of the topics of the next section: the omissibility of the complement. When the patient of the action is in the partitive form, the complement cannot be left out:

(37) a. Tämä   kirja   on   helppo.
        this.NOM book.NOM be.3SG easy
        'This book is easy.'

    b. *Tä-tä   kirja-a   on   helppo.
        this-PART book-PART be.3SG easy
        'This book is easy.'

In Finnish, the inflected nominal requires a verb to assign its case, and in the absence of such a verb, the partitive topic is not allowed, rendering (37b) ungrammatical.

3.4 Relationships between elements in the TC and the possibility of omitting the complement

According to Reider (1993: 161), the *tough* construction in Spanish is not as frequent as in English, because, according to him, 'the adjectives that govern the *tough* construction are relatively few'. In order to test this fact, Reider proceeds to a more comprehensive analysis of the *tough* construction in Spanish by carrying out a survey with 16 native speakers (8 from Spain and 8 from Latin America). The results give a surprisingly heterogeneous view of the construction in Spanish and, moreover, the judgements of some of the informants appear quite astonishing for most native speakers. For instance, *alcanzable*, one of the items in the survey, is not accepted in the TC by speakers from Spain, but three Latin American speakers find it acceptable in the

TC. *Alcanzable* in the TC does not seem to be widely used (non-existent in large corpora like CORPES XXI and CREA); the only hit found by Google is from a Colombian site (38):

(38)   Para iniciar nuestro negocio contamos con un préstamo de $500.000, el cual es alcanzable de pagar, debido a la producción de galletas.[8]
'In order to launch our business we count on a loan of $500.000, which is possible to pay, due to the production of biscuits.'

In the Spanish corpora there are no occurrences of the negative *inalcanzable* as a constitutive element of the *tough* construction. Google finds a few hits, such as (39):

(39)   Cómo reparar el error 'Red inalcanzable de resolver' en CentOS[9]
'How to fix the error "Net impossible to resolve" in CentOS'

The above-mentioned phenomenon illustrates the linguistic variation in the Spanish-speaking world; it is very probable that the verb *alcanzar* and the derived adjectives *alcanzable* and *inalcanzable* have slightly different meanings in Colombian Spanish compared with other varieties of Spanish.

One of the main problems in Reider's analysis is the fact that he seems to consider the adjectives under study as having a global meaning. This is clearly not the case.[10] He (1993: 164) states, commenting on Zierer's (1974) definition of *tough* adjectives, that Zierer's analysis 'incorrectly predicts that *lento* and *rápido* can govern the *tough* construction'. While this is certainly true with nouns like *canción* 'song', it is not true with nouns that are construed with affected or effectuated objects:

(40)   *Esta canción es lenta de tocar.
'This song is slow to play.'

(41)   Esta torta es rápida de preparar.
'This cake is quick to prepare.'

(42)   V es el sensacional cepillo que [...] desenreda con solo una pasada. EURO V es sumamente fácil y rápido de usar. (CORPES XXI, 3 de marzo de 2014)
'V is the sensational brush that [...] disentangles with only one sweep. EURO V is extremely easy and quick to use.'

In English and Finnish the same applies to *fast/nopea* and *slow/hidas* – they only occur with verbs that entail a progressive process in which the object somehow is affected or effectuated. In order to make a comprehensive survey of the *tough* construction in Spanish (and in any language), it is necessary to take into consideration the compatibility of the adjective with the other elements of the proposition.

Reider's survey highlights the differences between Spanish and Latin American speakers of Spanish, but with only 16 subjects, the survey is not broad enough to make any definite judgements about the TC in Spanish. In order to give a complete coverage of the functions and use of the *tough* construction in Spanish it is necessary to consult large corpora that include material from all Spanish-speaking countries. Only in this way can we obtain a clearer view of the prototypical properties of the *tough* construction in Spanish. However, this type of large-scale study is beyond the scope of the present chapter.

One of the most important issues when studying the *tough* construction is to establish the cognitive relationship of the adjective with the other elements of the proposition. The adjective can potentially relate to the syntactic subject of the construction or to the action expressed by the infinitive. According to Langacker (1999: 66), 'it is only by engaging in some process [...] that an individual can be located on a scale [of, for instance, difficulty]'. It then depends on the saliency of the process whether it can be expressed explicitly (with a verb). Consider the examples in (43):

(43) a. The book is blue.
      b. Chess is easy.

(43′) a. ?? The book is blue to look at.
       b. Chess is easy to play.

With adjectives like *blue*, even though in principle there is a process connected to the adjective (someone has to look at the book), we perceive them as innate or inherent properties, and that is why the explicitly mentioned process renders (43′a) unnatural. However, with *tough* adjectives the process is very salient and an integral part of the proposition. That is why the explicit mention of the process in (43′b) is natural and perhaps expected. Sometimes the explicitly expressed process is even obligatory with *tough* adjectives, and this is further discussed below.

According to Bosque (1999: 264–9), there are 'relational preferences' which are contained in the lexicon and which are not based solely on discursive or pragmatic factors. This means that there are prototypical relations between a lexical element and its complements. For instance, whereas *camino* 'road, track' may be difficult to find or difficult to describe, *camino difícil* is by default *camino difícil de recorrer*, which means 'a road difficult to travel' (Bosque 1999: 267).[11] The relational preferences explain in certain cases the possibility of omitting the complement. For example, *un libro fácil* 'an easy book' is most naturally interpreted as *un libro fácil de leer/comprender* 'a book easy to read/understand'. This seems to be possible when the relational preferences are encoded in the mental lexicon and there is a prototypical process associated with the notional object. If this is not the case, the presence of the complement is obligatory. For instance, in *una mesa fácil* 'an easy table', *mesa* has no prototypical process associated with it and thus the sentence has no spontaneous interpretation.[12] Langacker (1999: 340) illustrates this point well with his example *Wombats are easy*. This is a case in which the complement is necessary (cf. Langacker 1984: 183–4). Without any context the sentence would be nonsensical, or at least highly ambiguous, and an average person could not decipher the meaning. However, in the proper context such as in a marsupial washing facility the correct interpretation would be instantly available.

Some adjectives that occur in the *tough* construction behave somewhat differently than prototypical *tough* adjectives. Let us take the adjective *rápido* 'quick, fast' as an example. First of all, *rápido* is not very frequently used in impersonal constructions of the type *ser* + adj. + inf. In CORPES XXI there are only two occurrences of this kind of an expression with the adjective *rápido*:

> (44) a. Le tapan la boca con cinta adhesiva porque es rápido hacerlo y porque le dolerá al serle retirada.
> 'They cover the mouth with tape, because it is fast to do it and because it hurts when taken off.'
>
> b. Encontrar lo que estamos buscando es rápido.
> 'To find what we are looking for is fast.'

The difference between adjectives like *fácil* and those like *rápido* becomes even clearer when we compare their compatibility with the impersonal construction *ser* + adj. + completive clause. Whereas *fácil* is quite naturally used in these kinds of constructions, albeit with a slight change of meaning, *rápido* is not:

> (45) a. Es fácil que uno se equivoque al intentar descifrar el texto.
> 'It is easy to make a mistake when trying to decipher the text.'
>
> b. ?? Es rápido que se prepare una tarta de fresas.
> 'It is fast that one makes a strawberry cake.'

This means that the adjective *rápido* practically never has a propositional scope. Its main function is to qualify a noun (*una melodía rápida* 'a quick melody') or an action (*tocar rápido/rápidamente una melodía* 'to quickly play a melody').[13] When referring to a noun, it describes the inherent properties of the entity (*una melodía rápida* 'a quick melody') or its potential qualities (*un coche rápido* 'a fast car'). In these cases with the explicit infinitive complement the structure has a very high level of ungrammaticality:[14]

(46) a. ?? Es una melodía rápida de tocar.
'It is a melody quick to play.'

b. ?? Es un coche rápido de conducir.
'It is a car fast to drive.'

When *rápido* refers to the process expressed by the verb, the infinitive complement is obligatory:

(47) a. ?? La papilla es rápida.
'Porridge is fast.'

b. [...] la mayoría de madres mencionaron que la papilla les había ayudado en su trabajo cotidiano, generalmente porque era 'rápida y fácil de preparar', 'es instantánea en su preparación',
'[...] most of the mothers mentioned that the porridge had helped them in their everyday work, mostly because it was "fast and easy to prepare", "its preparation is instantaneous"'. (Creed-Kanashiro et al. 2007: 71)

(48) a. ?? El análisis es rápido.
'The analysis is quick.'

b. El análisis, con una especificidad de un 90%, es muy sencillo y rápido de realizar con lo que puede llevarse a cabo, incluso, en atención primaria. (CREA)
'The analysis, with an accuracy of around 90 per cent, is very simple and quick to make and can thus be carried out during the primary health care.'

(49) a. ?? Este tipo de fuego es rápido.
'This type of fire is quick.'

b. Este tipo de fuego es muy rápido de hacer y da buenos resultados. (CREA)
'This type of fire is very quick to make and gives good results.'

It seems, then, that the difference between adjectives like *fácil* and *difícil*, on one hand, and *rápido* and *lento*, on the other, is the fact that the former have some generally interiorized relational preferences when connected with certain subjects, but the latter do not.

There are adjectives like *necesario* 'necessary' and *indispensable* 'indispensable' that typically have a propositional meaning. They are frequently used to qualify a noun, for instance *un libro necesario* 'a necessary book'. In European

Spanish, however, these adjectives are not frequently constitutive elements of the *tough* construction:

(50) a. ? Es un libro necesario de leer.
'It is a book necessary to read.'

b. ? Son personas indispensables de conocer.
'They are people indispensable to know.'

In English, *indispensable* is not as common as in Spanish (BNC 4.6 PMW, Corpus del Español 19.2 PMW) and no instances of *indispensable* in the TC were found in the BNC or COCA. However, it occasionally enters the *tough* construction (51a). *Necessary*, on the other hand, is very frequent in English and the pattern *necessary* + *to* + V occurs 4958 times in the BNC. Of these, a 10 per cent sample (496 tokens) was examined and no instances of the TC were found. On the Internet, however, examples such as (51b) can be found:

(51) a. What tests are indispensable to take?[15]
b. This seems to be a book necessary to read, not only for enjoyment, but [...][16]

In sum, there are some differences regarding the interpretation of the *tough* construction depending on the adjective. The prototypical adjectives expressing the level of difficulty are semantically free to occur with basically any kind of verb and thus with any kind of nominal in the TC. They do not have any other semantic input besides placing the process of the verb on a scale of difficulty. Some other, more peripheral, *tough* adjectives like *fast* and *slow* have more semantic content and they only select semantically compatible verbs as complements. Further, sometimes in the TC it is possible to leave out the syntactic manifestation of the process, that is, the verbal complement. This is possible if there is a prototypical process that is associated with the subject nominal in question or if the process is clear in the particular context of the utterance. However, even in the cases in which the overt complement can be and is omitted, the process is present in the conceptualization of the event.

3.5 Conclusion

In this chapter, we have investigated the *tough* construction in general, and also cross-linguistically in three different languages. It was argued that the main function of the TC is to put an entity on a scale of difficulty or pleasantness in relation to some action performed on the said entity. That is, whether an entity is difficult/easy or pleasant/unpleasant when it comes to performing an action on it. This seems to be a cross-linguistically valid notion, and from this point of view, the TC can be said to have a semantico-functional interpretation. Each of the three languages (and many others we know of) have some way of expressing the same or very similar kind of proposition. In English, Spanish and Finnish the syntactic constructions that convey the TC meaning are very similar with only small differences, but for instance in Romanian (cf. example 22) the verb form differs from the standard infinitive. In English, the passive infinitive used to be an option, but is now encountered only with non-prototypical *tough* adjectives, and in Spanish, although grammatically possible, the passive infinitive is not normally used. In Finnish the TC complement does not have a complementizer as in English and Spanish, and the adjective is directly followed by an infinitive form.

It seems that the adjectives that are allowed in the TC are semantically defined, and the less semantic content they have, the more easily they occur in the TC. This is demonstrated by the fact that the three languages examined here have more or less the same preferences as to which adjectives can easily occur in the TC and which are marginal or non-existent in the construction. In the same vein, the possibility of omitting the infinitive is defined by relational preferences, which pertain to semantics and are defined by convention and cultural considerations, and also by contextual factors. If the process in the complement is such that it is tightly and prototypically associated (in general or in the particular context) with the notional object entity, then the omission is possible. Otherwise the complement is obligatory. Finally, it is only in Finnish that there are also syntactic restrictions for the omission of the complement (cf. example 37b), but in English and Spanish the restrictions are purely semantic.

Notes

1. NPs also occur; see Table 3.1.
2. *Corpus of Early American Literature* (1690–1920). For further information, see Höglund and Syrjänen (2010) and Höglund (2014b).
3. The four most frequent *tough* adjectives, *difficult, easy, hard* and *impossible*, were used in the corpus search.
4. The reflexive constructions have been widely commented on by a number of scholars. From the point of view of the diathesis they include at least (i) real reflexive structures (where the reflexive pronoun is the object of the action, co-referential with the subject), *Juan se lavó* 'J. washed (himself)'; (ii) constructions transforming a transitive verb into an intransitive one as in *Juan se levantó* 'J. got up'; (iii) inchoative expressions as in *Juan se durmió* vs *Juan durmió* 'J. fell asleep' vs 'J. slept'; (iv) ambiguous cases of the type *se abrió la puerta*, which can mean either 'the door opened' or 'the door was opened'; (v) active impersonal sentences, *se habla español* 'Spanish is spoken'. For further information, see Mendikoetxea (1999).
5. Where other Romance languages have a construction of the type verb (+ relational element) + infinitive, Romanian prefers structures like verb + conjunctive: *Vreau să pleci* 'I want you to leave' and *Vreau să plec*, literally 'I want me to leave'.
6. For the sake of simplicity, we use the distinction made by Vendler (1957), although it has been supplemented and modified by various research works after his original article.

7. In standard spoken Finnish, no distinction is made between third person singular and plural forms. This means that one can find examples like (i):

> (i) Nämä　　kirja-t　　on　　helppo　avata　　satunnaise-sta
> kohda-sta [...]
> this.NOM.PL book-NOM.PL be.3SG easy.NOM open.INF random-ELAT
> point-ELAT
> 'These books are easy to open at a random place.'
> (http://www.kaleva.fi/uutiset/kulttuuri/kevyen-trivian-kolmas-tuleminen/
> 243159/)

However, in spoken Finnish the negated *tough* sentences are identical with those of the normative language.

8. http://galletasdemaizyfruta.blogspot.fi/2012/11/estrategia-de-promocion.html
9. http://www.ehowenespanol.com/reparar-error-red-inalcanzable-resolver-centos-como_187004/
10. This is in fact recognized by Reider himself (1993: 169) when he comments on the adjective *duro* 'hard'. He observes that further research is needed in order 'to determine just what role semantics does play in screening every *tough* construction that the syntax generates'.
11. It is clear that there are considerable differences between languages. It is not altogether clear what would be the default complement in English (a difficult road to travel, to walk, to drive, to get somewhere, etc.).
12. In very specific contexts, e.g. in a carpenter's workshop, the expression *una mesa fácil* might be naturally interpreted as something like *una mesa fácil de reparar* 'a table easy to repair'. The relational preferences may thus vary according to contextual and pragmatic factors.
13. About the difference between *rápido* and *rápidamente* used as adverbial modifiers, see De Miguel and Fernández Lagunilla (2004).
14. Sentences like (46) are non-existent in the large corpora of Spanish. On two reliable Internet sites we have found two occurrences with the verb *conducir* 'to drive':

> (i) Es un coche rápido de conducir en carreteras de montaña [...] (http://autosportplus.es/book/export/html/357)
> (ii) [...] la experiencia en competición es clave para hacer del 599 GTO un coche rápido de conducir [...]
> (http://www.diariomotor.com/2010/12/28/premios-diariomotor-2010-los-mejores-deportivos/)

These examples may of course be due to certain carelessness in writing or (although less likely) mark a new tendency in Spanish.
15. http://www.edusystemsinternational.com/aboutESI.htm
16. http://www.amazon.com/Ship-Death-Voyage-Changed-Atlantic/dp/0300194528

Bibliography

Bosque, I. (1999) 'El sintagma adjetival. Modificadores y complementos' in I. Bosque and V. Demonte (eds), *Gramática descriptiva de la lengua española* (Madrid: Espasa), pp. 217–310.

Chae, H.-R. (1992) 'Lexically Triggered Unbounded Discontinuities in English: an Indexed Phrase Structure Grammar Approach'. Doctoral dissertation, Ohio State University.

Chomsky, N. (1964) *Current Issues in Linguistic Theory* (The Hague: Mouton & Co).

Chomsky, N. (1970) 'Remarks on Nominalization' in R. A. Jacobs and P. S. Rosenbaum (eds) *Readings in English Transformational Grammar* (Waltham, Mass.: Ginn and Company), pp. 184–221.

Chung, Y.-S. (2001) *'Tough* Construction in English: a Construction Grammar Approach'. Doctoral dissertation, University of California, Berkeley.

Creed-Kanashiro, H., N. Espinola and G. Prain (2007) *Fortaleciendo la nutricion infantil en Peru: Desarrollo de una papilla a base de camote*, s.l. (CIP-Urban Harvest).

Dik, S. C. (1978) *Functional Grammar* (Amsterdam: North-Holland).

Fischer, O., A. Van Kemenade, W. Koopman and W. Van Der Wurff (2000) *The Syntax of Early English* (Cambridge: Cambridge University Press).

Givón, T. (1985) 'Iconicity, Isomorphism and Non-Arbitrary Coding in Syntax' in J. Haiman (ed.) *Iconicity in Syntax* (Amsterdam: John Benjamins), pp. 187–219.

Höglund, M. (2014a) 'Active and Passive Infinitive, Ambiguity and Non-Canonical Subject with *Ready*' in K. Davidse, C. Gentens, L. Ghesquière and L. Vandelanotte (eds) *Corpus Interrogation and Grammatical Patterns* (Amsterdam: John Benjamins), pp. 239–62.

Höglund, M. (2014b) '"Self-Discipline Strategies Were Easy to Design but Difficult to Adhere to" – a Usage-Based Study of the *Tough* Construction in English'. Doctoral dissertation, University of Tampere.

Höglund, M. and K. Syrjänen (2010) 'Towards a Corpus of Early American Literature: on the Challenges of Compiling a Comparable Diachronic Corpus' in I. Moskowich-Spiegel Fandiño, B. Crespo García, I. Lareo Martín and P. Lojo Sandino (eds) *Language Windowing through Corpora* (A Coruña: Universidade da Coruña), pp. 429–42.

Langacker, R. W. (1984) 'Active Zones'. *Proceedings of the Tenth Annual Meeting of the Berkeley Linguistics Society*, 172–88.

Langacker, R. W. (1999) *Grammar and Conceptualization* (Berlin: Mouton de Gruyter).

Lasnik, H. and R. Fiengo (1974) 'Complement Object Deletion'. *Linguistic Inquiry*, 5 (4): 535–71.

Mahieu, M.-A. (2007) 'Cas structuraux et dépendances syntaxiques des expressions nominales en finnois'. Thèse de doctorat en Linguistique théorique, descriptive et automatique, Université de Paris 7.

Mendikoetxea, A. (1999) 'Construcciones con *se*: medias, pasivas e impersonales' in I. Bosque and V. Demonte (eds) *Gramática descriptiva de la lengua española* (Madrid: Espasa), pp. 1631–722.

Nanni, D. L. (1980) 'On the Surface Syntax of Constructions with Easy-Type Adjectives'. *Language*, 56 (3): 569–81.

Postal, P. M. (1971) *Cross-Over Phenomena* (New York: Holt, Rinehart and Winston).

Reider, M. (1993) 'On *Tough* Movement in Spanish'. *Hispania*, 76 (1): 160–70.

Rosenbaum, P. S. (1967) *The Grammar of English Predicate Complement Constructions* (Cambridge: The MIT Press).

Ross, J. R. (1967) 'Constraints on Variables in Syntax'. Doctoral dissertation, MIT, Cambridge, Mass.

Van Der Wurff, W. (1990) 'The Easy-to-Please Construction in Old and Middle English' in S. Adamson, V. Law, N. Vincent and S. Wright (eds) *Papers from the 5th International Conference on English Historical Linguistics* (Amsterdam: John Benjamins), pp. 519–36.

Vendler, Z. (1967 [1957]) 'Verbs and Times' in Z. Vendler (ed.) *Linguistics in Philosophy* (Ithaca: Cornell University Press).

Vosberg, U. (2011) 'Varianten und Varietäten im Wandel: Die Entwicklung von aktiven und passiven Infinitiven bei *tough*-Konstruktionen und verwandten Strukturen im britischen und amerikanischen Englisch' in M. Elmentaler (ed.) *Gute Sprache, Schlechte Sprache* (Frankfurt a.m.: Lang), pp. 121–38.

Zierer, E. (1974) *The Qualjfying Adjective in Spanish* (The Hague: Mouton).

Part II
Variation

4

Variability in Clausal Verb Complementation: the Case of *Admit*

Hubert Cuyckens* and Frauke D'hoedt**
KU Leuven* and KU Leuven/Research fund – Flanders**

4.1 Introduction[1]

Descriptive surveys of clausal verb complementation in English (see, for instance, Quirk et al. 1985: 1170–220, Declerck 1991: 468–87, 501–13) show that different complement-taking predicates (CTPs) (or, matrix verbs) may combine with different complement types; in other words, that 'the different complement types in a language distribute differently over the inventory of complement-taking predicates' (De Smet 2013: 19). As such, the matrix verb *ask* takes the *to*-infinitive, while the verb *anticipate* combines with a gerundial -*ing*-clause.

(1) So I'm going to have to ask you **to get out of your car and accompany us to the station.** (Wordbanks Online, British Books, *The Execution*, 2002)

(2) I anticipate **having to travel considerably in my investigations.** (Wordbanks Online, British Books, *To His Just Desserts*, 1986)

This distribution does not work along clear-cut dividing lines, whereby each matrix verb uniquely pairs up with a particular complement type. In particular, a matrix verb may combine with two (or more) complementation types. The verb *remember*, for instance, may take a *to*-infinitive clause (3a) or a gerundial -*ing*-clause (3b) as clausal verb complement, while the verb *regret* in (4) shows alternation between the *that*-clause and the gerundial -*ing*-clause.

(3) a. *He remembered* **to thank her for everything.**
    b. *I remember* **reading about it in the newspaper.** (Declerck 1991: 511)
(4) a. *I don't regret* **helping her start out.**
    b. *I don't regret* **that I helped her start out.**

The two alternation patterns differ, however, in that in (3), language users cannot choose freely between one or the other pattern; rather, the variation

77

in (3) is *categorically* defined. In the case at hand, the variation can be characterized as functional differentiation, whereby the *to*-infinitive encodes a situation which is not yet actualized at the time of remembering, whereas the gerundial *-ing*-clause encodes the situation as actualizing before or at that time. In (4), however, it would appear that both variants are freely interchangeable; the variation is therefore *non-categorical* or *probabilistic*.

In this chapter, we will be concerned with the alternation pattern with the verb *admit*, which, interestingly, allows five complementation types (three non-finite types and two finite types):

(5) a. gerundial *-ing*-clause: So far no group has admitted **carrying out the murder.** (Wordbanks Online, British – spoken, *BBC World Service*, 1990)

b. gerundial *to-ing*-clause: The East German Housing Minister (...) admitted **to having worked for the former secret police** and announced that he was resigning. (Wordbanks Online, British – spoken, *BBC World Service*, 1990)

c. *to*-infinitive clause: The Prisoner admitted **the note in question to be his own hand-writing.** (OBC, 1740)

d. *that*-clause: Meanwhile you will perhaps admit **that a little charity greases the wheels.** (CLMET, M.A. Ward, *Marcella*, 1894)

e. zero-complement clause: But even you must admit **there are different standards of oddity.** (Wordbanks Online, British Books, E. Ferrars, *The Other Devil's Name*, 1986)

The case of *admit* is all the more interesting because it features categorical as well as non-categorical variation. In particular, when the subject of the matrix clause and of the complement clause (CC) are different, only the finite variants or the *to*-infinitive are possible (5c, 5d, 5e); on the other hand, when the matrix subject and the CC-subject are identical, all complement types in (5) are possible, that is, there is no single factor categorically triggering one of the variants. In addition, non-categorical variation also occurs between *that*-clause, zero-complement clause, and *to*-infinitive when matrix subject and CC-subject are different.

In this chapter, we wish to offer a corpus-based analysis of CC-variation in the Late Modern English (LModE) and Present-day English (PDE) periods with the verb *admit*. In examining the factors co-determining this variation, we focus on the *probabilistic* nature of complement choice with *admit*. Another aim is to examine to what extent general hypotheses about complement choice can be informed by our results on the changing/varying distributions of finite versus non-finite complement clauses.

The chapter is organized as follows: section 4.2 presents a short survey of clausal verb complementation, which serves as a backdrop to our study of CC-variation. Section 4.3 details the goals of this chapter, while section

4.4 presents the data and methodology. Section 4.5 is devoted to the multivariate and probabilistic analysis of three types of CC-choice with *admit*. In section 4.6, we discuss the results of our analysis and confront them with earlier claims in the literature on (changing) CC-preferences. Section 4.7 summarizes and details the contribution our study makes to the body of previous research.

4.2 A short survey of clausal verb complementation

Clausal verb complementation (i.e. structures of the type [CTP + *to*-infinitive clause/gerundial *-ing*-clause/*that*-clause/*for* ... *to*-infinitive clause]) has been an important research topic within generative as well as cognitive-functional linguistic frameworks. Indeed, complementation phenomena have been a concern of generative linguists (Rosenbaum 1967, Bresnan 1970) since Chomsky's seminal *Aspects of the Theory of Syntax* (1965), and important work in this domain has continued ever since (Bresnan 1979, Warner 1982, Chomsky 1986, Rizzi 1990, Radford 1997, Felser 1999). From the 1980s onwards, the scope of complementation research was expanded by functional-typological linguists (e.g. Givón 1980, Noonan 2007 [1985], Dixon 1991). While the generative literature on verb complementation has largely focused on synchronic, syntactic issues, such as the constituent structure of different complement types, synchronic research within the cognitive-functional tradition to date has been concerned with the question of how CCs are distributed over the various CTPs (or main/matrix verbs). Much of this cognitive-functional research is semantic in orientation, and has been informed by Noonan's observation that across languages 'complementation is basically a matter of matching a particular complement type to a particular complement-taking predicate' (2007: 101) (see Wierzbicka 1988, Duffley 1992, 1999, Langacker 1991, Achard 1998, Smith 2002). However, as De Smet (2013: 20–33) points out, a satisfactory synchronic account of complementation needs to envisage additional, non-semantic determining principles, such as the role of information structure (Noël 2003), the *horror aequi* principle (Rudanko 2000, Vosberg 2003), the cognitive complexity principle (Rohdenburg 1995), social and regional stratification (Mair 2002, 2003), and register (Mindt 2000).

Significantly, though, this synchronic work has tended to neglect the fact that the synchronic matches between the CTP and the CC can be subject to change over time. It is only in the last 15 or 20 years that diachronic studies have appeared which present broad accounts of change and variation in complementation patterns in different periods of the history of English (see Fischer 1995, Fanego 1996, 1998, Rudanko 1998, 2006, 2010, 2012, Miller 2001, Los 2005, Rohdenburg 2006, De Smet 2008, 2013), attesting to a distributional reorganization of CCs over time.[2] It has thus been shown that new complement types have made their way into the English language (e.g. the gerundial -*ing*-CC and the *for* ... *to*-infinitive construction are relatively recent), or that long-existing types have spread to new CTP-contexts (e.g. the *to*-infinitive) or, conversely, have become increasingly restricted (e.g. the bare infinitive). These changes have led to competition between CC-types; in particular, in some CTP-contexts, one CC-type may have been replaced by another (e.g. with verbs of volition, the *that*-clause has largely been supplanted by the *to*-infinitive; see Croft 2000, Los 2005); in other contexts, a situation of variation may have come about. Sometimes, as in (3), this CC-variation results in functional differentiation, whereby the domain of operation of one CC-type can be differentiated in a clear-cut, that is, categorical fashion from that of the other. Often, though, this variation is non-categorical, and unstable, in that CC-types coexist (e.g. *regret* patterns with a *that*-clause, a gerundial -*ing*-clause, and a *to*-infinitive; verbs such as *like* and *love* alternate between the *to*-infinitive and the gerundial -*ing* form) and show varying/shifting patterns of preference across speakers and over time. While replacement of CC-types as well as CC-variation characterized by functional differentiation have been well documented, the type of competition between CC-types resulting in unstable variation (or changing patterns of preference over time) – though attested in the literature – is still largely underexplored, and it is this non-categorical variation that this chapter focuses on.

4.3   Goals

In this chapter, we wish to focus on the non-categorical or probabilistic variation with the verb *admit*, as exemplified in (5) above and in (6):

> (6) a. gerundial -*ing*-clause: Those who admitted **feeling abandoned by God**, or who blamed God or the Devil for their poor health, increased their risk of death. (Wordbanks Online, British Books, D. Rowe, *Beyond Fear*, 2002)
>
> b. gerundial *to-ing*-gerund: The poet, though never admitting **to taking the poppy**, wrote the next day how he had slept in, felt languid, and was indifferent to pain and pleasure. (Wordbanks Online, British Books, Leavesley & Biro, *The Medical Mysteries: Omnibus*, 2001)
>
> c. *to*-infinitive clause: I told him Duncan was in custody, and partly admitted **himself to be guilty**. (OBC, 1849)
>
> d. *that*-clause: Mr. Luker admitted **that he had no evidence to produce of any attempt at robbery being in contemplation.** (CLMET, W. Collins, *The Moonstone*, 1868)
>
> e. zero-complement clause: Well I must admit **I'm only seventeen yes.** (Wordbanks Online, British – spoken, British Spoken Corpus, Cobuild, 1991)

What characterizes this type of variation is the indeterminacy of choice; this indeterminacy does not occur at the abstract level of grammar – indeed, each of the CC-types with *admit* in (6) can be independently motivated (see, for instance, the semantic characterization of CCs in Langacker 2008: 429–45) – but at the usage level, that is, at the level of actual, online choices speakers make in discourse (see De Smet 2013: 27–9). Our concern is with these online choices: by fitting a logistic regression model, we aim to isolate the factors significantly predicting, in terms of odds or probability ratios, this CC-variation.

Finally, the factors that turn out to be instrumental in predicting CC-choice feed into an assessment of (some of the) earlier claims made in the literature on (changing patterns in) CC-choice (see section 4.2; De Smet 2013: 20–33). Thus, we are able to explore to what extent CC-choice is affected (i) by Noonan's semantic characterization of CCs in terms of 'dependent time reference' versus 'independent time reference' (2007: 102), and (ii) by various types of structural complexity consonant with Rohdenburg's (1995, 1996) notion of 'cognitive complexity'. Further, we examine whether any changes in CC-choice observed over time tie in with Denison's claim that 'a long-term trend in English has been the growth of nonfinite complement clauses at the expense of finite clauses' (1998: 256).

4.4   Data and methodology

4.4.1   Data selection

In our selection of matrix verbs, we chose a verb that allows variation between finite and non-finite CCs, and these are relatively few in number. We selected the verb *admit* from Quirk et al.'s (1985: 1182–4) list of factual verbs which allow the finite/non-finite CC-alternation. Finite CCs are introduced either by the complementizer *that* or by 'zero', as in (7a, 8a) and (7b, 8b), respectively, and their subjects may be denotationally identical to, or different from, the matrix subject (see (7a, 7b) and (8a, 8b)):

(7) a. I changed a five-pound note for him, he afterwards admitted **that he had taken it from his master.** (OBC, 1812)
   b. I must admit **I have never ever felt there was any need to read the Bible though.** (Wordbanks Online, British – spoken, British Spoken Corpus, Cobuild, <1990)

(8) a. British Rail has admitted **that two of its busy commuter lines in Kent have failed to meet its punctuality standards under the Passengers' Charter.** (Wordbanks Online, British – spoken, British Spoken Corpus, Cobuild, 1992)
   b. I must admit **the down-to-earth joy of living and being with one another and enjoying one another is more important.** (Wordbanks Online, British Books, S. Boston, *Too Deep for Tears*, 1994)

Non-finite CCs include (i) the subjectless (controlled) gerundial *-ing*-CC (as in (9a)), (ii) the subjectless *to*-gerundial *-ing*-CC (9b), (iii) the subjectless *to*-infinitive[3] (9c), (iv) the *to*-infinitive-CC with expressed subject (9d). No *-ing*-gerundials with expressed subject were attested in our database (but there is one *to*-gerundial with expressed subject).[4] In addition, it was ensured that matrix verbs occurred sufficiently frequently with the CC-variants to allow statistically significant results.

(9) a. I admit **using snuff occasionally**, but not tobacco. (OBC, 1907)
   b. Some of my friends who claimed to have been untouched by the threats of anthrax attacks or 9/11 admit **to being deeply uneasy now**. (Wordbanks Online, British – spoken, British Spoken Corpus, Cobuild, 1991)
   c. Surely he's admitted **to be highly attractive** – to women? (Wordbanks Online, British Books, E. Townsend, *In Love and War*, 1989)
   d. The prisoner admitted **this to be the same shirt that he pledged with me**. (OBC, 1767)

The data for this study were extracted from the *Old Bailey Corpus* (OBC, Huber et al. 2012), the *Corpus of Late Modern English Texts* (CLMET3.0) and *Wordbanks Online*. The OBC is based on the proceedings of London's criminal court and documents speech-based English from 1720 to 1913 (see Culpeper and Kytö 2010: 16–17).[5] For its PDE spoken correlate, we made use of the spoken component of Wordbanks Online. The CLMET searches were confined to the fiction component; its PDE correlate was the 'British Books' component of Wordbanks Online. A simple search for the string *admit* (and its spelling variants) was carried out; that is, we extracted all attestations of the matrix verbs (including those with NP complements). After manual pruning of all spurious hits, we were left with the following numbers of [CTP – CC] patterns – they are presented in Table 4.1. Observations were then coded, as described below.

4.4.2 Coding of the data

Each corpus attestation, consisting of [subject + *admit* + CC], was entered into an Excel database with the following descriptors: (i) N: number of the attestation in the Excel table; (ii) CONCORDANCE: the entire concordance comprising the corpus attestation (in order to provide the necessary context); (iii) FILE: corpus in which the example was attested. Each attestation was obviously also coded for COMPLEMENTATION TYPE. Five types of CC are distinguished:

- *-ing*-CC (includes present as well as perfect gerundials)
- *to-ing*-CC
- *to*-infinitive-CC (includes present as well as perfect infinitives)
- *that*-clause
- zero-complementizer clause (a *that*-clause without a *that*-complementizer)

Table 4.1 Number of attestations of CCs with *admit*

Corpus	Period	Words	Total hits	Relevant hits
OBC	1720–1913	33,605,300	1,348	377
	→ 1720–1780	10,860,425	462	31
	→ 1780–1850	14,191,908	336	105
	→ 1850–1913	8,552,966	550	241
CLMET (fiction)	1710–1920	15,784,689	1,975	272
	→ 1710–1780	4,642,670	692	16
	→ 1780–1850	4,830,718	561	35
	→ 1850–1920	6,311,301	722	221
Wordbanks (British – spoken)	1990–2005	41,403,450	3,145 (→ sample of 1,000 hits was taken)	577
Wordbanks (British Books)	1990–2005	76,062,449	6,469 (→ sample of 1,400 hits was taken)	585

Each token was then coded for a number of factors determining CC-choice and describing characteristics of the CTP/matrix verb, the CC, or the combined [CTP – CC] structure. Importantly, our selection of potentially significant factors of CC-variation was informed by the relevant literature (see section 4.2; De Smet 2013: 20–33) and comprises semantic, structural, genre-related and periodization-related factors; it also includes a number of factors not typically discussed in the literature.[6,7] In what follows, we discuss the factors used in this study.

(i) Semantic factors

The only semantic factor coded for was *the meaning of the matrix verb* (MEAN-ING). For the semantics of *admit*, the distinction was made between *admit* as a speech act verb and *admit* with the meaning of 'admitting to wrongdo-ing'. In the former case, *admit* is a verb of 'saying', and merely introduces an utterance without adding a negative connotation to it (see (10)). In the case of semantics of 'wrongdoing', on the other hand, *admit* is synonymous to 'owning up to something/coming clean about something/confessing something' and is typically used when someone admits to having done something wrong (see (11)). As becomes clear from the examples, each semantic value can occur with each of the different complementation types (both finite and non-finite).

(10) a. I must admit **I do like listening to the radio when I'm in the car.** (Wordbanks Online, British spoken, *John Taynton radio show phone-in*, 1991)

     b. Normally Rose had an even temper; she was rarely irritable, and had no hesitation in admitting **that she felt unwell.** (Wordbanks Online, British books, J. Penn, *Unto the Grave*, 1986)

     c. The Prime Minister visited EMI's Abbey Road recording studios – of Beatles' fame – yesterday and tried her hand at drumming; she admitted **being a fan of the group's.** (Wordbanks Online, British spoken, *BBC World Service*, 1990)

     d. I examined the prisoner's box, which he admitted **to be his,** and found these three duplicates, (...) (OBC, 1797)

(11) a. Confess the truth, and admit **you have very rarely spared a thought to the person to whom you fancy yourself at this moment so passionately devoted.** (CLMET, B. Disraeli, *Venetia,* 1837)

     b. So you're admitting **that you killed Dexter?** (Wordbanks Online, British books, S. Harrison, *Better than This,* 2002)

     c. Stella was ashamed to admit **to feeling slightly jealous.** (Wordbanks Online, British books, K. Cathy, *Just between Us,* 2002)

     d. The twenty-one-year-old French driver alleged to have admitted **falling asleep at the wheel** has been charged with manslaughter and other offences. (Wordbanks Online, British Spoken Corpus, Cobuild, <1990)

(ii)   *Structural factors*

(iia) NEGATIVE_MARKER_PRESENT. This factor has the values 'Yes' and 'No'; it indicates whether a negative form (*not, never,* etc.) occurs in the CC.

(iib) MODAL_PRESENT. Indicates whether a modal auxiliary is present in the CC.

(iic) CC_SUBJECT. This factor has the following two values:
- 'complex NP', comprising [noun + postmodifier] and [noun + noun]
- 'other', comprising the following types of subject: pronoun, noun, *there,* (pro)noun in the genitive, proper name, and no subject (when no subject is expressed in control environments).

(iid) FORM_MATRIX_SUBJECT. This factor has the following two values:
- '3/n', comprising third-person pronouns and nouns;
- 'other', comprising first- and second-person pronouns, and none (none when an explicit main clause subject is missing ('You know, admitting I've had lots to drink and all that (...) (Wordbanks Online, British Books, A. Masters, *Stuart: A Life Backwards,* 2005)).

(iie) FORM_CC. The CC may show the following types of predicate structure:
- verbs without argument/modifier: 'Verb'
- verbs with either an object or an adjunct: 'verbobjadj'
- verbs with an object and an adjunct: 'verb + obj + adj'
- copula verbs with a nominal predicate: 'verb + predicate'.

(iif) INTERVENING MATERIAL IN WORDS. Indicates the number of words between the CTP and the subject of the complement (when the complement is finite) or between the subject and the non-finite verb form.[8]

(iii) Genre-related factor

The following genre-related factor was distinguished:

MODE. The attestation belongs to the 'speech-based', 'the spoken', or the 'written' mode. Attestations from the CLMET, which contains formal prose and from British Books (WordBank online) were classified as 'written', attestations from the OBC as 'speech-based', and attestations from British-spoken (WordBank online) as 'spoken'. The speech-based and spoken modes were collapsed for the logistic regression.

(iv) Periodization-related factor

Periodization is captured by the following factor:

PERIOD. This factor locates the attestation within two time bands:
– Late Modern English (between 1710 and 1920)
– Present-day English (from 1990 to the present)

(v) Additional semantic and structural factors

Finally, a number of additional semantic and structural factors were distinguished which are not typically addressed in the literature.

(va) ANIMACY SUBJECT CC. The subject may be:
– animate
– inanimate
(vb) VOICE VERB CC
– active
– passive
– copula
(vc) DENOTATION. Two values are distinguished:
– 'different': main clause subject and CC subject denote different entities (as in (12))
– 'same': main clause subject and CC subject denote the same entity; in this condition, the CC subject may be controlled by the matrix subject (as in (13a)) or not (as in (13b))

(12) **The government** admitted that **the miners** had perpetrated some excesses against innocent people but it did not express regret for these actions. (Wordbanks Online, British – spoken, BBC World Service, 1990)

(13) a. He half admitted **having** rushed to the palace on his road to me. (CLMET, G. Meredith, *The Adventures of Harry Richmond*, 1870)

b. I admitted before the Magistrate that **I should not be surprised if he did not turn up.** (OBC, 1902)

(vd) TEMPORAL RELATION. Indicates the temporal relation between the CC and the time of the CTP:
- anteriority (14a)
- simultaneity (14b)
- posteriority (14c)
- simant (14d) (simultaneous in form (no explicit past marker) but semantically anterior)

(14) a. Although I must admit **I thought they'd changed the titles.** (Wordbanks Online, British – spoken, Lecture at the University of Birmingham, 1990)

b. In his last paper on cocaine, Freud finally admitted **that it did harm morphine addicts.** (Wordbanks Online, British Books, Leavesley and Biro, *The Medical Mysteries: Omnibus*, 2001)

c. But he admitted **the next eighteen months would be difficult and possibly dangerous.** (Wordbanks Online, British – spoken, BBC World Service, 1990)

d. No group has yet admitted **carrying out the attack.** (Wordbanks Online, British – spoken, BBC World Service, 1990)

4.5   A probabilistic analysis of complement choice

It can be observed that none of the factors proposed uniquely conditions one outcome or the other (finite *that*-clause or zero-CC; non-finite *to*-infinitive clause, gerundial *-ing*- or *to-ing*-clause). Consider in this respect (15a) and (15b). While the condition DENOTATION = 'same' triggers a non-finite *-ing*-CC in (15a), it also allows a finite *that*-CC, as in (15b):

(15) a. President Mladenov of Bulgaria has admitted **making controversial remarks about bringing in tanks** (…). (Wordbanks Online, British – spoken, BBC World Service, 1990)

b. I changed a five-pound note for him, he afterwards admitted **that he had taken it from his master.** (OBC, 1812)

Similarly, while the condition FORM_MATRIX_SUBJECT = 'non-complex' in (16a) may be hypothesized to trigger an *-ing*-CC (a hypothesis in line with Rohdenburg's complexity principle; see below), attestations such as (16b) show that this condition is not sufficient to predict the -*ing*-CC because it also allows a finite *that*-clause.

(16) a. 'I'd be ashamed to admit **feeling jealous**,' Janice says. (Wordbanks Online, British Books, N. Friday, *Jealousy*, 1986)
b. Well I have to admit **that one of my motivations is just that building the smallest robots possible is just such a neat idea** that I can't resist the temptation of doing it. (Wordbanks Online, British – spoken, BBC World Service, 1990)

Then again, *that*-clauses can be hypothesized to be associated with the condition DENOTATION = 'different' (that is, different denotation of matrix subject and CC-subject) (see 17a), but not uniquely so, as our data show that this condition can also be observed in non-finite *to*-infinitive-CCs, as in (17b):

(17) a. Microsoft has admitted **patch 65 may not be fully effective in certain circumstances.** (Wordbanks Online, British – spoken, British spoken Corpus, Cobuild, 1991)
b. I then asked him whether he meant the one in the yard to be the second or third, and he admitted **that to be the second.** (OBC, 1827)

While it can be seen that none of the factors uniquely conditions/determines one (or more) of the variants of *admit*, it may not be inferred that each of the factors co-predicts/conditions *all* of the variants. For instance, the condition DENOTATION = 'different' only allows *that*/zero-CCs and the *to*-infinitive but does not allow gerundial -*ing*- and *to*-*ing*-CCs. This is different from the complementation types with *regret/remember/deny*, where each of the predictive factors could trigger the entire range of complementation types (see Cuyckens et al. 2014). The verb *admit*, then, shows a mixture of categorical and non-categorical or probabilistic variation, whereby probabilistic variation is restricted to the *that*-clause, zero-CC and the *to*-infinitive. When DENOTATION = 'same', *admit* features non-categorical variation.

Let us first examine the complementation types with *admit* under the condition DENOTATION = 'same'. The factors identified in section 4.4.2 are predictors[9] of the non-finite as well as the finite CC-types following *admit*. In particular, each condition within a particular factor/predictor favours non-finite as well as finite CCs. Importantly, these patterns of preference vary across factors; in other words, the relative weight or impact of one factor on the choice of finite versus non-finite CC-type may differ from another factor. As was pointed out in Cuyckens et al. (2014), frequency distributions alone cannot sufficiently inform us about the relative strength of each of the variables/factors. In a situation such as this, where we are dealing with probabilistic complementation choice in a context where various factors are at play, it is advisable to fit a regression model.

To probe the multivariate and probabilistic nature of complementation strategy choice, we fit a *binary logistic regression model* with fixed effects (Pinheiro and Bates 2000).[10] Logistic regression modelling is the closest a corpus analyst can come to conducting a controlled experiment: the technique models the combined contribution of all the conditioning factors considered in the analysis, systematically testing the probabilistic effect of each factor while holding the other factors in the model constant. Ideally, the factors should be independent of each other, but in practice a certain degree of overlap (*collinearity*) is admissible.[11]

Our response variable is binary, distinguishing between finite complementation (*that-* and zero-CC) and non-finite complementation (gerundial *-ing* and *to-ing*-CC and *to*-infinitive). Predicted odds are for non-finite complementation. We observed the customary steps to obtain a minimal adequate regression model. We began by fitting the maximal model including all potentially important factors. Subsequently, the model was simplified by removing factors lacking significant explanatory power (for instance, we removed the predictor FORM_MATRIX_SUBJECT and CC_SUBJECT, because they did not turn out to have a significant effect). The resulting model is of good quality.[12] The regression output is presented in (18):

(18)
Fixed effects:

	Estimate Std.	Error	z value	Pr(>|z|)	
(Intercept)	-1.3219	0.8125	-1.627	0.103764	
meaningwrongdoing	0.9946	0.2667	3.728	0.000193	***
negative_marker_presentyes	-1.7425	1.1927	-1.461	0.144030	
modal_presentyes	-1.0310	0.4340	-2.375	0.017537	*
intervening_material	-0.8471	0.2466	-3.435	0.000592	***
periodPDE	-0.1673	0.2195	-0.762	0.446131	
negative_marker_presentyes: periodPDE	2.7349	1.3441	2.035	0.041878	*

Signif. codes: 0 '***' 0.001 '**' 0.01 '*' 0.05 '.' 0.1
'.' 1

In short, this means that the condition MEANING = 'wrongdoing' significantly favours non-finite CCs. Factors significantly disfavouring non-finite CCs are MODAL_PRESENT = 'yes' and PRESENCE INTERVENING MATERIAL. The presence of a negative marker disfavours non-finites but not significantly so. Further, there exists an interaction effect between NEGATIVE_MARKER_PRESENT and PDE in that the presence of negative markers in PDE tends to favour non-finites (compared to the other periods).

A different explanatory technique to look at the data set, whereby various predictors can be seen to 'team up' to create linguistic outcomes, is 'Conditional inference trees' (for discussion, see Tagliamonte and Baayen 2012). Bernaisch et al. (2014: 14) succinctly sum up the essence of conditional inference trees as follows:

Conditional inference trees are a recursive partitioning approach towards classification and regression that attempt to classify/compute predicted outcomes/values on the basis of multiple binary splits of the data. Less technically, a data set is recursively inspected to determine according to which (categorical or numeric) independent variable the data should be split up into two groups to classify/predict best the known outcomes of the dependent variable [...] This process of splitting the data up is repeated until no further split that would still sufficiently increase the predictive accuracy can be made, and the final result is a flowchart-like decision tree.

With regard to the variation between non-finite and finite CCs (see Figure 4.1), we can observe that MEANING is a major discriminatory factor: finite CCs typically occur when the matrix verb is a speech act verb; when the meaning denotes 'wrongdoing', there is a higher incidence of non-finite CCs. Actually, non-finites occur most frequently when the 'wrongdoing' meaning occurs in PDE, and when the matrix subject is a third-person pronoun or a noun.

Second, when the denotation of matrix subject and CC-subject differ, complementation types occurring with *admit* are restricted to the *that*- and zero-CC as well as the *to*-infinitive. In other words, the condition DENOTATION = 'different' categorically excludes the *-ing-* and *to-ing-*CCs. The variation between the *that*- and zero-CC and the *to*-infinitive is, however, probabilistic. In theory, three binary models could be fitted here: (i) *to*-infinitive versus *that*-/zero-CC; (ii) zero-CC versus *that*-CC + *to*-infinitive; (iii) *that*-CC versus zero-CC + *to*-infinitive. The first model could not be fitted because the number of attestations of the *to*-infinitive was too low (42). We then fitted both models (ii) and (iii) with predicted odds for the zero-CC in (ii) and for the *that*-CC in (iii). The regression output for model (ii), with predicted odds for the zero-CC, is represented in (19).

90

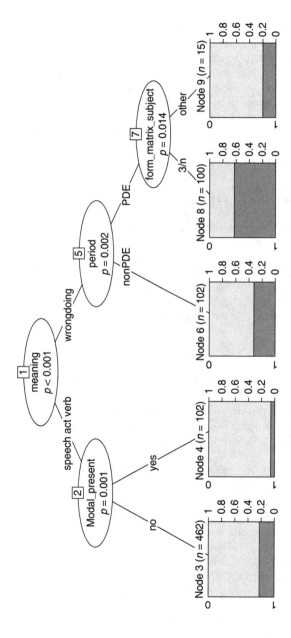

Figure 4.1 Conditional inference tree of non-finite versus finite complementation types with *admit*

(19)
Fixed effects:

	Estimate Std.	Error	z value	Pr(>|z|)
(Intercept)	-0.68552	0.22583	-3.036	0.00240 **
CC_subjectnon-complex	1.57153	0.14988	10.485	< 2e-16 ***
form_matrix_subjectthree_noun	-1.81973	0.22413	-8.119	4.70e-16 ***
negative_marker_presentyes	-1.57904	0.58807	-2.685	0.00725 **
model_presentyes	-0.63880	0.42793	-1.493	0.13550
intervening_material	-0.37106	0.09498	-3.907	9.36e-05 ***
periodPDE	0.91099	0.16078	5.666	1.46e-08 ***
modewritten	-1.34792	0.23136	-5.826	5.68e-09 ***
negative_marker_presentyes:period2PDE	1.64838	0.82796	1.991	0.04649 *
model_presentyes:periodPDE	1.13117	0.46578	2.429	0.01516 *
form_matrix_subjectthree_noun:modewritten	0.89287	0.27868	3.204	0.00136 **
intervening_material:modewritten	-0.51160	0.21864	-2.340	0.01929 *

Signif. codes: 0 '***' 0.001 '**' 0.01 '*' 0.05 '.' 0.1
'.' 1

As can be seen, non-complex CC-subjects favour zero; third-person pronouns or nouns as matrix subjects disfavour zero, as do the conditions MODAL_PRESENT = 'yes' and the written mode. In the PDE period, the conditions NEGATIVE_MARKER_PRESENT as well as MODAL_PRESENT tend to disfavour zero less; in the written mode, the aforementioned matrix subject types disfavour zero less, but intervening material disfavours zero more.

The regression output for model (iii), with predicted odds for the *that*-clause, is represented in (20):

(20)
Fixed effects:

	Estimate Std.	Error	z value	Pr(>|z|)	
(Intercept)	0.42522	0.24227	1.755	0.079234.	
CC_subjectnon-complex	-1.58903	0.14537	-10.931	< 2e-16	***
form_matrix_subjectthree_noun	1.64785	0.22062	7.469	8.08e-14	***
negative_marker_presentyes	0.75113	0.36926	2.034	0.041937	*
model_presentyes	0.60593	0.38383	1.579	0.114417	
intervening_material	0.36003	0.08859	4.064	4.82e-05	***
periodPDE	-0.43375	0.14997	-2.892	0.003824	**
modewritten	1.27531	0.22857	5.579	2.41e-08	***
model_presentyes:periodPDE	-1.14873	0.42547	-2.700	0.006936	**
form_matrix_subjectthree_noun:modewritten	-0.96025	0.27306	-3.517	0.000437	***
intervening_material:mode2written	0.59869	0.21961	2.726	0.006407	**

Signif. codes: 0 `***' 0.001 `**' 0.01 `*' 0.05 `.' 0.1 ` ' 1

This regression output presents a nice mirror image of the regression output in (19); in other words, we see the previous model confirmed: non-complex CCs subjects strongly disfavour *that*; third-person personal pronouns or noun subjects favour *that*. If a negative marker or a modal is present, there is a preference for *that*; intervening material favours *that*, and the written mode favours *that* (this is confirmed, for instance, in Van Bogaert et al., forthcoming). Further, in the written mode, the aforementioned matrix subject types (third-person personal pronouns or noun subjects) are less favouring, but intervening material is even more favouring. Finally, in PDE, the presence of a modal favours *that* less.

Figure 4.2 represents the conditional inference tree of model (iii). We can see from Figure 4.2 that CC-SUBJECT and FORM_MATRIX_SUBJECT are indeed important explanatory factors: the values CC-SUBJECT = 'complex' and FORM_MATRIX_SUBJECT = '3/n' yield a high proportion of *that*-clauses. Conversely, the combination of the values CC-SUBJECT = 'NON-complex' and FORM_MATRIX_SUBJECT = 'other' yields high number of zero-CCs (node 3).

Finally, we wish to address the variation between gerundial *-ing*-clauses and gerundial *to-ing*-clauses. While the low number of attestations keeps us from fitting a logistic regression model, we have drawn up a conditional inference tree (Figure 4.3).

The factor MODE appears to be a crucial factor distinguishing between gerundial *to-ing*-CCs and (bare) *-ing*-CCs, with the highest number of *to-ing*-CCs in the written mode. In the spoken mode, the copula verb form seems to be most important predictor of the gerundial *to-ing*-CCs. Then again, active verb forms appear to be the most important trigger of the bare gerund, with a higher share in PDE (so, this is a structure which is becoming increasingly frequent).

4.6 Discusssion

First of all, we can observe that across the three models, two types of factors are of paramount importance. On the one hand, under the condition DENOTATION = 'same' the meaning of the matrix verb plays a crucial role in the selection of finite versus non-finite CCs. Second, structural factors play a role in most of the regression models. In the first model (non-finite versus finite CCs), the presence of a modal verb in the CC favours increased presence of the finite CC-clause; furthermore, when teaming up with the meanings 'wrongdoing' in the PDE period, noun matrix subjects favour finites more than first- and second-person pronouns. In the regression models of zero-CC versus *that*-CC + *to*-infinitive (and its mirror image model), the *that*-CC is disfavoured when the CC-subject is non-complex and it is strongly favoured when there is intervening material.

Each of these observations can be accounted for in terms of earlier views expressed in the literature on complement choice. When *admit* denotes 'wrongdoing', the wrongful act that the subject admits to is likely to be situated in the past. In other words, the matrix verb itself specifies the particular temporal domain of the event in the CC, which is anterior to the temporal domain of the matrix verb. It is therefore not necessary to explicitly encode this anterior temporal domain again in the CC (e.g. by finite verbs with a

94

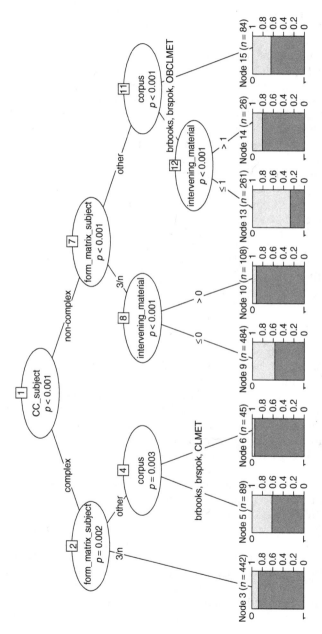

Figure 4.2 Conditional inference tree of *that*-clause versus zero-CC + *to*-infinitive with *admit*

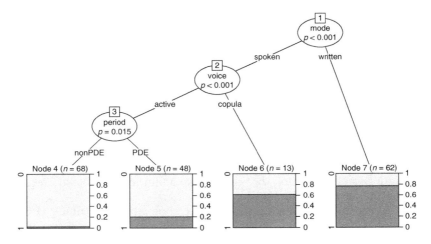

Figure 4.3 Conditional inference tree of gerundial -*ing*-clauses versus gerundial *to-ing*-clauses

tense marker). In contrast, when *admit* is used as a speech act verb (a 'say'-like verb), it does not specify a temporal domain of its CC. In this case, a finite CC detailing the temporal specifications is preferred. These preferences in CC-choice can be usefully linked up with Noonan's hypothesis about reduced CCs (2007: 111). Noonan points out that 'reduced complements, which are likely to lack tense distinctions ... are typically associated with predicates whose complements have DTR [dependent time reference]' (2007: 111). Our study shows that the reduced -*ing*-CCs typically occur with the 'wrongdoing' attestations of the matrix *admit*, which determine the temporal domain of their CCs. A similar view is expressed in De Smet (2012).

We can also usefully link up our observations about the correlation between the higher incidence of *that*-CC with *admit* and its structurally complex CCs with Rohdenburg's (1995, 1996) Cognitive Complexity Principle. This principle states that in a cognitively more complex environment, more explicit grammatical options tend to be favoured (see Rohdenburg 1996: 151). A cognitively more complex environment, in turn, is hypothesized by Rohdenburg as requiring more processing effort. Grammatical manifestations of cognitive complexity are, for instance, constituents of sizeable length and great distance between head and dependent (notably because of insertions); in other words, structurally complex entities or environments. If we take structural complexity as a measure of cognitive complexity, it follows that these structurally complex entities/environments will tend to favour the more explicit finite *that*-CCs (and less complex environments the less explicit non-finite CCs, namely gerundial -*ing*-clauses and *to*-infinitives).

That-CCs can here be seen as more explicit grammatically because they carry tense/mood distinctions and obligatorily have an expressed subject.

Our analysis has revealed that the factors INTERVENING MATERIAL and MODAL_PRESENT, each associated with structurally complex environments, significantly favour finite complementation. In the variation *that*-CC versus zero-CC, it has been observed that the structural complexity factors INTER-VENING MATERIAL, CC_SUBJECT, MODAL_PRESENT and NEGATIVE MARKER each favour the more complex *that*-clause rather than the zero-CC. As such, our results strengthen Rohdenburg's earlier findings: they are not only consonant with his observations (with respect to the variation *to*-infinitive versus *that*-clause) that INTERVENING MATERIAL has a disfavouring effect on non-finite complementation, but they reveal additional complexity factors having a similar disfavouring effect.

In addition to his findings on cognitive complexity, Rohdenburg (1995) observes that in the course of the seventeenth and eighteenth centuries, *that*-clauses are increasingly replaced by *to*-infinitives – a finding in line with Denison's finding (1998: 256). In a recent study on the evolutionary path of *that*-clauses versus gerundial -*ing*-clauses, however, Rohdenburg (2014) sketches a more balanced picture, in that any replacement of *that*-clauses by gerundial -*ing*-clauses varies with individual matrix verbs. An earlier study (Cuyckens et al. 2014) is in line with these results. The present study also attests to the fact that there is no across-the-board phasing out of the finite *that*-clause in favour of the non-finite gerundial -*ing*-CC. Compared to *that*-clauses (including zero-CCs), gerundial -*ing*-CCs only take up a share of 15 per cent in the period 1850–1920, for instance, and this share even decreases to 11 per cent in PDE.

4.7   Conclusions

In this chapter, we examined the probabilistic or non-categorical variation in LModE and PDE of the various finite and non-finite CCs with the matrix verb *admit*. To probe the multivariate nature of complementation strategy choice, we fit a *binary logistic regression model* with fixed effects to the data, thus shedding light on the factors favouring various complementation patterns. Finally, we considered the relevance of the observed preferences (i) for Rohdenburg's (1996) complexity hypothesis, (ii) for Denison's (1998) and Rohdenburg's (1995, this volume) views on the replacement of finite *that*-clauses by non-finite clauses, and (iii) for Noonan's (2007) views on reduced clauses. Our study provided corroborating evidence for Rohdenburg's complexity principle as well as for Noonan's claims on reduced clauses. It also showed that there is no across-the-board replacement of finite *that*-clauses by non-finite clauses.

While our analysis is, on the whole, not at odds with earlier claims on the differential patterns of preference and differential evolution of finite and non-finite CCs, it is important that it has made use of state-of-the-art methodology and involves a large data set, thus putting these earlier analyses on much more solid empirical ground. Further, while the focus in this chapter has been on non-categorical CC-variation, and on statistical modelling as a way to get a handle on this variation, the study of *admit* has also shown that due attention should be given to categorical CC-variation, and that one and the same verb may harbour the two types of variation. Finally, as has already been suggested in Cuyckens et al. (2014), it is only when a larger set of verbs will have been investigated that we will be able to get a good picture of the development of CC patterns, and the (changing) factors conditioning these patterns. This study is meant to be a further contribution to this research programme.

Notes

1. The second author gratefully acknowledges the financial support of the Research Foundation, Flanders. Both authors are very much indebted to Benedikt Szmrecsanyi for running the logistic regression models, and helping them with the interpretation.
2. Most linguists, also of the generative persuasion, are now agreed that the diachronic perspective is an important facet of a satisfactory account of complementation.
3. In the case of *to*-infinitives, 'subjectless' refers to instances where the subject is not expressed in the subclause, but includes examples like *The man, who is admitted to be the world's greatest author,(...)*, where the CC-subject is expressed in the matrix clause and functions as the antecedent of the relative clause.
4. This example runs as follows: 'He denied the legality of the first; he admitted to his marrying Miss Clark[;] he denied the legality of the marriage, with Miss Marshall' (OBC, 1851).
5. Culpeper and Kytö (2010: 17) classify trial proceedings as 'speech-based': '"Speech-based" genres, such as Trial proceedings, are those that are based on an actual "real-life" speech event. There is no claim here that such genres involve the accurate recording of a speech event. In the absence of audio or video recording equipment or even full systems of shorthand, most speech-based texts are reconstructions assisted by notes.'
6. Information-based factors (as discussed in Noël 2003) were not included, as the present study focuses on [CTP – CC] patterns only. Nor was *horror aequi* (Rudanko 2000, Vosberg 2003) or factors relating to geographical or social stratification (Mair 2000, 2003).
7. The information in SMALL CAPS indicates the factor, as it was labelled in the Excel database.
8. Initially a distinction was made for finite clauses with a *that*-complementizer between, on the one hand, intervening words between the matrix verb and *that* and, on the other hand, intervening words between *that* and the subject of the complement. In the statistical analysis, this distinction turned out to be impracticable and was given up.
9. In a statistical model (such as the one described below), the factors triggering a particular outcome are said to have a *predictive* value (see Gries 2012).
10. We utilize the lme4 package in the statistical software package R (R Development Core Team 2011).

11. Random factors were factors with more than three levels (FORM_CC, TEMPORAL RELATION) as well as the language-external factor FILE.
12. None of them turned out to be significant predictors. Goodness of fit is C 0.86 and predictive accuracy is 83.4.

References

Achard, M. (1998) *Representation of Cognitive Structures: Syntax and Semantics of French Sentential Complements* (Berlin: Mouton de Gruyter).

Bernaisch, T., S. T. Gries and J. Mukherjee (2014) 'The Dative Alternation in South Asian Englishes: Modelling Predictors and Predicting Prototypes'. *English World-Wide*, 35: 7–31.

Bresnan, J. (1970) 'On Complementizers: Toward a Syntactic Theory of Complement Types'. *Foundations of Language*, VI (3): 297–321.

Bresnan, J. (1979) *Theory of Complementation in English Syntax* (New York: Garland).

Chomsky, N. (1965) *Aspects of the Theory of Syntax* (Cambridge, Mass.: MIT Press).

Chomsky, N. (1986). *Barriers* (Cambridge, Mass.: MIT Press).

Croft, W. (2000) *Explaining Language Change* (London: Longman).

Culpeper, J. and M. Kytö (2010) *Early Modern English Dialogues: Spoken Interaction as Writing* (Cambridge: Cambridge: University Press).

Cuyckens, H., F. D'hoedt and B. Szmrecsanyi (2014) 'Variability in Verb Complementation in Late Modern English: Finite vs. Non-Finite Patterns' in M. Hundt (ed.) *Late Modern English Syntax* (Cambridge: Cambridge University Press), pp. 182–203.

Declerck, R. (1991) *A Comprehensive Descriptive Grammar of English* (Kaitakusha).

Denison, D. (1998). 'Syntax' in S. Romaine (ed.) *Cambridge History of the English Language*, Vol. 4 (Cambridge: Cambridge University Press), pp. 92–329.

De Smet, H. (2008) 'Diffusional Change in the English System of Complementation'. PhD dissertation, Department of Linguistics, University of Leuven.

De Smet, H. (2012) 'Review of Yoko Iyeiri. *Verbs of Implicit Negation and Their Complements in the History of English*. Amsterdam and Philadelphia: John Benjamins. 223p. ISBN 978-90-272-1170-5.' *ICAME-Journal*, 35: 138–43.

De Smet, H. (2013) *Spreading Patterns: Diffusional Change in the English System of Complemenation* (Oxford: Oxford University Press).

Dixon, R. W. (1991) *A New Approach to English Grammar on Semantic Principles* (Oxford: Oxford University Press).

Duffley, P. (1992) *The English Infinitive* (London: Longman).

Duffley, P. (1999) 'The Use of the Infinitive and the *-Ing* after Verbs Denoting the Beginning, Middle and End of an Event'. *Folia Linguistica*, XXXIII: 295–331.

Fanego, T. (1996) 'The Development of Gerunds as Objects of Subject-Control Verbs in English (1400–1700)'. *Diachronica*, XIII: 29–62.

Fanego, T. (1998) 'Developments in Argument Linking in Early Modern English Gerund Phrases'. *English Language and Linguistics*, 2: 87–119.

Felser, C. (1999) *Verbal Complement Clauses* (Amsterdam: John Benjamins).

Fischer, O. (1995) 'The Distinction between *to* and Bare Infinitival Complements in Late Middle English'. *Diachronica*, 12: 1–30.

Givón, T. (1980) 'The Binding Hierarchy and the Typology of Complements'. *Studies in Language*, 4: 333–77.

Gries, S. T. (2012) 'Statistische Modellierung'. *Zeitschrift für germanistische Linguistik*, 40: 38–67.

Huber, M., P. Maiwald, M. Nissel and B. Widlitzki (2012) *The Old Bailey Corpus. Spoken English in the 18th and 19th Centuries* (www.uni-giessen.de/oldbaileycorpus, date accessed 15 June 2012).

Langacker, R. W. (1991) *Cognitive Grammar,* Vol. 2 (Stanford: Stanford University Press).

Langacker, R. W. (2008) *Cognitive Grammar: a Basic Introduction* (Oxford: Oxford University Press).

Los, B. (2005) *The Rise of the To-Infinitive* (Oxford: Oxford University Press).

Mair, C. (2002) 'Three Changing Patterns of Verb Complementation in Late Modern English'. *English Language and Linguistics,* 6: 105–31.

Mair, C. (2003) 'Gerundial Complements after *begin* and *start*: Grammatical and Sociolinguistic Factors, and how they work against each other' in G. Rohdenburg and B. Mondorf (eds) *Determinants of Grammatical Variation in English* (Berlin: Mouton de Gruyter), pp. 329–45.

Miller, D. G. (2001) *Nonfinite Structures in Theory and Change* (Oxford: Oxford University Press).

Mindt, D. (2000) *An Empirical Grammar of the English Verb* (Berlin: Cornelsen).

Noël, D. (2003) 'Is There Semantics in All Syntax? The Case of Accusative and Infinitive Constructions vs. That-Clauses' in G. Rohdenburg and B. Mondorf (eds) *Determinants of Grammatical Variation in English* (Berlin: Mouton de Gruyter), pp. 347–77.

Noonan, M. (2007) [1985] 'Complementation' in T. Shopen (ed.) *Language Typology and Syntactic Description:* Vol. 2, *Complex Constructions* (Cambridge: Cambridge University Press), pp. 52–150.

Quirk, R., S. Greenbaum, G. Leech and J. Svartvik (1985) *A Comprehensive Grammar of the English Language* (London: Longman).

Pinheiro, J. C. and D. M. Bates (2000) *Mixed-Effects Models in S and S-PLUS* (New York: Springer).

R Development Core Team (2011) *R: a Language and Environment for Statistical Computing* (Vienna, Austria, http://www.R-project.org/).

Radford, A. (1997) *Syntactic Theory and the Structure of English* (Cambridge: Cambridge University Press).

Rizzi, L. (1990) *Relativized Minimality* (Cambridge, Mass.: MIT Press).

Rohdenburg, G. (1995) 'On the Replacement of Finite Complement Clauses by Infinitives in English'. *English Studies,* 76: 367–88.

Rohdenburg, G. (1996) 'Cognitive Complexity and Increased Grammatical Explicitness in English'. *Cognitive Linguistics,* 7: 149–82.

Rohdenburg, G. (2006) 'The Role of Functional Constraints in the Evolution of the English Complementation System' in C. Dalton-Puffer, D. Kastovsky, N. Ritt and H. Schendl (eds) *Syntax, Style and Grammatical Norms: English from 1500–2000* (Bern: Peter Lang), pp. 143–66.

Rohdenburg, G. (2014) 'On the Changing Status of *That*-Clause' in M. Hundt (ed.) *Late Modern English Syntax* (Cambridge: Cambridge University Press), pp. 155–81.

Rosenbaum, P. (1967) *The Grammar of English Predicate Complementation* (Cambridge, Mass.: MIT Press).

Rudanko, J. (1998) *Change and Continuity in the English Language: Studies on Complementation over the Past Three Hundred Years* (Lanham, Md: University Press of America).

Rudanko, J. (2000) *Corpora and Complementation* (Lanham, Md: University Press of America).

Rudanko, J. (2006) 'Watching English Grammar Change'. *English Language and Linguistics*, 10: 31–48.

Rudanko, J. (2010) 'Explaining Grammatical Variation and Change: a Case Study of Complementation in American English over Three Decades'. *Journal of English Linguistics*, 38: 4–24.

Rudanko, J. (2012) 'Exploring Aspects of the Great Complement Shift, with Evidence from the TIME Corpus and COCA' in Terttu Nevalainen and Elizabeth Closs Traugott (eds) *The Oxford Handbook of the History of English* (Oxford: Oxford University Press), pp. 222–32.

Smith, M. B. (2002) 'The Semantics of *to*-Infinitival vs. *-ing* Verb Complement Constructions in English' (with J. Escobedo) in M. Andronis, C. Ball, H. Helston, and S. Neuvel (eds) *The Proceedings from the Main Session of the Chicago Linguistic Society's Thirty-Seventh Meeting* (Chicago: Chicago Linguistic Society), pp. 549–65.

Tagliamonte, S. and R. H. Baayen (2012) 'Models, Forests, and Trees of York English: Was/Were Variation as a Case Study for Statistical Practice'. *Language Variation and Change*, 24: 135–78.

Van Bogaert, J., C. Shank and K. Plevoets (forthcoming) 'The Diachronic Development of Zero Complementation: a Multifactorial Analysis of the *That*/Zero Alternation with *Think, Suppose*, and *Believe*'. *Corpus Linguistics and Linguistic Theory*.

Vosberg, U. (2003) 'The Role of Extractions and Horror Aequi in the Evolution of *-ing* Complements in Modern English' in G. Rohdenburg and B. Mondorf (eds) *Determinants of Grammatical Variation in English* (Berlin: Mouton de Gruyter), pp. 329–45.

Warner, A. (1982) *Complementation in Middle English and the Methodology of Historical Syntax* (University Park: Pennsylvania State University Press).

Wierzbicka, A. (1988) *The Semantics of Grammar* (Amsterdam: John Benjamins).

Corpora

Old Bailey Corpus (OBC), pilot version, http://www.uni-giessen.de/oldbaileycorpus/

Corpus of Late Modern English Texts (CLMET 3.0), https://perswww.kuleuven.be/~u0044428/clmet3_0.htm

Wordbanks Online, http://wordbanks.harpercollins.co.uk

5

The Embedded Negation Constraint and the Choice between More or Less Explicit Clausal Structures in English

Günter Rohdenburg
University of Paderborn

5.1 Introduction

This chapter considers a wide range of embedded clausal structures that come in pairs and whose members may be described as representing more or less explicit choices.[1] Typical and presumably uncontroversial examples of such contrasts are found in (1a–b) and (2a–b):

(1) a. He pledged (that) he would reduce taxes.
   b. He pledged to reduce taxes.
(2) a. We helped those students to complete their course of study.
   b. We helped those students Ø complete their course of study.

So far, the prevailing approaches to such alternatives have focused on a variety of semantic, communicative and sociolinguistic/stylistic aspects. Over the last two decades, it has become clear, however, that this kind of grammatical variation is additionally controlled by several processing tendencies (see, for example, Berg 1998, Hawkins 1999, 2004, Gries 2003, Wasow 2002, Rohdenburg and Mondorf 2003, Lohse et al. 2004, Schlüter 2005, Vosberg 2006, Fanego 2007, Rohdenburg and Schlüter 2009, Mondorf 2009, Rudanko 2011, Berlage 2014). It has been shown, in particular, that a large number of contextual constraints can be subsumed under the so-called Complexity Principle. The principle represents a correlation between processing complexity and grammatical explicitness, and it has been described as follows:

> In the case of more or less explicit constructional options, the more explicit one(s) will tend to be preferred in cognitively more complex environments (see, for example, Rohdenburg 1995, 1996, 2000, 2006a/b, 2007, 2008, 2009a/b, Vosberg 2006, Mondorf 2009, Berlage 2014).

It is well known that semantic and communicative tendencies are slippery concepts which are extremely difficult to quantify empirically. By contrast, complexity effects generally translate into identifiable structural features, and as such they readily lend themselves to empirical research in (large) computerized corpora.

Consider, for instance, the contextual changes made to the a-examples in (1) and (2):

(1) c. He pledged that if he were elected he would reduce taxes.
(2) c. We helped those students who had undergone medical treatment for this disease to complete their course of study.

In (1c), an adverbial clause has been inserted between the superordinate and subordinate clauses. In (2c), the object-noun phrase has been expanded by a relative clause. The two kinds of complications, structural discontinuity and nominal complexity, are among the most intensively studied phenomena in this research paradigm, and in line with the Complexity Principle they have always been found to strikingly increase the shares of the more explicit variants (see, for example, Vosberg 2006, Mondorf 2009, Berlage 2009, 2014, Rohdenburg 2003: 225–8, 2006a: 148–9, 2006b, 2007: 225–7, 2008: 318–21, 2009a, b).

This chapter is concerned with the use of negation as a further important (though sorely neglected) complexity factor in subordinate clauses.[2] The inquiry was inspired by Horn (1978: 191–205), who points out by reference to minimal pairs like (3a–b) that negated complements are attracted cross-linguistically to maximally explicit clausal structures.

(3) a. ? I let/made/had him not smoke. (Horn 1978: 197)
    b. I allowed/forced/ordered him not to smoke. (Ibid.)

With the unmarked infinitive in (3a), negated complements are found to be very awkward at best. By contrast, complement negation is easily accommodated by the marked infinitive in (3b). Horn uses the term Embedded Negation Constraint to designate this tendency despite the fact that it is illustrated only by means of verb-dependent complement clauses.

The purpose of this chapter is to test the Embedded Negation Constraint on a large number of clausal rivals in present-day English and earlier stages of English. Instead of relying on acceptability contrasts such as (3), the argumentation will throughout be supported by distributional differences as discovered in large computerized databases. In other words, we will be testing the Performance-Grammar-Correspondence Hypothesis advanced by Hawkins (2004: 3): 'Grammars have conventionalized syntactic structures in proportion to their degree of preference in performance, as evidenced by patterns of selection in corpora and by ease of processing in psycholinguistic experiments.' Thus the expectation is that the kinds of acceptability contrasts discovered by Horn in various languages should be reflected in text-distributional preferences in those cases where both options are allowed in principle.

The notion of clausal explicitness informally introduced on the basis of the complements in (1a–b) and (2a–b) may be equated with the (degree of clausal) finiteness as expounded by Givón (1990: chs 13 and 19). In particular, Givón points out that 'The finiteness of a clause is expressed as the degree of its similarity to the prototype transitive main clause' (ibid.: 853). Accordingly, in English, all finite subordinate clauses including those featuring subjunctives rank higher on the scale of finiteness than any comparable infinitives or gerunds. Even *for … to*-infinitives and gerunds containing their own subjects (see sections 5.2.4 and 5.2.6–5.2.7) are clearly less finite than rival finite clauses. This is partly because – unlike finite clauses – their subjects are realized as less prototypical non-nominative phrases. This chapter deals with only four kinds of explicitness contrast in the English subordinate clause that are not covered by Givón's analyses and which will have to be considered more closely later on: *try* + marked infinitive versus *try and* + verbal base form (section 5.4), modal verb (e.g. *should*) + bare infinitive versus the subjunctive after mandative predicates (sections 5.5.1–5.5.2), the marked infinitive versus the gerund (sections 5.6.1–5.6.2), and the prepositional gerund versus the directly linked type (section 5.7).

In Tottie (1991), a distinction is drawn between *not*-negation (including, of course, contractions like *isn't*, *didn't* and so on) and all other forms of syntactic negation which have the negative element fused with different types of indefinites such as determiners, pronouns and adverbs as in *no* + N, *none*, *nothing*, *nowhere* and *never*. The latter are subsumed under the category of *no*-negation. This chapter focuses on *not*-negation, ideally contrasting this strategy with all other clauses of the relevant type not containing any forms of *no*-negation (in Tottie's terminology). As pointed out in later sections (5.2.1 and 5.8), some forms of *no*-negation exhibit a similar influence on the choice of clausal variants to that of *not*-negation. Therefore, I would have preferred to include a series of detailed analyses of at least some major types of *no*-negation. However, with the vast majority of embedded clauses to be presented below, *no*-negation is far too rare to be dealt with on its own. It follows that the basic syntactic contrast between *not*-negated and non-negated examples is in general not seriously affected if any occurring instances of *no*-negation are not explicitly excluded. However, it is only in a restricted number of case studies, supported by available older analyses, that the basic research strategy has been departed from in the following manner:

(a) The category of negated clauses may include the occasional example of *no*-negation, and
(b) the category of other than *not*-negated examples may include a negligible admixture of *no*-negation.

While concentrating on verb-dependent complement clauses, this chapter attempts to show that the Embedded Negation Constraint does indeed extend to other types of subordinate clauses including those introduced by complex conjunctions.

In addition to the quotations in OED2, the database used for this study consists of a large number of British and American newspapers (including a newsmagazine) from the 1990s and early 2000s (3,160,532,479 words), the BNC (100,000,000 words) and a collection of historical data sets provided by Chadwyck-Healey (NCF = 37,589,837 words) and the Gutenberg project (30,900,678 words).

5.2 Finite and non-finite clauses

5.2.1 Commissive verbs like *pledge* and *vow*

We start with the verb *pledge* as a typical representative of the class of commissive verbs. What, then, is the effect of *not*-negation on the choice of the two more or less explicit variants illustrated in (4a–b)?

(4) a. He pledged (that) he would not increase taxes.
    b. He pledged not to/to not increase taxes.

Compare the analysis shown in Table 5.1, which distinguishes between cases involving *not*-negated complements and all others.[3]

The evidence clearly confirms our expectations: in the absence of *not*-negation, the more explicit finite clause is used only very sparingly, in less than 6 per cent of all cases. However, the proportion of finite clauses rises conspicuously (to 25 per cent) in the case of complement negation.

This brings us to similar contrasts involving the verb *vow*, as shown in (5a–b):

(5) a. She vowed (not/never) to return.
    b. She vowed (that) she would (not/never) return.

The case of *vow* is complicated by the fact that *not*-negation is not just rivalled but clearly outnumbered by a functionally related strategy, the use

Table 5.1 Finite and infinitival complements associated with the verb *pledge* in British newspapers (t90–4, g90–4, d91–4, m93–4) (adapted from Table 2 in Rohdenburg 2000: 28)

	I finite	II *to*	III total	IV % finite
1 *not*-negation	47	142	189	24.9
2 remaining cases	217	~3823	~4040	~5.4

of the negator *never*. Comparing the two strategies in Table 5.2, we find that both of them increase substantially the proportions of the finite option, with *not*-negation producing a distinctly stronger effect than *never*-negation.[4]

5.2.2 Directive verbs associated with (personal) objects

A related kind of contrast used to be typical of directive verbs like *command*, *charge* and *entreat*. Consider the relevant variants in (6a–b):

(6) a. *The captain commanded them that they should (not) blow up the bridge.

b. The captain commanded them (not) to blow up the bridge.

Today, (6a) is no longer acceptable in English. In fact, with almost all directive verbs, type (6a) including a personal object has been ousted completely by type (6b) over the last few centuries (Rohdenburg 1995). On the basis of the Complexity Principle, we would now predict that finite complements as in (6a) should have survived much better under *not*-negation than elsewhere. This is exactly what the manual analysis in Table 5.3 has brought to light.

In the corpus of narratives used here, ranging from Gascoigne (1575) to Swift (1726), negated complements use the finite option roughly ten times as frequently as non-negated ones.

Table 5.2 Finite and infinitival complements associated with and immediately following the string *he vowed* in British newspapers (t90–00, g90–00, d91–00, m93–00)

	I finite	II *to*-inf.	III total	IV % finite
1 *not-/never*-negation	36 (15/21)	104 (26/78)	140 (41/99)	25.7 (36.5/21.2)
2 remaining cases (excluding any other forms of syntactic negation)	33	477	510	6.5

Table 5.3 Finite and infinitival complements after the sequence directive verb + (personal) object in 10 selected authors of the sixteenth to (early) eighteenth centuries (based on Rohdenburg 1995: 378–80)

	I finite	II *to*	III total	IV % finite
1 *not*-negation (and any examples of *no*-negation)	23	18	41	56.1
2 other cases (not involving any form of syntactic negation)	9	~145	~154	~5.8

5.2.3 Indefinite object deletion with directive verbs

Type (6a) is still common enough in most other European languages. In addition to (6a), and again unlike most other European languages, directive verbs in English have virtually lost the type of construction illustrated in (7a):

(7) a. *The captain commanded (not) to blow up the bridge.

Of course, indefinite object deletion is still possible with the finite rival as in (7b):

(7) b. The captain commanded that the bridge (should) (not) be blown up.

Type (7a) just about survives with two mild directive verbs, *advise* and *recommend*. In both cases, the receding infinitive has been largely replaced by the upcoming gerund. For the verb *advise*, this gives us the functional equivalents set out in (8a–c) (cf. also section 5.6.1):

(8) a. They advised that his instructions (should) (not) be followed.
 b. They advised (not) to follow his instructions.
 c. They advised (not) following his instructions.

In this section, we are comparing passive finite complements as in (8a), which leave the agent unspecified, with the two competing non-finite constructions in (8b–c). Consider now the corpus analysis summarized in Table 5.4, which collapses the two non-finite options.

As predicted by the Complexity Principle, there is a clear contrast between the two kinds of context under scrutiny, with *not*-negation triggering a larger proportion of finite complements than all other cases. Comparing the two national varieties, we note that the effect of *not*-negation is greatly enhanced in British English.

5.2.4 Finite clauses and rivalling *for ... to*-infinitives after mandative uses of *plead*

This section contrasts finite passive complements like (9a) with those like (9b), where the younger infinitival passive complement contains its own subject and might even be bulkier than the *that*-clause:

(9) a. They pleaded (that) she (should) (not) be notified.
 b. They pleaded for her (not) to be notified.

Nevertheless, as pointed out in the introduction, the non-prototypical realization of the subject in (9b) leaves no doubt that the finite complement in

Table 5.4 Finite and non-finite complements after the verb *advise* (used without personal object) in British and American English

			I *(should)* *be -ed* etc.	II *to/-ing*	III total	IV % *(should)* *be -ed* etc.
BrE	1	*not*-negation (BNC, t90–01, g90–00, d91–00, m93–00)	56	34	90	62.2
	2	remaining cases excluding *no*-negation* (BNC, t90, t95, t00, g90, g95, g00, d91, d95, d00, m93, m95, m00)	56	397	453	12.4
AmE	1	*not*-negation (L92–95, D92–5, W90–92, N01)	11	27	38	28.9
	2	remaining cases excluding *no*-negation† (L93–4, D93–4, W91–2)	29	279	308	9.4

*Here the analysis of non-finite structures has been confined to those examples immediately following the verb forms *advise/advises/advising*.
†Here the analysis of non-finite structures has been confined to those examples immediately following the verb *advise*.

(9a) represents a more finite or explicit grammatical alternative. Accordingly, we would expect the use of syntactic negation in the complement clause after *plead* to favour the selection of the finite option. As is seen in Table 5.5, the expectation is confirmed for (a) the aggregate of *not*-negation and *no*-negation and for (b) *not*-negation on its own.

5.2.5 Finite clauses and rivalling gerunds after mandative uses of *advocate*

In the case of *advocate*, the younger and more common gerundial construction as in (10a) may correspond to active as well as passive *that*-clauses as in (10b) and (10c):

(10) a. They advocate (not) treating us more respectfully.
  b. They advocate that everybody (should) (not) treat us more respectfully.
  c. They advocate that we (should) (not) be treated more respectfully (by everybody).

Again, it may be assumed that any occurrence of syntactic negation should be attracted to the more explicit finite structures, which – unlike the gerund — contain their own subjects. The assumption is borne out by the evidence in Table 5.6.

Table 5.5   The rivalry between passive finite complements and *for ... to*-infinitives after active uses of mandative *plead* in American newspapers (L92–9, D92–5, W90–2, N01) and *Time Magazine* for 1989–94*

	I finite complement	II *for ... to-* infinitive	III total	IV % finite complement
1 complements involving some form of syntactic negation following the verb *plead*				
(a) all examples	14 (11/3)	1	15	93.3
(b) *not*-negation	11 (9/2)	1	12	91.7
(c) *no*-negation (involving negated subject NPs)	3 (2/1)	–	3	
2 remaining examples not containing any form of syntactic negation				
(a) all examples	35 (34/1)	25	60	58.3
(b) prepositional arguments (= *with*-phrases) immediately preceding the complement clause	4	–	4	
(c) adverbial prepositional phrase intervening between the verb *plead* and the complement clause	2	2	4	
(d) all examples excluding intervening elements between the verb *plead* and the complement clause	29 (28/1)	23	52	55.8

*The bracketed figures distinguish between subjunctives and *should*-structures.

5.2.6   Finite and gerundial clauses dependent on nouns

Complement clauses typically function as core elements of a higher clause (Dixon 2006). Going beyond the prototypical domain of clausal complements, this section compares finite and gerundial clauses governed by nouns such as *risk*. The contrast is illustrated in examples (11a–b):

(11) a. There was the (great) risk that the Government would (not) take over the bank.

Table 5.6 The rivalry between finite complements and gerunds after active uses of mandative *advocate* in the *Los Angeles Times* for 1992–9*

	I finite	II gerunds	III total	IV % finite
1 complements involving some form of syntactic negation following the verb *advocate* (a) all examples	17 (9/5/3)	7	24	70.8
(b) *not*-negation	13 (7/5/1)	6	19	68.4
(c) *no*-negation involving *no* 1 *longer* (1x) and negated subject and object phrases	4 (2/0/2)	1 (*doing* *nothing*)	5	80
2 remaining examples not containing any form of syntactic negation	~275	~1,334	~1,609	~20.6

*The bracketed figures distinguish between subjunctives, *should*-structures and verb forms ambivalent between the subjunctive and the indicative.

Table 5.7 Finite and gerundial complements associated with the noun *risk* in British newspapers (Contextual restriction: use of subject expressions involving the definite article immediately following *risk that/Ø/of*)

	I finite	II of the ... -*ing*	III total	IV % finite
1 *not*-negation (t01–4, g01–5, d02, d04–5, i02–5)	70	6	76	92.1
2 remaining cases (excluding other forms of syntactic negation) (t04, g05, d05, i05)	206	127	333	61.9

b. There was the (great) risk of the Government('s) (not) taking over the bank.

As shown in (11a–b), the corpus analysis is confined to cases involving subjects introduced by the definite article. The evidence in Table 5.7 yields the expected result: examples displaying *not*-negation are much more frequently found in (the more explicit) finite clause than the remaining non-negated ones.

5.2.7 The rivalry between finite adverbial clauses and prepositional gerunds

Superficially similar contrasts have evolved in the course of the Early and Late Modern English periods with a number of (partly grammaticalized) prepositional structures. These include the items in (12), which are commonly treated as (emergent or obsolescent) complex conjunctions:

(12) on account, on the basis (Hopper and Traugott 2003: 185, Rohdenburg 2008: 320–1, Rohdenburg and Schlüter 2009: 407–8), on (the) condition (Quirk et al. 1972: 746, Biber et al. 1999: 844, Schlüter 2009), in the event (Biber et al. 1999: 844), for fear (Rohdenburg 2008: 328, Rohdenburg and Schlüter 2009: 407–9), by reason (Rohdenburg 2008: 326)

Accordingly, we are dealing in cases like (13) with (finite) adverbial clauses and their non-finite counterparts containing an explicit (notional) subject:

(13) a. In the event that the team is delayed we will have to make alternative arrangements.
    b. In the event of the team('s) being delayed we will have to make alternative arrangements.

Comparing in Table 5.8 the two options with respect to *not*-negation, we find in British English much the same situation as in Table 5.7. There is a clear-cut divergence between the two kinds of environment, and in the expected direction. The evidence for American English, however, remains inconclusive simply because the (older) gerundial alternative is hardly used at all.

Table 5.8 Finite and gerundial clauses associated with *in the event* in British and American newspapers*,†

			I finite	II *of* NP *-ing*	III total	IV % finite
BrE	1	*not*-negation (t90–00, g90–00, d91–00)	68	61	129	52.7
	2	non-negated clauses excluding *no*-negation as well (t95, g95, d95)	45	135	180	25
AmE	1	*not*-negation (L92–5)	48	–	48	100
	2	non-negated clauses excluding *no*-negation as well (L93)	108	2	110	98.2

*In the category of *not*-negation, the following contractions have been searched for in addition to non-contracted *not* and *cannot*: *don't, doesn't, didn't, hasn't, hadn't, isn't, aren't, ain't, aint, wouldn't, shouldn't, won't, can't, couldn't*.
†The analysis is confined to those cases where *in the event* (*that/Ø/of*) is followed immediately by (the subject of) the finite or gerundial clause.

5.3 Marked and unmarked infinitives

5.3.1 *to help* + direct object

This brings us to the rivalry between marked and unmarked infinitives. For practical purposes, and unlike earlier stages of English, there is only one (transitive) verb left today, namely *help* as in (2a–b), which still allows both options, even though the marked infinitive has been disappearing at a dramatic rate, in particular in American English (see, for example, Mair 1995, 2002, Berlage 2014, Rohdenburg 2009b: 316–19).[5] Concerning the use of *not*-negation in infinitival complements as in (14), received opinion has it that the *to*-infinitive is still obligatory.

(14) She helped me not (to) make a hash of things.

While no longer true at present even in British English, this certainly provides a valuable hint pointing in the right direction. The issue is settled by the evidence in Table 5.9, which contrasts examples involving *not*-negation with an available set of all uses in both British and American English.

Since *not*-negation is extremely rare in this area, the category of all uses may in fact represent a true complement set in the mathematical sense. In both British and American English, *not*-negation is seen to preserve the marked infinitive to a strikingly higher extent than all (other) uses. On this basis, it is safe to predict that the marked infinitive will still be found in *not*-negated complements long after it has been eliminated from most other environments.

5.3.2 *to bid* + direct object

In earlier stages of English, the rivalry between the marked and the unmarked infinitive was found with several other verbs governing direct objects (see, for example, Schlüter 2005: 185ff.). This section focuses on

Table 5.9 Marked and unmarked infinitives after the verb *help* + object in British and American periodicals

			I *to*	II Ø	III total	IV % *to*
BrE	1	*not*-negation (t90–4, g90–4, d91–4, m93–4)	34	5	39	87.2
	2	all uses (1st quarter of t92)	332	411	793	43.9
AmE	1	*not*-negation (L92–5, D92–5, W90–2)	26	22	48	54.2
	2	all uses (TAL90, TAL94)	25	445	468	5.3

Table 5.10 Marked and unmarked infinitives immediately following the verb *bid* + object in British authors born between 1800 and 1869 (NCF, MNC/B, LNC/B)*†

	I *to*	II Ø	III total	IV % *to*
1 *not*-negation	21	37	58	36.2
2 remaining cases excluding *no*-negation	120	2,380	2,500	4.8

*The object expressions studied are confined to the personal pronouns *me/you/him/her/it/us/them/ thee*.
†The analysis excludes the verbal mergers *beware* and *begone* (and their spelling variants), which virtually always occur without infinitive marking.

the obsolescent use of *bid* illustrated in (15a–b), which was still current in nineteenth-century narratives:

(15) a. She bade me (not) to leave the house.
     b. She bade me (not) Ø leave the house.

While the distribution of the infinitive marker in passive constructions has been found to be sensitive to the Principle of Rhythmic Alternation (Rohdenburg and Schlüter 2000: 484–8, Schlüter 2005: 203–6), very little is known concerning active uses like (15a–b). Visser's (1973: 2302) statement that '– *to* is normal, although here and there + *to* puts in an appearance, mostly, it would seem, for rhythmical or other stylistic reasons' has so far been neither supported nor refuted empirically. For our purposes, a more pertinent hint is found in an American usage book published over 90 years ago:

The verb *bid*, except before a negative or in the passive voice, takes the infinitive without *to*;...
1. They *bade* me go in; they *bade* me *not to go* in. ...(Ball 1923: 100)

Even though the contrast between the two environments has been exaggerated in both directions, we do find it essentially confirmed by the data analysed in Table 5.10.

5.4 Marked infinitives and pseudo-coordinated structures involving the verb stem *try*

Recently, there has been a spate of corpus-based studies analysing the two complement options found in examples like (16a–b) with the verb stem *try* (see, for example, Lind 1983, Kjellmer 2000, Rohdenburg 2003: 236–42, Vosberg 2006: 224–34, Hommerberg and Tottie 2007, Tottie 2009: 343–9, 2012).

(16) a. They made/asked us Ø/to try (not) to ignore the matter.
     b. They made/asked us Ø/to try and (not) ignore the matter.

Table 5.11 Marked infinitives and pseudo-coordinated structures associated with and immediately following the verb stem *try* in the BNC

	I *to*-inf.	II *and* + verb stem	III total	IV % *to*-inf.
1 *to try:* a *not*-negation	7	4	11	63.6
b remaining cases excluding *no*-negation in a representative sample	40	29	69	58.0
2 Ø *try:* a *not*-negation	327	–	327	100
b remaining cases excluding *no*-negation in a representative sample	103	32	135	76.3

However, negated complements have generally been neglected so far. The first question to be answered is which of the two variants should be regarded as the more explicit clausal type. No doubt, the *to*-infinitive represents an extremely pervasive class of non-finite complements. In addition, in cases like (16a), where it necessarily refers to a future event, the infinitive marker is felt to be closely related semantically to the preposition *to*. By contrast, no such connection exists in the case of pseudo-coordinated structures such as (16b). Moreover, the cue value of *and* + verb stem is relatively low: the string functions only very rarely as a clausal complement, and unlike *to* + verb stem it cannot be identified as a clausal structure in the absence of the governing verb. These facts alone suggest that the *to*-infinitive constitutes a more explicit clausal choice than the pseudo-coordinated structure. With this in mind, compare the corpus findings in Table 5.11, which are based on the complete BNC.

After *to* + *try*, we fail to find a significant contrast in the expected direction, presumably because the figures for the use of *not*-negation are simply too low. However, the predicted contrast does indeed occur with all other uses of the stem *try* lumped together. Here, a total of 327 instances of *not*-negated complements are exclusively realized by the *to*-infinitive.

5.5 Modal verb + infinitive versus the subjunctive

5.5.1 Complement clauses after directive or mandative predicates

As is shown in (8a) and (17a–b), the verbs *advise* and *suggest* – like many other directive or mandative predicates – may be associated with two competing kinds of finite complements, a modal construction usually involving *should* or the subjunctive:

(17) a. He suggested that the exam should (not) be repeated.
b. He suggested that the exam (not) be repeated.

In the recent past, we have learnt quite a lot about many regional contrasts relating to the choice of the two variants (see, for example, Övergaard 1995, Hundt 1998, 2009: 30–1, Crawford 2009, Kjellmer 2009, Schlüter 2009, Rohdenburg 2009b: 319–22). We know, for instance, that for well over a hundred years American English has witnessed a revival of the subjunctive, which is now spilling over into British English. By contrast, very little is known about any contextual constraints that might influence the use of the subjunctive or the near-equivalent *should*-construction in cases like (17a–b). In the following, I will show that the choice is also motivated by the Complexity Principle.

To apply the principle, we have to be able to distinguish clearly between more or less explicit variants. There are a number of reasons suggesting that the *should*-construction represents a more explicit or more finite complement than the subjunctive. These include the following five:

- Analytic structures tend to be more explicit than their synthetic rivals (see, for instance, the contrast between analytic comparatives like *more proud* and synthetic ones like *prouder* dealt with by Mondorf 2009).
- Unlike the subjunctive, which shares its form with the imperative, the infinitive and finite verbs, the *should*-structure unambiguously represents a finite verb form.
- The subjunctive behaves syntactically like a reduced form of the *should*-structure in at least two respects: *not*-negation does not trigger *do*-support (see example (18) below), and the negator occupies the position it has in the corresponding modal alternative (see also Kjellmer 2009).
- As indicated above, structural discontinuities generally promote the choice of the more explicit variant. In our case, discontinuities produced by inserted *if*-clauses as in (19) below have been shown to clearly favour the *should*-structure over the subjunctive (Hagemeier 2006).
- Complements involving structural discontinuities and/or subject complexity regularly favour the presence of the complementizer *that* over its absence. In (as yet) unpublished research, I have found that there is a special affinity between the occurrence of *that* and the use of *should*-structures, with subjunctives leaning towards the zero variant in both British and American English.

(18) They requested (that) she (should) not miss this opportunity.
(19) They demanded that if the money was available everyone (should) benefit.

There is no doubt, then, that the modal alternative should be treated as a more explicit clausal structure than the subjunctive. Accordingly, we would expect there to be a special affinity between the use of *not*-negation and the analytic *should*-type. This assumption has been confirmed in all of the relevant analyses carried out by Hagemeier (2006) and myself. In this chapter, we will have to confine ourselves to the verbs *advise* and *suggest*, whose behaviour is analysed in Tables 5.12 and 5.13.

In both cases, the more explicit *should*-construction has been preserved to a far greater extent in negated complements than elsewhere. In addition, American English is seen to live up to its reputation by using the subjunctive much more frequently than does British English.

5.5.2 Adverbial clauses after *(up)on (the) condition*

As shown by Schlüter (2009: 298–301), similar tendencies are displayed by (finite) adverbial clauses associated with *on condition* and its variants *on the*

Table 5.12 Passive complements after the verb *advise* in British and American newspapers

			I *should*	II subjunctive	III total	IV *% should*
BrE	1	*not*-negation (BNC, t90–00, g90–00, d91–00, m93–00)	54	2	56	96.4
	2	remaining cases excluding *no*-negation (BNC, t90, t95, t00, g90, g95, g00, d91, d95, d00, m93, m95, m00)	42	14	56	75
AmE	1	*not*-negation (L92–5, D92–5, W90–2, N01)	6	5	11	54.5
	2	remaining cases excluding *no*-negation (L93–4, D93–4, W91–2)	9	20	29	31.0

Table 5.13 Passive complements associated with directive uses of the verb *suggest* in British and American newspapers*

			I *should*	II subjunctive	III total	IV *% should*
BrE	1	*not*-negation (g90–02)	70	1	71	98.6
	2	remaining cases excluding *no*-negation (g90, g95, g04)	181	83	264	68.6
AmE	1	*not*-negation (L92–9, D92–5, W90–2)	37	29	66	56.1
	2	remaining cases excluding *no*-negation (L95, D95, W90-2)	43	168	211	20.4

*The analysis in rows 2 (for both British and American English) is confined to sequences of the form *be* + *V-ed*, *be* + *V-t*, and *be* + *V-n*.

Table 5.14   Competing verb forms in adverbial clauses introduced by *(up)on (the) condition* in a British and American newspaper database (adapted from Figure 15.7 in Schlüter 2009: 300)*

		I modal	II indicative	III ambiguous	IV subjunctive
BrE	1 *not*-negated clauses (*N* = 56)	25	75	0	0
	2 non-negated clauses (*N* = 426)	12	70	6	12
AmE	1 *not*-negated clauses (*N* = 36)	36	17	0	47
	2 non-negated clauses (*N* = 210)	11	14	7	68

*The category of non-negated clauses contains a number of instances involving *no*-negation.

condition and *upon (the) condition*. Since Schlüter deals with passive as well as active clauses, her analysis distinguishes four categories of verb forms given as percentages of the relevant totals: (1) modals (e.g. *should*) + infinitive, (2) unambiguous indicatives, (3) forms ambiguous between indicatives and subjunctives, and (4) unambiguous subjunctives. In her present-day newspaper database, these are distributed as shown in Table 5.14.

Abstracting away from indicative and ambiguous verb forms we note that in both British and American English, *not*-negation promotes the use of *should* and other modals and disfavours the subjunctive compared to non-negated clauses. In addition, it is seen that British English is again lagging behind American English in the establishment of the subjunctive.

5.6   Marked infinitives and gerunds

5.6.1   Unspecified object control with directive verbs

One of the most important changes in the English complementation system concerns the spread of gerunds at the expense of infinitives in several types of constructions with an increasing number of verbs, adjectives and nouns (see, for example, Fanego 1996, 2007, Rudanko 1999, 2000, 2002, 2011, Vosberg 2003, 2006, 2009, Rohdenburg 2007). In the following, we will consider some of these ongoing changes.

We may begin by taking a closer look at the contrast involving the verb *advise* in examples (8b–c), which are repeated here for convenience:

(8)   b. They advised (not) to follow his instructions.
　　　c. They advised (not) following his instructions.

Remember that in these cases the object slot has been left empty. Let us now compare the evidence adduced in Table 5.15.

It is seen immediately that – in other than *not*-negated complements – only a trickle of infinitives have been preserved in both British and American English.[6] However, in *not*-negated complements, the older infinitive is still

Table 5.15 Infinitival and gerundial complements immediately following the verb *advise* (used without a personal object) in British and American English

			I *to*	II *-ing*	III total	IV *% to*
BrE	1	*not*-negation (BNC, t90–01, g90–00, d91–00, m93–00)	23	11	34	67.6
	2	remaining cases excluding *no*-negation* (BNC, t90, t95, t00, g90, g95, g00, m93, m95, m00)	10	387	397	2.5
AmE	1	*not*-negation (L92–9, D92–5, W90–2, N01)	14	13	27	51.9
	2	remaining cases excluding *no*-negation[†] (L93–4, L97–8, D93–4, W91–2, N01)	8	421	429	1.9

*Here, the analysis has been confined to those examples immediately following the verb forms *advise*, *advises*, and *advising*.
[†]Here, the analysis has been confined to those examples immediately following the verb *advise*.

used as often as the gerund in American English and twice as frequently even in British English.

A number of arguments presented by Vosberg (2003, 2006) and Fanego (2007: 213–21) suggest that the (marked) infinitive represents a more explicit clausal complement than the gerund. Accordingly, it is found again and again that structural discontinuities are particularly attracted to the *to*-infinitive rather than the gerund. Thus the data in Table 5.15 could also be said to conform to the Complexity Principle. Obviously, any other assessment would automatically weaken an important generalization.

5.6.2 Subject control verbs

Similar observations have been made with many subject control verbs including the two verbs of inception, *begin* and *start*, which are illustrated in (20) and (21):

(20) a. People began (not) to/to (not) pay attention.
  b. People began (not) paying attention.
(21) a. She started (not) to/to (not) eat breakfast.
  b. She started (not) eating breakfast.

The two verbs no doubt belong to the best researched ones in English. It has been pointed out, for instance, that the gerund has progressed further in American English than in British English and that the informal verb *start* is – in both British and American English – further advanced than the more staid *begin* (see, for example, Mair 2002, 2003, Vosberg 2006: 205–10). These observations are, of course, confirmed by the analyses summarized in Tables 5.16 and 5.17. Concentrating on non-negated complements, we find that the infinitive has been preserved much better in British English, and in both varieties with the verb *begin*. Beyond these corroborative findings, we can see that the use of *not*-negation invariably increases the shares of the *to*-infinitive.

Two further examples of verbs displaying a similar contrast between the marked infinitive and the gerund are provided by *prefer* and *feign*. Relevant examples are given in (22a–b) and (23a–b), respectively:

(22) a. We prefer (not) to talk about it in public.
    b. We prefer (not) talking about it in public.
(23) a. He feigned (not) to take an interest in the matter.
    b. He feigned (not) taking an interest in the matter.

Table 5.16 Infinitival and gerundial complements immediately following the verb *begin* in British and American newspapers*

			I to	II -ing	III total	IV % to
BrE	1	*not*-negation (t90–01, g90–00, d91–00, m93–00)	38 (36/2)	3	41	92.7
	2	remaining cases excluding *no*-negation (representative sample drawn from t95, g95, d95, m95)	65	25	90	72.2
AmE	1	*not*-negation (L92–9, D92–5, W90–2, N01)	17 (11/6)	2	19	89.5
	2	remaining cases excluding *no*-negation (representative sample drawn from L96, D94, W91, N01)	45	52	97	46.4

*The bracketed figures distinguish between the orderings *not to* + infinitive and *to not* + infinitive.

Table 5.17 Infinitival and gerundial complements immediately following the verb *start* in British and American newspapers*

			I to	II -ing	III total	IV % to
BrE	1	*not*-negation (t90–01, g90–00, d91–00, m93–00)	32 (27/5)	15	47	68.1
	2	remaining cases excluding *no*-negation (representative sample drawn from t95, g95, d95, m95)	34	52	86	39.5
AmE	1	*not*-negation (L92–9, D92–5, W90–2, N01)	17 (13/4)	14	31	54.8
	2	remaining cases excluding *no*-negation (representative sample drawn from L96, D94, W91, N01)	20	63	83	24.1

*The bracketed figures distinguish between the orderings *not to* + infinitive and *to not* + infinitive.

Prefer happens to be one of those rare verbs where the *-ing* complement was established earlier than the infinitive (Egan 2012). Even so, as is seen in Table 5.18, the infinitive has by now overtaken the gerund in both national varieties, with American English lagging behind British English. Crucially, the infinitive is more common in *not*-negated complement clauses than in non-negated ones.

A similar, though much more dramatic, regional contrast is found with *feign*, where the establishment of the infinitival complement preceded that of the gerund, thus following the usual pattern (see, for example, Vosberg 2006). The distribution of the two rivalling constructions in British and American newspapers is documented in Table 5.19.

Again we find that, unlike British English, American English shows a pronounced affinity for the gerund. Unfortunately, the negation figures

Table 5.18 Infinitival and gerundial complements immediately following the verb *prefer* in British and American newspapers*

			I to	II -ing	III total	IV % to
BrE	1	*not*-negation (i93–4)	179 (179/0)	–	179	100
	2	remaining cases excluding *no*-negation (i94)	972	52	1,024	94.9
AmE	1	*not*-negation (L92–9)	735 (727/8)	14	749	98.1
	2	remaining cases excluding *no*-negation (L92)	1,171	228	1,399	83.7

*The bracketed figures distinguish between the orderings *not to* + infinitive and *to not* + infinitive.

Table 5.19 Infinitival and gerundial complements associated with and immediately following the verb *feign* in British and American newspapers (t90–04, g90–05, d91–00, d02, d04–5, i93–4, i02–5, m93–00; L92–9, D92–5, W90–92, N01, TAL89–94)

			I to-inf.	II -ing	III total	IV % to-inf.
BrE	1	*not-/never*-negation	27 (26/1)	–	27 (26/1)	100
	2	remaining cases (excluding any other forms of syntactic negation)	124	32	156	79.5
AmE	1	*not*-negation	2	–	2	
	2	remaining cases (excluding any other forms of syntactic negation)	2	23	25	8

Table 5.20 Prepositional gerunds and directly linked ones immediately following the verb *admit* in American newspapers (L92–9, D92–5, W90–2)

		I *to -ing*	II *Ø-ing*	III total	IV *% to -ing*
1	*not*-negation	26	15	41	63.4
2	remaining cases excluding *no*-negation (representative sample drawn from L92, D92, W90)	128	208	336	38.1

are too low for American English to provide a clear-cut contrast between *not*-negated complements and all other environments. In British English, however, there is a robust contrast in the expected direction: as yet, the incoming gerund is not found at all in the case of *not*-negation.

5.7 Prepositional gerunds and directly linked ones

In a number of case studies, Vosberg (2006) has found that structural discontinuities are much more easily tolerated by prepositional gerunds than directly linked ones. In line with the preceding findings, this would suggest that the prepositional gerund represents a more explicit structure than the zero variant. Be that as it may, we can point to similar asymmetries in this area between negated and non-negated complements, as in (24a–b):

(24) a. He admitted (not) carrying out those instructions.
  b. He admitted to (not) carrying out those instructions.

The results in Table 5.20 neatly tie in with the effects produced by structural discontinuities elsewhere.

5.8 Conclusion

In this chapter, a total of 14 pairs of embedded clause types have been scrutinized, whose members may for various reasons be distinguished as constituting more or less explicit grammatical options. In conformity with Horn's Embedded Negation Constraint, which is treated as a special manifestation of the Complexity Principle, the negated clauses analysed have always been shown to gravitate towards the more explicit alternative. In addition, it has been demonstrated that the negation effects extend beyond the domain of verb-dependent complement clauses to include various types of dependent clauses governed by nouns (e.g. *risk*) and complex conjunctions (e.g. *in the event* or *on (the) condition*).

As an alternative explanation of the range of facts surveyed, it has been suggested to me that the negator *not* might simply be attracted to the historically older construction. It is true that with most of the clausal rivals analysed in this chapter there is a clear evolutionary trend towards the less explicit variant in question, with American English typically being further advanced than British English. In these cases, and in line with the Complexity Principle as well as the alternative hypothesis, *not*-negation will remain a major stronghold of the more explicit variant long after the less explicit one has generally supplanted it.

However, a closer scrutiny of the variation phenomena described identifies two sets of examples which are problematic or clearly incompatible with the alternative hypothesis. To begin with, there are those cases which involve U-turn developments or revivals of earlier constructions. As was pointed out above, the earlier subjunctive, which was later replaced by modal constructions including *should*, in particular, has been reasserting itself after directive or mandative predicates and certain conjunctions. It is not clear, therefore, which of the two variants concerned (the subjunctive or the modal construction) should be regarded as the older one. It is only when an attribute like 'recessive at present' is added that the hypothesis can be tested at all. The case of *prefer* presented in section 5.6.2 may also belong here, since the older infinitival complement has reasserted itself after having been largely replaced by the gerund in the nineteenth century (Egan 2012).

What is more, the alternative hypothesis is directly refuted by three kinds of clausal rivalry (where an earlier and less explicit variant has been increasingly replaced by a more explicit one): the prepositional gerund versus the (finite) *that*-clause after the noun *risk* (section 5.2.6), the (emergent) complex conjunction *in the event* (section 5.2.7) also governing prepositional gerunds and *that*-clauses, and, in the case of the form *try*, the pseudo-coordinated construction *and* + verbal base form alternating with the marked infinitive (section 5.4). Crucially, in all three cases, *not*-negation is attracted to the more explicit and more recent option, the finite clause after *risk* and *in the event* as well as the marked infinitive after *try*. Tottie (2012) argues convincingly that with *try* the establishment of the (more explicit) *to*-infinitive was preceded by that of the pseudo-coordinated construction. Furthermore, the historical evidence assembled in the quotations database of the *OED* leaves no doubt that, with both the noun *risk* and the conjunction *in the event*, the finite clause originated and became established later than the gerund (Rohdenburg 2013: sections 2.2 and 6). Obviously, the Complexity Principle is a synchronic constraint, which is perfectly neutral with respect to any particular direction of change.[7]

Of course, the subject matter is not exhausted by this study. For a start, there are several other complement pairs yet to be sorted out. They include those listed in (25):

(25) a. the presence or absence of *that* introducing complement or other subordinate clauses

    b. optional *to be*-deletion, as in *want/order X (to be) V-ed*
    c. the optional use of *from* in examples like *prevent X (from) doing Y* in British English
    d. the choice between finite complements and (prepositional) gerunds governed by verbs like *admit*

And here the Complexity Principle should allow us to make a number of predictions. The more explicit alternatives expected to be especially accommodating of *not*-negation should include the following:

- the presence of *that* in (25a)
- the presence of *to be* in (25b)
- the presence of *from* in (25c)
- the finite complement in (25d)

Other avenues for further research relate to the use of alternative forms of syntactic negation, referred to as *no*-negation following Tottie (1991). In the case of *vow*, we have already seen that negation by means of *never* promotes the use of finite complements like *not*-negation, though less strongly (section 5.2.1). Similarly, phrasal negation using the determiner *no* as in (26) has been shown to display a weaker tendency to select the *should*-construction than does *not*-negation (Hagemeier 2006):

(26) They demanded that no changes (should) be made to the current guidelines.

It remains to be seen, however, whether the various forms of *no*-negation show a uniform behaviour and to what extent they favour the more explicit variant less strongly than *not*-negation.

Notes

1. Previous versions of this chapter were presented at the universities of Bonn, Uppsala, Mainz, Jena and Bamberg. I wish to thank the audiences for their stimulating questions and suggestions.
2. Other kinds of grammatical (and cognitive) complexity accounted for by the Complexity Principle include the following:

   - voice contrasts (see, for example, Rohdenburg 1999: 107, 2002: 82–5, 89–91)
   - the contrast between finite and infinitival interrogative complements (see, for example, Rohdenburg 1999: 108–9, 2002: 89–90, 2003: 228–32)
   - the length of complement clauses (Rohdenburg 2006b: 55)
   - number contrasts (see, for example, Rohdenburg 2002: 80–1, 87, 93, 2003: 223–5, 2006b: 56)
   - gapping (Postal 1974: 129–31)
   - right node raising (Postal 1974: 125–8)

3. In this and all following analyses, any second (and third) conjuncts of the embedded clauses concerned have been excluded from consideration.
4. Similar negation effects to those found with *pledge* and *vow* have been observed in the case of *promise* (Rohdenburg 1999: 105–6).
5. Owing to the increasing use of the unmarked infinitive after *assist* + direct object, in particular in American English, a further contrast of this kind is now becoming established (Rohdenburg 2012: 149).
6. In present-day grammars the obsolescent infinitive as in (8b) tends to be disregarded. Thus Sammon (2002: 150) describes the situation as follows: 'The verbs *advise, allow, permit, encourage, recommend* take the infinitive with a personal object, but the gerund when there is no such object [...]'
7. The literature on the Complexity Principle refers to several other changes resulting in a statistical strengthening of the more explicit variant. They include the following:

- the replacement of *with* by *on/upon* in *prevail with/(up)on* NP + *to*-infinitive in the seventeenth to early nineteenth centuries (Rohdenburg 2000: 34–5, 2007: 223–4)
- the increase of *than* at the expense of *from* after *different* (Rohdenburg 2002: 94–6)
- in the case of *prefer* (see also Egan 2012), the increase of *over* at the expense of *to* in the type *prefer* NP$_1$ *to/over* NP$_2$ (Rohdenburg and Schlüter 2009: 387–8)
- the large-scale replacement of the zero link introducing dependent interrogatives as in *the question (of) whether this is true* by prepositional links (Rohdenburg 1999: 108–10, 2002: 86–90, 2003, 2007: 227–8, Rohdenburg and Schlüter 2009: 385–7)
- the replacement of the zero-linked beneficiary by a prepositionally linked one in (regular or primary) passives like *the money was given (to) her on her birthday* (Rohdenburg 2009a: 203–7, 2009b: 307–9)
- the replacement of the zero-linked experiencer by a prepositionally linked one after *unbecoming* (Rohdenburg 2009a: 195–6).

Bibliography

Electronic corpora

BNC	British National Corpus 1995. Version 1.0. BNC Consortium/ Oxford University Computing Services.
d91–00, 02, 04–05	*The Daily Telegraph* and *The Sunday Telegraph* on CD-ROM 1991– 2000, 2002,2004–5 Chadwyck-Healey/ProQuest.
D92–5	Detroit Free Press on CD-ROM 1992-5 Knight Ridder Information Inc.
g90–05	*The Guardian* (including *The Observer* 1994–2005) on CD-ROM 1990–2005, Chadwyck-Healey/ProQuest.
i93–4, 02–5	*The Independent* and *The Independent on Sunday* on CD-ROM 1993-4, 2002–5 ProQuest.
L92–5	*Los Angeles Times* on CD-ROM 1992–5 Knight Ridder Information Inc.
L96–9	*The Los Angeles Times* 1996–9 (courtesy of The Los Angeles Times Editorial Library).

LNC   Late Nineteenth-Century Corpus – a selection of British and American writings (complementary to the EAF and the NCF) by authors born between 1830 and 1869. Source: Project Gutenberg compiled in the Research Project 'Determinants of Grammatical Variation in English', University of Paderborn.

LNC/B   British writings in the LNC.

m93–00   *Daily Mail* and *The Mail on Sunday* on CD-ROM 1993–2000 Chadwyck-Healey.

MNC   Mid-Nineteenth Century Corpus – a selection of British and American writings (complementary to the EAF and the NCF) by authors born between 1803 and 1829. Source: Project Gutenberg compiled in the Research Project 'Determinants of Grammatical Variation in English', University of Paderborn.

MNC/B   British writings in the MNC.

N01   *The New York Times* on CD-ROM 2001 ProQuest.

NCF   *Nineteenth-Century Fiction* 1999–2000 Chadwyck-Healey.

t90–04   *The Times* and *The Sunday Times* on CD-ROM 1990–2004 Chadwyck-Healey/ProQuest.

TAL89–94   *Time Magazine* for 1989–94.

W90–92   *The Washington Times* (including *Insight on the News* 1990–2) on CD-ROM 1990–2 Wayzata Technology.

References

Ball, F. K. (1923) *Constructive English: a Handbook of Speaking and Writing* (Boston, etc.: Ginn).

Berg, T. (1998) *Linguistic Structure and Change: an Explanation from Language Processing* (Oxford: Clarendon Press).

Berlage, E. (2009) 'Prepositions and Postpositions' in G. Rohdenburg and J. Schlüter (eds) *One Language, Two Grammars? Differences between British and American English* (Cambridge: Cambridge University Press), pp. 13–48.

Berlage, E. (2014) *Complex Noun Phrases in English* (Cambridge: Cambridge University Press).

Biber, D., S. Johansson, G. Leech, S. Conrad and E. Finegan (1999) *Longman Grammar of Spoken and Written English* (Harlow: Longman).

Crawford, W. J. (2009) 'The Mandative Subjunctive' in G. Rohdenburg and J. Schlüter (eds) *One Language, Two Grammars? Differences between British and American English* (Cambridge: Cambridge University Press), pp. 257–76.

Dixon, R. M. W. (2006) 'Complement Clauses and Complementation Strategies in Typological Perspective' in R. M. Dixon and A. Y. Aikhenvald (eds) *Complementation. Explorations in Linguistic Typology* (Oxford: Oxford University Press), pp. 1–48.

Egan, T. (2012) 'Prefer: the Odd Verb out' in Irén Hegedüs and A. Fodor (eds) *English Historical Linguistics 2010: Selected Papers from the Sixteenth International Conference on English Historical Linguistics (ICEHL 16)*, Pécs, 23–27 August 2010 (Amsterdam and New York: Benjamins), pp. 215–28.

Fanego, T. (1996) 'The Development of Gerunds as Objects of Subject-Control Verbs in English (1400–1700)'. *Diachronica*, 13: 29–62.

Fanego, T. (2007) 'Drift and the Development of Sentential Complements in British and American English from 1700 to the Present Day' in J. Pérez-Guerra, D. González-Álvarez, J. L. Bueno-Alonso and E. Rama-Martínez (eds) *'Of Varying*

Language and Opposing Creed': New Insights into Late Modern English (Bern, etc.: Lang), pp. 161–235.

Givón, T. (1990) *Syntax: a Functional-Typological Introduction*. Vol. II (Amsterdam and Philadelphia: Benjamins).

Gries, S. T. (2003) *Multifactorial Analysis in Corpus Linguistics: a Study of Particle Placement* (New York: Continuum International Publishing Group Ltd).

Hagemeier, V. (2006) 'Der Einfluß struktureller/kognitiver Komplexität auf die Wahl alternativer Komplementstrukturen nach direktiven Ausdrücken im britischen und amerikanischen Englisch'. MA thesis, University of Paderborn.

Hawkins, J. A. (1999) 'Processing Complexity and Filler-Gap Dependencies across Grammars'. *Language*, 75: 244–85.

Hawkins, J. A. (2004) *Efficiency and Complexity in Grammars* (Oxford: Oxford University Press).

Hommerberg, C. and G. Tottie (2007) '*Try to* or *try and*? Verb Complementation in British and American English'. *ICAME Journal*, 31: 45–64.

Hopper, P. J. and E. C. Traugott (2003) *Grammaticalization*, 2nd edn (Cambridge: Cambridge University Press).

Horn, L. R. (1978) 'Some Aspects of Negation' in J. H. Greenberg (ed.) *Universals of Human Language*, Vol. 4 (Stanford: Stanford University Press), pp. 127–210.

Hundt, M. (1998) 'It is Important that this Study (*Should*) be Based on the Analysis of Parallel Corpora: on the Use of the Mandative Subjunctive in Four Major Varieties of English' in H. Lindquist, S. Klintborg, M. Levin and M. Estling (eds) *The Major Varieties of English: Papers from MAVEN 97* (Växjö: Acta Wexionensia), pp. 159–75.

Hundt, M. (2009) 'Colonial Lag, Colonial Innovation, or Simply Language Change?' in G. Rohdenburg and J. Schlüter (eds) *One Language, Two Grammars? Differences between British and American English* (Cambridge: Cambridge University Press), pp. 13–37.

Kjellmer, G. (2000) 'Auxiliary Marginalities: the Case of *try*' in J. M. Kirk (ed.) *Corpora Galore: Papers from the Nineteenth International Conference on English Language Research on Computerised Corpora (ICAME 1998)* (Amsterdam and Atlanta: Rodopi), pp. 115–24.

Kjellmer, G. (2009) 'The Revived Subjunctive' in G. Rohdenburg and J. Schlüter (eds) *One Language, Two Grammars? Differences between British and American English* (Cambridge: Cambridge University Press), pp. 246–56.

Lind, Å. (1983) 'The Variant Forms *try and*/*try to*'. *English Studies*, 64: 550–63.

Lohse, B., J. A. Hawkins and T. Wasow (2004) 'Processing Domains in English Verb-Particle Constructions'. *Language*, 80: 238–61.

Mair, C. (1995) 'Changing Patterns of Complementation, and Concomitant Grammaticalisation, of the Verb *help* in Present-Day British English' in B. Aarts, B. and C. F. Meyer (eds) *The Verb in Contemporary English: Theory and Description* (Oxford: Oxford University Press), pp. 258–72.

Mair, C. (2002) 'Three Changing Patterns of Verb Complementation in Late Modern English: a Real-Time Study Based on Matching Text Corpora'. *English Language and Linguistics*, 6: 105–31.

Mair, C. (2003) 'Gerundial Complements after *begin* and *start*: Grammatical and Sociolinguistic Factors and How They Work against Each Other' in G. Rohdenburg and B. Mondorf (eds) *Determinants of Grammatical Variation in English*. Topics in English Linguistics 43 (Berlin and New York: Mouton de Gruyter), pp. 329–45.

Mondorf, B. (2009) *More Support for More-Support: the Role of Processing Constraints on the Choice between Synthetic and Analytic Comparative Forms*. Studies in Language Variation (Amsterdam and Philadelphia: Benjamins).

Övergaard, G. (1995) *The Mandative Subjunctive in American and British English in the 20th Century.* Studia Anglistica Upsaliensia 94 (Uppsala: Acta Universitatis Upsaliensis and Stockholm: Almqvist & Wiksell).

Postal, P. M. (1974) *On Raising: One Rule of English Grammar and its Theoretical Implications* (Cambridge, Mass.: MIT Press).

Quirk, R., S. Greenbaum, G. Leech and J. Svartvik (1972) *A Grammar of Contemporary English* (London: Longman).

Rohdenburg, G. (1995) 'On the Replacement of Finite Complement Clauses by Infinitives in English'. *English Studies,* 76: 367–88.

Rohdenburg, G. (1996) 'Cognitive Complexity and Increased Grammatical Explicitness in English'. *Cognitive Linguistics,* 7: 149–82.

Rohdenburg, G. (1999) 'Clausal Complementation and Cognitive Complexity in English' in F.-W. Neumann and S. Schülting (eds) *Anglistentag 1998 Erfurt* (Trier: Wissenschaftlicher Verlag), pp. 101–12.

Rohdenburg, G. (2000) 'The Complexity Principle as a Factor Determining Grammatical Variation and Change in English' in I. Plag and K. P. Schneider (eds) *Language Use, Language Acquisition and Language History: (Mostly) Empirical Studies in Honour of Rüdiger Zimmermann* (Trier: Wissenschaftlicher Verlag), pp. 25–44.

Rohdenburg, G. (2002) 'Processing Complexity and the Variable Use of Prepositions in English' in H. Cuyckens and G. Radden (eds) *Perspectives on Prepositions* (Tübingen: Niemeyer), pp. 79–100.

Rohdenburg, G. (2003) 'Cognitive Complexity and *horror aequi* as Factors Determining the Use of Interrogative Clause Linkers in English' in G. Rohdenburg and B. Mondorf (eds) *Determinants of Grammatical Variation in English.* Topics in English Linguistics 43 (Berlin and New York: Mouton de Gruyter), pp. 205–49.

Rohdenburg, G. (2006a) 'The Role of Functional Constraints in the Evolution of the English Complementation System' in C. Dalton-Puffer, D. Kastovsky, N. Ritt and H. Schendl (eds) *Syntax, Style and Grammatical Norms: English from 1500–2000* (Bern, etc.: Lang), pp. 143–66.

Rohdenburg, G. (2006b) 'Processing Complexity and Competing Sentential Variants in Present-Day English' in W. Kürschner and R. Rapp (eds) *Linguistik International: Festschrift für Heinrich Weber* (Lengerich: Pabst Science Publishers), pp. 51–67.

Rohdenburg, G. (2007) 'Functional Constraints in Syntactic Change: the Rise and Fall of Prepositional Constructions in Early and Late Modern English'. *English Studies,* 88: 217–33.

Rohdenburg, G. (2008) 'On the History and Present Behaviour of Subordinating *that* with Adverbial Conjunctions in English' in E. Seoane and M. J. López-Couso (eds) *Theoretical and Empirical Issues in Grammaticalization* (Amsterdam and Philadelphia: Benjamins), pp. 315–31.

Rohdenburg, G. (2009a) 'Nominal Complements' in G. Rohdenburg and J. Schlüter (eds) *One Language, Two Grammars? Differences between British and American English* (Cambridge: Cambridge University Press), pp. 194–211.

Rohdenburg, G. (2009b) 'Grammatical Divergence between British and American English in the Nineteenth and Early Twentieth Centuries' in I. Tieken-Boon van Ostade and W. van der Wurff (eds) *Current Issues in Late Modern English* (Bern, etc.: Lang), pp. 301–29.

Rohdenburg, G. (2012) 'Britisches und Amerikanisches Englisch: Eine Sprache, zwei Grammatiken?' in L. Anderwald (ed.) *Sprachmythen – Fiktion oder Wirklichkeit?* (Frankfurt a. M., etc.: Lang), pp. 137–60.

Rohdenburg, G. (2013) 'Using the OED Quotations Database as a Diachronic Corpus' in M. Krug and J. Schlüter (eds) *Research Methods in Language Variation and Change* (Cambridge: Cambridge University Press), pp. 136–57.

Rohdenburg, G. and B. Mondorf (eds) (2003) *Determinants of Grammatical Variation in English*. Topics in English Linguistics 43 (Berlin and New York: Mouton de Gruyter).

Rohdenburg, G. and J. Schlüter (2000) 'Determinanten grammatischer Variation im Früh-und Spätneuenglischen'. *Sprachwissenschaft*, 25: 443–96.

Rohdenburg, G. and J. Schlüter (eds) (2009) *One Language, Two Grammars? Differences between British and American English* (Cambridge: Cambridge University Press).

Rudanko, J. (1999) *Diachronic Studies of English Complementation Patterns: Eighteenth Century Evidence in Tracing the Developments of Verbs and Adjectives Selecting Prepositions and Complement Clauses* (Lanham: University Press of America).

Rudanko, J. (2000) *Corpora and Complementation: Tracing Sentential Complementation Patterns of Nouns, Adjectives and Verbs over the Last Three Centuries* (Lanham: University Press of America).

Rudanko, J. (2002) *Complements and Constructions: Corpus-Based Studies on Sentential Complements in English in Recent Centuries* (Lanham: University Press of America).

Rudanko, J. (2011) *Changes in Complementation in British and American English: Corpus-Based Studies of Non-Finite Complements in Recent English* (Basingstoke: Palgrave Macmillan).

Sammon, G. (2002) *Exploring English Grammar* (Berlin: Cornelsen).

Schlüter, J. (2005) *Rhythmic Grammar: the Influence of Rhythm on Grammatical Variation and Change in English*. Topics in English Linguistics 46 (Berlin and New York: Mouton).

Schlüter, J. (2009) 'The Conditional Subjunctive' in G. Rohdenburg and J. Schlüter (eds) *One Language, Two Grammars? Differences between British and American English* (Cambridge: Cambridge University Press), pp. 277–305.

Tottie, G. (1991) 'Lexical Diffusion in Syntactic Change: Frequency as a Determinant of Linguistic Conservatism in the Development of Negation in English' in D. Kastovsky (ed.) *Historical English Syntax*. Topics in English Linguistics 2 (Berlin and New York: Mouton de Gruyter), pp. 439–67.

Tottie, G. (2009) 'How Different are American and British English Grammar? And How are They Different?' in G. Rohdenburg and J. Schlüter (eds) *One Language, Two Grammars? Differences between British and American English* (Cambridge: Cambridge University Press), pp. 341–63.

Tottie, G. (2012) 'On the History of *try* with Verbal Complements' in S. Chevalier and T. Honegegger (eds) *Words, Words, Words: Philology and Beyond. Festschrift for Andreas Fischer on the Occasion of his 65th Birthday* (Tübingen: Narr Francke Attempto), pp. 199–214.

Visser, F. T. (1973) *An Historical Syntax of the English Language*. Part III, 2nd Half: *Syntactical Units with Two and with More Verbs* (Leiden: E. J. Brill).

Vosberg, U. (2003) 'The Role of Extractions and *horror aequi* in the Evolution of -*ing* Complements in Modern English' in G. Rohdenburg and B. Mondorf (eds) *Determinants of Grammatical Variation in English*. Topics in English Linguistics 43 (Berlin and New York: Mouton de Gruyter), pp. 197–220.

Vosberg, U. (2006) *Die Große Komplementverschiebung: Außersemantische Einflüsse auf die Entwicklung satzwertiger Ergänzungen im Neuenglischen* (Tübingen: Narr).

Vosberg, U. (2009) 'Non-Finite Complements' in G. Rohdenburg and J. Schlüter (eds) *One Language, Two Grammars? Differences between British and American English* (Cambridge: Cambridge University Press), pp. 212–27.

Wasow, T. (2002) *Postverbal Behavior* (Chicago: The University of Chicago Press).

6

'Wheedled Me into Lending Him My Best Hunter': Comparing the Emergence of the Transitive *into -ing* Construction in British and American English

Juhani Rudanko
University of Tampere

6.1 Introduction and background

Consider sentence (1), abbreviated from an authentic sentence in the second part of the new version of the Corpus of Late Modern English Texts (CLMET3.0):

> (1) ... who wheedled me into lending him my best hunter ... (CLMET2
> 1796–1801, *The Parent's Assistant*)

In (1) the matrix verb *wheedle* selects three arguments. The first is the subject argument, realized by the NP *who*. The second is the direct object argument, realized by the NP *me*. The third is the oblique argument, realized by the PP *into lending him my best hunter*, which consists of the preposition *into* and a following gerund or *-ing* clause. It is assumed here that the latter has its own covert or understood subject. (For one consideration supporting the postulation of such an understood subject, see Jespersen [1940] 1961: 140–2.) The direct object of the main clause receives a semantic role from the matrix verb, and the construction in question is clearly one of control. More specifically, the construction is one of object control. To characterize the semantic roles of the three arguments, Sag and Pollard (1991: 66) proposed the labels 'Influence', 'Influenced' and 'SOA-ARG' (State of Affairs argument). These labels are self-explanatory and appropriate, but the more traditional labels of Agent, Patient or Undergoer, and Goal may also be used.

To represent the syntactic structure of the pattern for the purposes of the present study, the following representation may be used:

> (1′) [[who]$_{NP1}$ [[wheedled]$_{Verb}$ [me]$_{NP0}$ [[into]$_{Prep}$ [[[PRO]$_{NP2}$ [lending him my best hunter]$_{VP}$]$_{S2}$]$_{NP}$]$_{PP}$]$_{VP}$]$_{S1}$

(1´) makes use of the traditional notion of nominal clause in that the lower clause is represented as a sentence dominated by an NP node.

The pattern of (1´) is here termed the transitive *into -ing* pattern. *Into -ing* complements may also be found in an intransitive pattern, as in (2):

(2) And two people didn't, I thought, drift into talking like that after knowing each other for such a short while ... (BNC, BP9 1271)

Clearly the matrix verbs selecting the two patterns are not necessarily the same. The intransitive pattern of (2), which is one of subject control, deserves study, but is left for a later treatment.

In this connection consider also sentence (3):

(3) Just as he once battled for supreme fitness, he has poured his energy into learning to speak again. (BNC, CBC 14468)

In (3) the matrix verb selects a direct object, and from the point of view of argument structure, the pattern is superficially similar to (1). However, in (3) the direct object designates a resource at the disposal of the referent of the higher subject, and the pattern may be viewed as one of subject control. It can be set aside in the study of the object control pattern of (1).

The object may also sometimes be a reflexive, as in (4):

(4) She had been tricking herself earlier into thinking that ... (BNC, H9H 2573)

Trick of course also easily permits non-reflexive direct objects, as in (5):

(5) I could not prevent my father from tricking him into marrying me instead of Rachel. (BNC, HD6 479)

In view of the similarity of sentence (4), in respect of argument structure, to a sentence such as (5), it seems appropriate to include the reflexive pattern here.

Similarly passive versions of the pattern of (1) are of course also included, as in (6):

(6) Stuart had once been coerced by her into delivering food parcels for old people at Christmas ... (BNC, HDC 1449)

As regards the grammar of the transitive *into -ing* pattern, the semantic labels of the three arguments shed light on the interpretation of the pattern, but it is helpful to view the pattern as a type of the caused motion construction in the sense of Adele Goldberg's (1995) work. In this framework the matrix verb is the source of verb-specific participant role labels. For instance, in the case of *coerce*, as in (6), these might be given as Coercer, Coercee and Content of Coercion. For their part, the semantic role labels Agent, Patient and Goal designate the role labels of the construction, corresponding to the labels Influence, Influenced and SOA argument in Sag and Pollard (1991: 66). The participant roles are then matched with or mapped onto the argument roles corresponding to them. Thus the Coercer participant role is naturally mapped onto the Agent argument role of the caused motion construction.

The analysis of the transitive *into -ing* pattern as a caused motion construction gains traction from verbs that are often used with two arguments only. For instance, consider *frighten*, which is found with the transitive *into -ing* pattern, as in (7a). The verb is also commonly found with a simple NP object, as in (7b):

(7) a. 'Before I frightened you into running away from me.' (BNC, HH1 6357)
    b. 'I'm sorry if I frightened you.' (BNC, JY8 3568)

When using the caused motion approach, it is possible to say that the verb retains its basic meaning of 'to throw into a fright; to terrify' (*OED*) even in (7a), and that the participant roles of the verb are Frightener and Frightened in both (7a) and (7b). What distinguishes (7a) from (7b) is that the former represents an instance of the caused motion construction, but the latter does not. In the caused motion construction the third argument, introduced by the spatial preposition *into*, is supplied by the construction. What makes the constructional analysis insightful is the point made by Goldberg and Jackendoff (2004: 538) that there are two subevents involved and that the relation between the two subevents is not random or indeterminate in nature. Instead, it is regular and of a specific type:

> ... the meaning of a resultative sentence contains two separable subevents. One of them, the VERBAL SUBEVENT, is determined by the verb of the sentence. The other subevent, the CONSTRUCTIONAL SUBEVENT, is determined by the construction. A resultative sentence means more than just the conjunction of the verbal subevent and the constructional subevent. ... That is, for the bulk of cases ... the verbal subevent is the MEANS by which the constructional subevent takes place. (Goldberg and Jackendoff 2004: 538; emphasis in the original)

In the quotation Goldberg and Jackendoff refer to 'resultatives', but in their usage the term may be understood in a broad sense, and it also includes causatives such as the transitive *into -ing* construction. The third argument supplied by the caused motion construction in (7a) has the semantic role of Goal. Taking advantage of the caused motion construction, it is then possible to analyse the meaning of sentence (7a) along the lines 'before I caused you to run away from me by means of frightening you', with the verb *frighten* retaining its basic meaning even in sentence (7a).

The caused motion analysis of the transitive *into -ing* pattern gains additional traction from a verb such as *talk*. This verb only assigns one participant role, Talker, and the other two roles of the caused motion construction are supplied by the construction. The interpretation of the resulting sentences is as expected. For instance, a sentence such as *I talked you into going to London* may be paraphrased 'I caused you to go to London by means of talking to you'.

The Goal argument of the transitive *into -ing* construction is introduced by the preposition *into*. In a broad sense *into* is a spatial or locative preposition. Illustrating its use with a concrete NP complement of *into*, as in *We got into the car*, Lindstromberg (1998: 30) observes that it 'seems to give movement and result about equal emphasis'. It expresses the crossing of a boundary, and in a study that similarly focuses on concrete NP complements of *into*, Tutton (2009: 19) likewise observes that *into* gives prominence to the path followed by the moving entity to the goal. In the transitive *into -ing* construction under discussion here the complement of *into* is an *-ing* clause, and it designates an action or a state that is more abstract in nature than an NP like *the car*, but the construction still gives prominence to both the movement, or the path, of the moving entity and to the resulting end point of the movement.

The transitive *into -ing* pattern has been investigated in a number of studies in recent years, including Rudanko (2000) and Wulff et al. (2007). As Mark Davies (2012: 164) has noted, earlier studies have mostly concerned the properties of the pattern in current English. However, his study raises the question of how the pattern established itself in American English, with data from COHA. The present study starts from the discussion of Davies (2012), with further information and illustration of American English data, but another objective is to consider data in British English, from the perspective opened up by Davies's important study. A further objective of the present study is to compare the early history of the transitive *into -ing* pattern in these two regional varieties, in order to shed light on the question of whether the pattern might have emerged and spread more rapidly in one of them.

6.2   The transitive *into -ing* pattern in the early years of COHA

Davies (2012: 164) terms what is here called the transitive *into -ing* pattern the 'construction [V NP into V-ing]', and investigates the construction in the entire course of COHA, providing frequency information on the pattern in every second decade of COHA starting with the 1820s. On the basis of his investigation, Davies makes these important observations on the emergence and early history of the pattern:

> In terms of semantics, we might briefly consider an issue that may relate to the origin and initial extension of the [V NP into V-ing] construction. In the early 1800s there are many cases of [V NP into N]: *he bullied himself into power, you have driven him into exile, he was carrying it into effect,* etc. In the earliest stages of [V NP into V-ing], a high percentage of all tokens occur with the subordinate clause verb *being* (*called them into being, start others into being, brought this banquet into being, quickened such intention into being,* etc.). Note that *being* is a semantically rather simple verb and—although it can be analyzed as a verb in these case[s]—it also has a strong nominal feel to it. Rather than have the construction created 'ex nihilo', it apparently started where [V NP into V-ing] would be least noticeable—where [into V-ing] could also be analyzed as a noun, as with the pre-existing [into N]. And then once the [into V-ing] construction was firmly 'established' in about the 1850s, the percentage of *being* decreased markedly. (Davies 2012: 165–6)

The form *being* does lend itself to the dichotomous analysis suggested by Davies, and the present author regards his comments as insightful. It may be added that the V-*ing* string that follows the preposition *into* may be considered a nominal clause, as a sentence dominated by an NP, which is in harmony with the early nominal pattern of '*into* N', identified by Davies as a factor favouring the emergence and spread of the sentential *into* -*ing* construction. (The present author would prefer to view the pattern as '*into* NP', rather than as '*into* N', since the constituent in question is invariably phrasal, but this is a matter of terminology, and does not affect the point.) Indeed, this factor may well have played a general role in furthering the emergence and spread of sentential -*ing* complements or gerunds, as was suggested in the case of a different gerundial pattern in Rudanko (1998).

It seems appropriate here to supplement Davies's account with some illustrations of the *into being* construction from the first decades of COHA. Such illustrations are given in (8a–d):

(8) a. ... the one which stood there before that republic was called into being. (1851, MAG)

b. But they had outlived the causes which brought them into being. (1853, MAG)

c. It was not ushered into being by the warmth of popular excitement, ... (1824, MAG)

d. ... then I possess it already, and do not will it into being, since it had gained existence anterior to my willing. (1846, NF)

Call and *bring*, illustrated in (8a–b), respectively, are the most frequent higher verbs selecting the *into being* construction, but *usher*, as in (8c), and *will*, as in (8d), testify to the variety of the higher verbs found.

The present author also wants to add further information on the frequencies of the *into being* construction in relation to 'true' V-*ing* complements, or more clearly sentential *into* -*ing* complements, in the early years of COHA. Regarding the selection of a search string, insertions between *into* and the following verb seem unlikely, given the status of the -*ing* clause as a complement, and the string 'into *ing' may be used to collect tokens. This search string retrieves a number of irrelevant tokens, for instance of the type *into something*, and these have been set aside manually.

The first decade of COHA, the 1810s, is only 1.2 million words in size. As a curiosity, it can be mentioned that one token of the 'Verb NP *into being*' pattern is found in that decade, but no tokens of the more clearly sentential pattern are retrieved. Because of the small size of the subcorpus for the 1810s, this decade is omitted from further consideration here. Table 6.1 gives information on the frequencies of the two constructions for the four decades from the 1820s to the 1850s. (The size of each subcorpus has been rounded to the nearest 100,000 words. The numbers in parentheses indicate the normalized frequencies per million words. The searches were conducted in March 2013.)

The figures in Table 6.1 confirm that the transitive *into* -*ing* construction was firmly established in American English in the 1850s. The normalized frequency of the 'Verb NP *into being*' pattern seems relatively constant during the first four decades, but as far as the more clearly sentential pattern is concerned, its frequency goes up considerably during the decades under review. The frequency is very low in the 1820s, but goes up noticeably even in the 1830s, almost reaching the level of the 'Verb NP *into being*' pattern during that decade. In the 1840s the frequency of the more clearly sentential pattern surpasses that of the 'Verb NP *into being*' pattern. Finally, in the 1850s the frequency of the latter pattern stagnates, but the frequency of the more clearly sentential pattern rises sharply once more, making this pattern considerably more frequent than the other one.

An obvious task in the study of any syntactic pattern of complementation is to identify the matrix predicates that select the pattern. In his study, when

Table 6.1 Frequencies of the 'Verb NP *into being*' and 'Verb NP *into* -*ing*' patterns in four decades of COHA

Decade	Size	Verb NP *into being*	Verb NP *into* -*ing*
1820s	6.9	12 (1.7)	3 (0.4)
1830s	13.8	20 (1.4)	19 (1.4)
1840s	16.0	30 (1.9)	36 (2.3)
1850s	16.5	31 (1.9)	57 (3.5)

discussing the Brown Corpus, Davies (2012: 164) characterized some verbs as 'basic verbs of influence or force', including *coax, deceive, force* and *persuade,* and these can also be found in the early decades of COHA, along with a number of other verbs that may also be viewed as 'basic verbs of influence or force', including *betray, bully, cajole, entrap, scare* and *scold.* Here are some illustrations:

(9) a. ... the baseness of this man, on whom they had been cajoled into relying, ... (1856, FIC)
   b. The department chiefly forced into serving this dishonest purpose was that of Public Works; ... (1858, MAG)
   c. ... would sit still to see if the flame could not be scolded into going out of itself. (1838, FIC)

In his discussion of COHA, Davies (2012: 165) gives another list of matrix verbs, labelling them as 'some of the more interesting ones'. For the 1840s he lists *cheat, quicken* and *wake* in this class, and for the 1850s he lists *irritate, natter* and *starve.* Here are examples of *natter* and *starve*:

(10) a. ... a desire to please an unknown correspondent who nattered you into flattering me. (1859, NF)
   b. Truly, sir, he is starved into flattering his patrons. (1858, FIC)

Davies does not appear to consult the *OED* in his study, but it may be noted that for *natter*, which has a sense of 'to nag' (*OED*, sense 2) and 'to chat (in an aimless manner)' (*OED*, sense 1.b), the *OED* has no illustration of a pattern remotely resembling the transitive *into -ing* construction, and the usage of (10a) is therefore certainly interesting. Interpreting the transitive *into -ing* pattern in (10a) as an instance of the caused motion construction yields the paraphrase 'who caused you to flatter me by means of nagging or chatting', which seems appropriate for the sentence. Regarding *starve,* the *OED* does not illustrate *into -ing* complements under the entry, but it does offer the sense 'to force *into* (a course of action) by starvation', and illustrations under this sense include an *into* NP complement in *They ... were to be starved into compliance* (*OED*, 1775, Marq. Rockingham, *Hansard*). Still the causative use of (10b) remains interesting.

In addition to the lists in Davies (2012), two other interesting verbs in the data from the early decades of COHA may be noted here. These are the verbs *quiz* and *nose-lead*:

(11) a. 'You talk riddles, Mr. Ellison; but I will not be quizzed into believing this little castaway scrap of paper can be of any import.' (1835, FIC)
   b. ... we merely nose-led our good simple cousin Jonathan into making that treaty for the purpose of preventing him from getting any thing for himself. (1856, MAG)

Quiz and *nose-lead* are of course illustrated with two arguments in the *OED* or in *OED Online*, as in *So far forgot his good manners as to quiz Mrs. Disraeli at the dinner-table* (1928, *OED*, Sykes, *Mary Anne Disraeli*), but they are of interest in the present context because the *OED* apparently does not illustrate a causative use under these verb entries.

It may be added that the constructional approach offers a suitable analysis for verbs such as *starve, quiz* and *nose-lead*. For instance, we may consider *starve*. For the purposes of discussion, (10b) may be turned into the active, as in (10′).

> (10′) They starved him into flattering his patrons.

In the analysis of (10′) it is then possible to identify a verbal and constructional subevent. The constructional subevent is one of causation and the verbal subevent expresses the means of causation, similarly to earlier examples. (10′) may then be paraphrased along the lines of 'they caused him to flatter his patrons by means of starving him (or almost starving him)'. Analogous analyses are available for (11a–b).

To sum up this section, the present discussion confirms the finding in Davies (2012) that it was around the 1850s that the transitive *into -ing* pattern established itself in American English. Further, it is observed on the basis of the evidence of verbs such as *natter, quiz* and *nose-lead* that even in the early years of the nineteenth century the pattern was capable of being used in ways that can be viewed as unexpected, given the evidence of the *OED*. It is argued here that the analysis of the transitive *into -ing* pattern as a construction sheds light on the interpretation of such unexpected usages.

6.3 The transitive *into -ing* pattern in eighteenth- and early nineteenth-century British English

The finding in Davies (2012) that the transitive *into -ing* pattern established itself around the 1850s provides a point of departure for the investigation of the history of the pattern in British English. Unfortunately, there is no corpus of the type of COHA available for British English at the present time, but the newest version of the CLMET suggests itself as a corpus to be consulted here. (For discussion of the original version of the CLMET, see de Smet 2005.) This corpus cannot match the size and the balance of COHA, but it is relatively large, and it contains texts from fiction and non-fiction. It also has the added advantage that it reaches into the eighteenth century, affording the opportunity to examine the transitive *into -ing* pattern in that century.

The first part of the corpus contains approximately 10.4 million words, from the period of 1710–80. The search string used was 'into *ing', and it retrieved 97 tokens. Among them there are numerous intransitive 'Verb *into* NP' constructions, of the type *go into mourning* and *vanish into nothing*, but there are also transitive constructions found. Many of them are of the 'Verb NP *into* NP' type, as in *plunge both body and soul into everlasting misery, crush a worm into nothing, turn virtue into nothing*, but of more immediate interest is the question of the 'Verb NP *into being'* pattern in relation to the transitive *into -ing* pattern. The frequencies of these are given in Table 6.2.

Recalling the discussion of the data from American English above, it is rather surprising that there are only 6 tokens of the 'Verb NP *into being'* pattern, while the number of tokens of the more clearly sentential pattern is as high as 13. Most of the 13 are from major authors, with 5 each from Henry Fielding and Robert Walpole, and 2 from Samuel Richardson. Here are two examples of each type:

(12) a. ... that Power which first brought Nature into Being, established Laws ... (1751, TREAT, Brown, *Essays on the Characteristics*)

   b. ... it is rescued from the violence of the wave, and is called into being, by the sun beam. (1777, FIC, Pratt, *Charles and Charlotte*)

(13) a. ... and then you have charged me with bullocking you into owning the truth. (1749, FIC, Henry Fielding, *Tom Jones*)

   b. The Duke of Argyll has drawn the ministry into accommodating him with a notable job, ... (1735–69, LET, Walpole)

The frequency of the transitive *into -ing* pattern is therefore as high as 1.3 instances per million words even at this early stage. On the other hand, the frequency of the 'Verb NP *into being'* construction is only 0.6 per million. However, in addition to the six tokens of the pattern 'Verb NP *into being'*, there are seven other examples where the *-ing* form is neither a prototypical verb nor a prototypical noun. *Take* NP *into keeping* is particularly frequent, with four tokens. Here is one example:

(14) ... three married Ladies whom he has taken into keeping, and who eloped to him from young and good looking Husbands. (1765–70, FIC, Brooke, *The Fool of Quality*)

The prominence of constructions such as the one in (14) may also have been a factor promoting the emergence and spread of the transitive *into -ing* pattern, with the pattern emerging precisely where it was the least conspicuous (Davies 2012: 166).

Table 6.2 Frequencies of the 'Verb NP *into being'* and 'Verb NP *into -ing'* patterns in the first period of the CLMET3.0

Period	Size	Verb NP *into being*	Verb NP *into -ing*
1710–80	10.4	6 (0.6)	13 (1.3)

The verbs selecting the transitive *into -ing* pattern in this section of the corpus are: *betray, blind, bullock, compliment, deceive* (two tokens), *draw* (two tokens), *reason, set* (two tokens), *soften, terrify*. Most of these, including *betray, bullock, deceive* and *set*, may be viewed as verbs of 'basic influence or force', to use a characterization from Davies (2012: 164), but in the list there are also some more interesting verbs. *Blind* and *compliment* are prominent among them. Here are the tokens:

(15) a. The Duchess complimented him into dining before his search, and in the meantime the woman was spirited away, ... (1735–9, LET, Walpole)

  b. ... even when he has not that candour, he is sometimes blinded into discovering truth unawares; ... (1735–69, LET, Walpole)

Both tokens are thus from the work of the same author, but they are still interesting, indicating that the transitive *into -ing* pattern was used in unexpected ways even in eighteenth-century British English. In the case of *blind*, which of course has the basic sense of 'render blind', there does not appear to be any illustrations of a usage comparable to that of (15b) in the *OED*. As for *compliment*, the *OED* records the nominal pattern of *compliment* NP *into* NP, as in *Complimenting me into a better opinion of my self than I deserve* (1705, Pope *Let. Wycherley*), but no sentential complement is illustrated in that standard work of reference. The unexpected usages involving the two verbs are accounted for easily enough when the transitive *into -ing* pattern is viewed as a construction. For instance, in the case of (15a) it is observed that one of the senses of *compliment* in the *OED* is 'to flatter with polite and delicate praise' (*OED*, sense 2), and thus for (15a) a paraphrase of the type 'The Duchess caused him to dine before his search by means of flattering him with polite praise' suggests itself.

Turning to the second period of CLMET3.0, covering the period from 1780 to 1850, the same search string 'into *ing' was used, with 175 tokens retrieved. Information on the frequencies of the 'Verb NP *into being*' and 'Verb NP *into -ing*' patterns is given in Table 6.3.

The 'Verb NP *into being*' construction is thus relatively rare, with only four tokens, and other 'inconspicuous' constructions are similarly rare. Such constructions are now only a fraction of the total of the tokens of the transitive *into -ing* pattern, for there are now as many as 61 tokens of the latter.

Table 6.3 Frequencies of the 'Verb NP *into being*' and 'Verb NP *into -ing*' patterns in the second period of the CLMET3.0

Period	Size	Verb NP *into being*	Verb NP *into -ing*
1780–1850	11.2	4 (0.4)	61 (5.4)

This represents a frequency of 5.4 per million. It is also worth noting that the 61 tokens are spread among a large number of authors. Here are some illustrations:

(16) a. ... he hoped to surprise you into believing there was no help for it, ... (1782, FIC, Burney *Cecilia*)
  b. ... you had been hurried into accepting his hand, ... (1838, FIC, Bulwer-Lytton, *Alice*)

Most of the verbs selecting the pattern may be classed as 'basic verbs of influence or force', to use Davies's label, but among the more interesting matrix verbs *laugh* and *sentimentalize* stand out. Here are the tokens:

(17) a. Be kind to your companions, but be firm. Do not be laughed into doing that which you know to be wrong. (1837, FIC, Disraeli, *Venetia*)
  b. Let not members of Parliament be lectured and sentimentalized into voting for such a law, ... (1839, OTHER, *Political Pamphlet*, Norton)

Laugh has a basic intransitive use with a sense that is defined in the *OED* as follows:

intr. to manifest the combination of bodily phenomena ... which forms the instinctive expression of mirth. (*OED*, part of the definition of sense 1.a)

In a somewhat similar way, *sentimentalize* is used intransitively with the sense 'to indulge in sentimental thoughts or expressions' (*OED*, sense 1.a), and transitively with the sense of 'to imbue (a person, work of art, etc.) with sentiment or sentimental qualities' (*OED*, sense 2). Both of these verbs are also recognized in resultative uses in the *OED*, taking the *Shorter OED* into account. The relevant gloss for *laugh* is 'bring into a given state or position by laughing; *esp.* persuade (a person) *out of* a belief, a solemn mood, etc., by laughter or mockery' (*Shorter OED*, sense 4) or 'to bring (a person or (occas.) thing) into a particular state or position by laughing' (*OED Online*, sense 5), and that for *sentimentalize* is 'bring *into* or *out of* a condition by the expression of sentiment' (*Shorter OED*, sense 2). The caused motion analysis of the constructions in question is attractive because it captures the similarity of the glosses, including the instrumentality expressed by the *by* phrases in them. For instance, if (17a) is turned into an active, a sentence such as *They laughed them into doing something wrong* may be paraphrased along the lines of 'they caused them to do something wrong by means of laughing at them'.

6.4 Conclusion

The present study argues that the recent history of the transitive *into -ing* pattern supports the hypothesis, originally put forward on the basis of current English in Rudanko (2000: 86, n. 2), that the pattern may be seen as a type of the caused motion construction. Verbs such as *frighten* commonly select two arguments, and when they occur with the *into -ing* pattern, the caused motion construction supplies the third argument. For their part, verbs of the *laugh* type generally only take one argument, and for them the caused motion construction supplies two arguments. The case for considering the transitive *into -ing* pattern as a type of the caused motion construction is strengthened by the specific interpretation of the construction, where it is possible to identify a constructional subevent and a verbal subevent and to establish a regular relationship between the two.

This study also sheds light on the emergence and the early history of the transitive *into -ing* pattern. A convenient point of departure is provided by Davies (2012). He argued on the basis of data from COHA that the transitive *into -ing* pattern established itself around the 1850s. He further linked the emergence of clearly verbal *-ing* complements to the relatively high frequency of 'inconspicuous' constructions where the *-ing* form also had a 'strong nominal feel to it', especially constructions of the type 'Verb NP *into being*'. The present study points to the presence of relatively large numbers of unambiguously verbal *into -ing* complements even in the 1830s and in the 1840s in COHA, but agrees with Davies's (2012) general finding about the high frequency of the emerging construction in American English in the 1850s. It is also noted that even in the early decades of the emergence of the transitive *into -ing* pattern, examples of the pattern occasionally include tokens where the higher verb is worth noting in that it is not from among 'basic verbs of influence or force', to use Davies's (2012: 164) formulation. *Quiz* and *nose-lead* are examples of such verbs.

The present chapter also examines the early history of the transitive *into -ing* pattern in British English on the basis of the new version of the CLMET, to shed further light on the emergence and spread of the pattern in the two main regional varieties of English. The CLMET3.0 corpus also makes it possible to examine the pattern in eighteenth-century British English. Unambiguously verbal tokens of the transitive *into -ing* construction are encountered in the first period of the corpus and their frequency surpasses that of the inconspicuous 'Verb NP *into being*' pattern. At the same time, there are also fairly frequent inconspicuous tokens. A more striking finding concerns the transitive *into -ing* construction in British English in the second period of CLMET3.0, that is, in the period of 1780–1850. In these decades 'inconspicuous' constructions of the 'Verb NP *into being*' type have become relatively rare, whereas the frequency of unambiguous verbal complements has risen considerably from the first period. It is thus suggested here that in this area of English grammar

British English may have been in the lead as regards the spread of a new pattern. At the same time, there is clearly a need for additional work on the early history of the pattern, especially when larger corpora of different text types of British English become available, and such larger corpora may allow a fuller comparison of the two regional varieties in the early history of the transitive *into -ing* pattern.

Acknowledgements

The author is indebted to Ian Gurney for his comments (private communication) on the meaning of the transitive *into -ing* construction and to Terhi Uusi-Mäkelä and Veera Saarimäki for their help with the chapter. All remaining shortcomings in the chapter are the author's responsibility.

References

Davies, M. (2012) 'Some Methodological Issues Related to Corpus-Based Investigations of Recent Syntactic Changes in English' in T. Nevalainen and E. Traugott (eds) *The Oxford Handbook of the History of English* (Oxford: Oxford University Press), pp. 157–74.

De Smet, H. (2005) 'A Corpus of Late Modern English Texts'. *ICAME Journal*, 29: 69–82.

Goldberg, A. (1995) *Constructions: a Construction Grammar Approach to Argument Structure* (Chicago: University of Chicago Press).

Goldberg, A. and R. Jackendoff (2004) 'The English Resultative as a Family of Constructions'. *Language*, 80: 532–68.

Jespersen, O. (1940) *A Modern English Grammar on Historical Principles*. Part V. *Syntax*, Vol. IV. Reprinted 1961 (London and Copenhagen: G. Allen and Unwin/E. Munksgaard).

Lindstromberg, S. (1998) *English Prepositions Explained* (Amsterdam: John Benjamins).

OED = The Oxford English Dictionary (1989) 2nd edn (Oxford: Clarendon Press).

OED Online = The OED Online. Includes the full text of the 2nd edn (1989) and the three additions. Available through www.oed.com. Consulted in March 2013.

Rudanko, J. (1998) 'To Infinitive and *to -ing* Complements: a Look at Some Matrix Verbs in Late Modern English and Later'. *English Studies*, 79: 336–49.

Rudanko, J. (2000) *Corpora and Complementation* (Lanham, Md: University Press of America).

Sag, I. and C. Pollard (1991) 'An Integrated Theory of Complement Control'. *Language*, 67: 63–113.

Shorter OED = The New Shorter Oxford English Dictionary on Historical Principles (1993) edited by Leslie Brown (Oxford: Oxford University Press).

Tutton, M. (2009) 'When *In* Means *Into*: Towards an Understanding of Boundary-Crossing *In*'. *Journal of English Linguistics*, 37: 5–27.

Wulff, S., A. Stefanowitsch and S. Gries (2007) 'Brutal Brits and Persuasive Americans' in G. Radden et al. (eds) *Aspects of Meaning Construction* (Amsterdam: John Benjamins), pp. 265–81.

7

Prepositions and Sentential Complements: the Case of *Waste* and *Spend*

Paul Rickman
University of Tampere

7.1 Introduction and background

The topic of the optional use of various grammatical items in English, such as prepositions and complementizers, enjoys a fair amount of attention in the literature (Rohdenburg 1996: 168–70, 2002, 2007: 223–5; Dixon 2005: 257–8 and 299–300; Mair 2006: 130–5; Leech et al. 2009: 193–5; Sellgren 2010, among many others), yet much work remains to be done. To this end, the present study aims to shed light on the matrix verb *waste*, in the pattern *waste* + NP + (*in/on*) + V-*ing*, where in present-day English the preposition is becoming a rarity. Earlier work on the matrix verb *spend* in the same pattern (Rohdenburg 1996, 2002, 2007), noted that the preposition, having at one time been a more or less obligatory component, has decreased in frequency over the course of the twentieth century, with AmE at the forefront of this change. This earlier work also noted that, in the vast majority of cases, the NP component falls into one of three semantic categories: expressions of TIME, EFFORT or MONEY, with TIME NPs being less likely than either of the other two to be followed by the preposition today (Rohdenburg 2002: 83, 2007: 225). This point, while interesting, will not be the main focus of the present research.

The present chapter assumes a broadly functional approach to this type of variation, in that, rather than being simply random, it is seen instead as being motivated by factors related to cognitive complexity; when given the option of two competing forms, the speaker tends to select the more explicit option in more complex environments, in order to facilitate the exchange of information. The Complexity Principle (Rohdenburg 1996) plays a key theoretical role in (some of) the earlier research, as it does here, since it has been proved highly relevant, in much of Rohdenburg's other work, in providing motivation for the retention in certain environments of an otherwise receding form. The principle runs as follows:

In the case of more or less explicit grammatical options the more explicit one(s) will tend to be favored in cognitively more complex environments. (Rohdenburg 1996: 151)

The present study is divided into two main areas of analysis, with the first seeking to build, to some small extent, upon the work on *spend*, and adding to that some new information on the related verb *waste*. As suggested above, the Complexity Principle comprises the main theoretical background, and it will be determined whether *waste* follows *spend* in falling in line with the principle's general predictions. Thus the first section begins by looking into the semantic and syntactic similarities evident between *spend* and *waste*, before going on to document the progress of preposition use with both verbs in BrE fiction over the late modern English period.

The second part of the analysis focuses on the idiomatic pattern *waste no time* + (*in*) + *V-ing*, as this follows naturally from the findings of *waste* in its more general use. This pattern accounts for only a small percentage of the overall use of *waste,* but is clearly providing an environment in which the preposition has held its position longer than it has in other, more typical environments. It will be shown that this follows the Complexity Principle's predictions in a less obvious manner than the behaviour of *spend*. For reasons that will be explained further below, the data set for this second analysis is widened to encompass all genres of BrE and AmE.

7.2   *Spend* and *waste*

7.2.1   Data and methods

The data for this section were obtained from the Corpus of Late Modern English Texts (extended version) and the prose fiction subsection of the British National Corpus.[1] BrE fiction was selected due to the availability of appropriate corpora reaching back to 1710. The BNC data on *spend* comprise a sample of 500 tokens taken at random from the 3728 hits obtained in the search for the lemma *spend*. Of the 500, the amount of relevant tokens was 163. Given that the precise details of *spend* are of secondary importance here, this data set was judged sufficient in providing a general overview of its behaviour in present-day English. Apart from this, all other available data were utilized.

Regarding the identification and removal of irrelevant tokens, the main issue in the present case involved the differentiation of the more nominal -*ing* forms from the more sentential ones. Consider examples (1a–b) below:

(1) a. We did not waste time (in) discussing the matter.
    b. We did not waste time *(in) discussion.

In (1a) the preposition preceding the sentential -*ing* clause is optional for many speakers, but its presence before the NP *discussion* in (1b) is obligatory for all speakers of standard English. This division relates to the concept of nouniness outlined in Ross (2004: 352–3), where it is shown that the preposition *at* is omissible before the more sentential complement in *I was surprised (at) how far I could throw the ball*, but must remain before the more nominal complement in *I was surprised *(at) Jim ('s) retching* (both examples from Ross 2004: 353). This criterion has been used here in sorting out *-ing* type complements that approach the often fuzzy borderline between the sentential and the nominal, as in *I did zip the tent flap shut, but wasted no other time on housekeeping* (BNC, CFK 2561). In this case the omission of *on* yields a less than acceptable result, and *housekeeping* is judged to be more nominal then sentential. Tokens that did not pass this test were disregarded.

Numerous tokens similar to (2a–b) were also eliminated from the data, being examples of *-ing* clauses acting as free adjuncts, rather than complements (see e.g. Kortmann 1991):

(2) a. I thought we'd spend the next few days in Monaco, getting to know each other. (BNC, HGM 1476)
   b. When I think of all the time they've wasted, trying to prove me guilty while the real killer goes free. (BNC, HNJ 3264)

In cases such as these, the comma and the tone unit boundary that would naturally accompany it in spoken English are among the relevant criteria differentiating free adjuncts from complements.

7.2.2 Common ground

The verbs in question have a number of similarities: it can, for example, be seen that the same patterns are possible for both: the prepositions *in* (3a–b) and *on* (3c–d) may be included, or omitted (3e–f):[2]

(3) a. This isn't good enough for me, I shall get further if I'm pulled, I can't waste time in going first. (BNC, EFP 839)
   b. She had spent her lunch-hours of the two previous days in talking to letting agents. (BNC, JY1 1339)
   c. If duplicity was his genius why waste it on deceiving husbands and mistresses? (BNC, CRE 537)[3]
   d. ... at least as far as amusing themselves by helping her to spend money on having her hair done and buying clothes. (BNC, APM 722)
   e. Why are you wasting your precious money paying me to look an absolute fool on your behalf, Roman? (BNC, GUE 2801)
   f. He had spent the afternoon teaching Sun Tzu to his senior officers. (BNC, G04 3619)

The examples given above also illustrate the three semantic types of NP – TIME, EFFORT and MONEY – with which *spend* and *waste*, for the most part, tend to co-occur (the skill or talent of *duplicity* in [3c] is counted here as EFFORT). Rohdenburg (2002) found that, in the case of *spend*, when a preposition is selected in present-day English, MONEY NPs tend to prefer *on*, while TIME and EFFORT NPs attract *in*. Analysis of the distribution of the three NP types and the prepositions they prefer falls somewhat outside the scope of the present investigation, but it can be stated that for the most part the observations above in connection with *spend* also hold true for *waste*, with the exception that *on* does not seem to be quite so restricted to MONEY NPs (as (3c) shows). Also, the BrE fiction data show NPs of TIME to be far more common than either of the other two types, with only small numbers of tokens found for EFFORT and MONEY in all the subcorpora.

There is also clear semantic overlap of *spend* and *waste*, as the following definitions from the *Oxford English Dictionary* (*OED*) help to illustrate:

(4) a. *Spend, OED* sense 4.a. To employ, occupy, use or pass (time, one's life, etc.) *in* or *on* some action, occupation, or state. *Christophe de Beaumont, who has spent his life in persecuting hysterical Jansenists.* (1837 T. Carlyle)

    b. *Waste, OED* sense 9. To spend, consume, employ uselessly or without adequate result. *We need not waste words in coming to our point.* (1905 R. Bagot)

Both verbs denote the use or consumption of a commodity, but each is located at opposite ends of the scale of positivity. The difference can be appreciated by considering the implication of each of the following (prototypical) sentences:[4]

(5) a. We spent the morning discussing politics.

    b. We wasted the morning discussing politics.

(5a) has the positive, or arguably neutral, implication that the discussion has yielded worthwhile results, while (5b) carries the undeniably negative implication that the time would have been better used in other ways.

In terms of control, both verbs are subject control predicates, as the following examples help to illustrate:

(6) a. We$_i$ spent the morning [PRO$_i$ discussing politics].

    b. We$_i$ wasted the morning [PRO$_i$ discussing politics].

The subject of the superordinate clause, *we*, is co-referential with the understood subject of the subordinate clause, represented by PRO.[5] Rudanko

(1999: 23) finds subject control to be typical of the *in + V-ing* pattern as it appears in patterns such as *He delights in perplexing me* (example from Rudanko 1999: 23), and there appears to be no problem in assigning subject control status to both *spend* and *waste* in the NP + *in* + *V-ing* pattern.

7.2.3 Preposition use

Turning now to preposition presence in the diachronic data, Tables 7.1 and 7.2 show the progress of *in* and *on* with the pattern over the past three centuries.

The results in Table 7.1 for *spend* support what was noted in the past: there has been a clear trend away from the use of the preposition in this pattern over the twentieth century. A significant rise in the overall use of the verb is also clearly indicated. The data in Table 7.2 on *waste* point to a similar trend away from the more explicit prepositional option, as well as an increase in general usage, but the numbers remain lower than those for *spend*. Given the low numbers for the preposition *on*, no further attention will be paid to it in this work, and focus will rest instead on the variation between *in* and the zero preposition.

Consideration of the BNC data in light of the Complexity Principle shows that, in the case of *spend*, the five tokens containing *in* also contain features that contribute to cognitive complexity, thus supporting the principle's general predictions: there are three cases of long and complex NPs (exemplified in (7a)), one of *wh*-movement (7b), and one passive (7c).

(7) a. ... they were a bunch of gilded pederasts who spent what little time they could spare from betraying the country's secrets in stealing the Security Service's territory, influence and share of the Secret Funds. (BNC, H86 292)

    b. How much time, spent in climbing over stiles and so on, had to elapse before you could proclaim one, and then one, rather than two? (BNC, GUK 2018)

Table 7.1 Prepositions in the **spend** + NP + (*in/on*) + *V-ing* pattern across three centuries

	in	*on*	**zero**
CLMETEV1	9.2 (28)	–	0.3 (1)
CLMETEV2	16.9 (97)	–	0.5 (3)
CLMETEV3	17.6 (110)	0.5 (3)	9.3 (58)
BNC	2.3 (5)	0.5 (1)	73.1 (157)

Numbers outside brackets represent normalized frequencies per 1 million words; bracketed numbers represent raw figures.

Table 7.2 Prepositions in the **waste** + *NP* + (*in/on*) + *V-ing* pattern across three centuries

	in	*on*	*zero*
CLMETEV1	0.3 (1)	–	–
CLMETEV2	1.9 (11)	–	0.5 (3)
CLMETEV3	3.8 (22)	–	1.9 (11)
BNC	1.7 (28)	0.2 (4)	6.9 (111)

Numbers outside brackets represent normalized frequencies per 1 million words; bracketed numbers represent raw figures.

c. The remainder of Cynthia's visit was spent in supporting Dorothy's arm while she wrote a letter ... (BNC, FS1 2288)

These are, of course, not the sole examples containing complexity features to be found in the data, but it is certainly of some significance that all five explicit tokens are matched with complex structures.

The data for *waste* in the BNC do not, at first glance, appear to comply quite so explicitly with the Complexity Principle's general predictions, as all (11 in total) tokens carrying features that increase cognitive complexity are matched with the less explicit complement type,[6] and among the 28 cases of the more explicit type, there is little in the way of (structural) complexity features to be found.

One particular type of pattern, however, is prominent in the 28 cases of *waste* + *NP* + *in* + *V-ing*, and this is shown in the illustration below.

(8) She'd been so sure that Marianne would waste no time in spreading her poison. (BNC, HA9 3313)

Of the 28 explicit tokens, 20 are of the type shown above. (Negation itself may be seen as a contributing factor here, but for the moment I set that aside to focus on another aspect of complexity.) This pattern is focused on in more detail in the following section, where, with discussion of its origins and development, it will be argued that the *waste no time* string constitutes an idiomatic pattern with a level of semantic opacity sufficient to trigger the use of the more explicit option more often than the less explicit, in present-day English.

7.3   *Waste no time* + (*in*) + *V-ing*

This section investigates the pattern noted at the close of the previous section, which, in a surprisingly high number of cases in the BNC data, appears in its explicit form, with the preposition *in*. The aim here is to establish the relevant complexity factors inherent in the pattern – since they do not appear to be explicitly structural in nature – in order to provide a link to the Complexity Principle, and an explanation for the continuing use of the preposition.[7] The scope is now widened to encompass both AmE and BrE, since it appears that AmE was the variety in which this pattern first gained currency. Thus, data from the Corpus of Historical American English and the Corpus of Contemporary American English[8] will supplement that of the BNC, and, with the aim of obtaining a more complete picture, all subsections of the relevant corpora are used, rather than just the fiction subsections. CLMETEV material contains no examples of the relevant pattern, and will no longer be used.

7.3.1 Sense

By way of illustration, consider the following tokens, taken from the BNC and a recent decade of COHA:

(9) a. Six minutes later, Shearer collected his fifth Coca-Cola goal of the campaign when a harmless looking corner from Jason Wilcox ricocheted off two bodies and fell nicely for Shearer, who wasted no time in sending the ball into the back of the net. (BNC, CBG 8206)

b. 'Hurry up and change back into your regular clothes. I've got a plan.' Hannah wasted no time in peeling herself out of the dress and handing it out the door to Claire. (COHA 2009, FIC)

Discussion of *waste no time* is not widespread in the literature, nor in grammars of English. It is mentioned, however, in a number of dictionaries (*Oxford Dictionary of Current Idiomatic English* (ODCIE) 1988: 366, *Oxford Advanced Learner's Dictionary* (OALD) 2010: 1737, *Collins Cobuild Advanced Dictionary of English* (COBUILD) 2014: 1641), a well-known reference work on English complementation patterns (Herbst et al. 2004: 938), and by de Smet (2013: 109), who describes it as a 'verbal idiom specifying a relation of immediate (unhesitating) and intentional realization between its subject and an action of which the subject is the agent'. Like de Smet, the reference works cited above all state the meaning of the pattern as something along the lines of: *do what is denoted by the lower verb immediately, without delay.* Thus, if you *waste no time in telling your story,* you tell your story immediately, without doing anything else first. This meaning will henceforth be referred to as Sense 1.

The corpus data show that a second interpretation is also possible. This alternative sense can be expressed as: *do not do what is denoted by the lower verb because it is counterproductive; do something else instead.* The two tokens below, one each from modern AmE and BrE, illustrate this alternative interpretation:

(10) a. With one accord they broke for the cabin, making for where a thin pencil of light hinted at a door. They wasted no time

fumbling for the knob, but put all the strength of their shoulders against the opening. (COHA 1999, FIC)
   b. Jacob wasted no time giving detailed explanations. 'A friend of mine – a good friend – has got trouble.' (BNC, HHC 851)

Here time is not wasted on performing the lower verb actions of *fumbling for the knob* and *giving detailed explanations*, which are seen as being pointless; a different course of action is taken instead. It can be seen that (10a–b) do not include the preposition – a point which will be discussed further below. This second meaning will be referred to as Sense 2.

It is obvious that Sense 2 is not as common today as Sense 1; this is made clear both by the predominance of Sense 1 in the corpus evidence taken from the most recent decades, and the lack of information in the literature on Sense 2. The diachronic AmE data, however, show that this was not always the case: Sense 2 was the more common meaning when the pattern first began to appear, which, according to the corpus evidence, was around the middle of the nineteenth century. Discussion of the semantic development of the pattern over the last 150 years is taken up in section 7.3.3 below, following a discussion of the idiom status of *waste no time* in section 7.3.2.

7.3.2   Idiomaticity

This section discusses the pattern in question from the perspective of idiomaticity, and looks into the effects of various insertions, substitutions and movement, on the semantic interpretation. Huddleston and Pullum (2002: 273) define an idiom as 'an expression larger than a word whose meaning cannot be systematically derived from meanings that the parts have when used independently of each other'. The literature on idioms (see e.g. Makkai 1972: 148–55, Fillmore et al. 1988, 504–5) generally differentiates between idioms that are lexically open, and allow some substitution of their elements without loss of meaning, and those whose elements are more or less fixed, but may allow for morphological freedom without a loss of meaning. Fillmore et al. (1988: 505) point out that between the two types we have a 'gradient or cline rather than a two-way distinction', and, as will be shown below, *waste no time* can be located within the general proximity of the more fixed end of this cline.

As we have seen, *waste no time* allows for two possible readings, with Sense 1 being more common than Sense 2. The insertion of *more* into the string causes the balance to swing in favour of Sense 2: of the seven tokens for *waste no more time* + *(in)* + *V-ing* found in the data, only one carries the Sense 1 meaning. Here is the token in question, followed by one of the six Sense 2 tokens:

(11) a. This administration has left America undefended from missile attack. My administration will not make the same mistake.

(APPLAUSE) If I become the president, we will waste no more time preparing to defend the American people. (Sense 1) (COCA 2000, SPOK)

b. Blood gushed from the deep wound. Booth wasted no more time finishing off Rathbone. The clock in his head was still ticking down. If he was going to escape the theater, he had to get out of the box at once. (Sense 2) (COCA 2009, ACAD)

(11a) is from (written to be) spoken English, and it is unclear whether the speaker, George W. Bush, was aware of the ambiguity associated with the phrase. In any case, here I assume an intended Sense 1 interpretation; it seems obvious that Bush is promising, upon election, to immediately make preparations to defend the American people.

A second variant, in which the verbal element *waste* is replaced by *lose*, is relatively common in the corpora:

(12) Ilona deposited the Cristal she'd been toting onto the center of the table. 'How extravagant,' Joyce murmured appreciatively. 'Thank you, Ilona.' Bill lost no time in motioning a waiter to uncork the liquid treasure. (COCA 2008, FIC)

With this substitution, a Sense 2 interpretation is all but ruled out. That is, *immediate performance of the lower verb action* is the meaning in almost all cases of *lose no time + (in) + V-ing* found in the data. A search of COHA returns several hundred tokens of the *lose no time* type, some of which go back to the earliest decades of the nineteenth century. A very small number of Sense 2 tokens are to be found though, the earliest being from 1823 – some 30 years earlier than the first *waste no time* token. This is given in (13):

(13) ... the one which arrived first, was to lose no time in waiting for the other, since it could not be far off with its assistance. (COHA 1823, FIC)

The link between *lose no time* and *waste no time*, compelling as it is, will not be explored in any more detail here, but will be set aside for future research.

It can also be seen that the pattern does not easily passivize, and when in the rare cases it is found in the passive voice, Sense 2 is more common than Sense 1. Three passive tokens are found in COCA, six in COHA[9] and three in the BNC (four of these are Sense 1, and eight are Sense 2).

(14) a. Because of the sickly geshe, no time was wasted returning to the abbey. Father Leon proved to be pushy and difficult about all the arrangements, just as Antoine had feared. (Sense 1) (COCA 2000, FIC)

    b. Since individual characters are downloaded rather than entire font files, no time is wasted sending and processing unnecessary data. (Sense 2) (COHA 1993, MAG)

    c. In Section 11.3, we described two possibilities: depth-first and frontier search. The first has the advantage that no time is wasted in finding a first feasible solution. (Sense 2) (BNC, CA4 1181)

There are of course many examples of constructions in English that either do not allow a change of voice, or change meaning or become ambiguous when passivized. Several of the passive tokens (e.g. (14b–c)) appear to express a meaning more in line with *we are not required to waste time doing sth*. Of the tokens that do retain the original meaning, true ambiguity can arise, and it is often extremely difficult to decide on the intended reading (as in (14a)), and the wider context becomes all-important.

One apparent substitution, on the other hand, appears to be possible without a significant change in meaning; *little* can replace *no*, with the following tokens – one of each sense, and one of each prepositional variant – among those found for this pattern:

(15) a. However, with Sarah Bentley making her singles debut for Surrey, the holders wasted little time in establishing a winning 5–1 lead to retain their title. (Sense 1) (BNC, CKL 867)

    b. Douglas, disappointed, had of course been prepared for this also, and wasted little time in cursing. He divided his force into three, one division under Fraser to sack the village and set it on fire. (Sense 2) (BNC, CD8 811)

    c. There was enough light seeping in from the living room to see the big black automatic. Since it takes less than a second to pull a trigger I wasted little time grabbing the barrel and pushing it toward the ceiling. (Sense 1) (COCA 2009, FIC)

    d. Folk customs and Viking history were supremely unimportant to this choice, and missionsfolk wasted little time writing about them. When they did write about the past, it was in the context of individual life histories ... (Sense 2) (COCA 1995, ACAD)

The relative proportions of Sense 1 and 2 tokens for *waste little time + (in) + V-ing* are very similar to those for *waste no time + (in) + V-ing*. Given this fact, and the fact that the overall meanings of the two variants are very similar (although *waste no time* could imply a higher level of immediacy than *waste little time*), it seems appropriate to view this as the substitution of an element in the *waste no time* string – suggesting that *waste no time* is close to, but still some distance from, the more fixed end of the cline mentioned above – rather than viewing *waste little time* as a separate idiom.

7.3.3 Preposition use

Omission of the preposition from this pattern did not get underway until around the early twentieth century, which is roughly the same time that preposition omission from the more general *waste* + *NP* + (*in/on*) + *V-ing* pattern began to pick up speed. As the closing comments of section 7.2 suggest, preposition omission from the *waste no time* pattern has not yet reached the level observed with *waste* in the more general pattern (at least in BrE fiction). COHA provides the diachronic data in Table 7.3, which shows the development of preposition use in AmE over 150 years.

The decades in COHA are of course different in size, and no valid comparison can be made between them based on the raw frequencies given above. Rather, Table 7.3 is intended to show the ratio of preposition use against omission within each decade. With this in mind, it can be seen that, according to the COHA data, in all decades apart from the 1980s, preposition use has been more common than omission.

A synchronic perspective employing more data gives a somewhat different picture of AmE usage, with a summary of the data from COCA and the BNC given in Table 7.4.

As Table 7.4 shows, the much higher volume of data on the past few decades available in COCA yields results that are, unfortunately, at odds with the less detailed data from the comparable decades of COHA. Table 7.4 also indicates that AmE favours preposition omission more than BrE does, which allows us to tentatively extend Rohdenburg's observation regarding *spend* – that preposition omission is a change that is being led by AmE – to the case of *waste*. The time frames of COCA and the BNC are, however, not the same, so any comment can be only a generalization at this stage.

Table 7.3 Preposition use with *waste no time* + (*in*) + *V-ing* over 150 years in COHA

DECADE	1850s	1860s	1870s	1880s	1890s	1900s	1910s	1920s	1930s	1940s	1950s	1960s	1970s	1980s	1990s	2000s
in	3	2	–	4	3	7	11	6	9	10	6	10	9	5	12	15
zero	–	–	–	–	–	1	5	2	5	9	5	9	6	6	10	10

All numbers indicate raw frequencies.

Table 7.4 Preposition use with *waste no time* + (*in*) + *V-ing* in COCA and the BNC

	COCA	BNC
in	0.30 (134)	0.51 (51)
zero	0.38 (170)	0.12 (12)

Numbers outside brackets represent normalized frequencies per 1 million words; bracketed numbers represent raw figures.

The link between preposition use and sense in the case of *waste no time* + (*in*) + *V-ing* is striking: of the relatively few modern English Sense 2 tokens (AmE and BrE), the majority omit the preposition ((10a–b) above are examples of this). COHA does, however, contain one clear Sense 2 token from 1999 which retains the preposition:

(16) The bank was lined with great boulders through which a day-time path wound a difficult way. Jerry wasted no time in trying to follow it, but skirted far around through a waist-high cornfield. (COHA 1999, FIC)

It should be pointed out that this token was produced by an author who, in the same work, produced two other Sense 2 examples without the preposition.

Looking at the shift in meaning across the decades shown in COHA, Figure 7.1 shows the competition between the two senses since 1850 in the more explicit variant. It can be seen that up until the twentieth century, Sense 2 was more common than Sense 1 with this pattern. From 1900 onwards, coinciding with the increase in preposition omission, Sense 1 became more frequent, with the latter half of the twentieth century seeing the predominant modern sense take over almost completely (it should be added as a reminder that unfortunately the raw numbers for each decade are not high, particularly the numbers for the decades of the nineteenth century – these were given in Table 7.3).

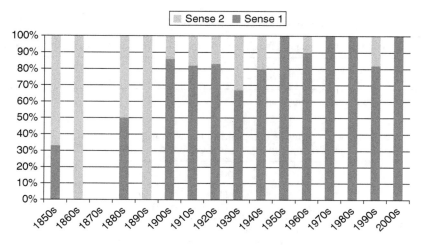

Figure 7.1   The semantic shift of *waste no time* + ***in*** + *V-ing* in AmE over 150 years

Figure 7.2 depicts the same development in the less explicit variant, and it can be seen here that the shift towards a total dominance of Sense 1 over Sense 2 appears to be occurring somewhat more gradually in the less explicit *waste no time + V-ing* variant.

It should be pointed out that there are numerous examples in the data of the more common pattern, the NEG + *waste* + *NP* + (*in*) + *V-ing* string, and that tokens of this type almost always carry a Sense 2 meaning. The following examples illustrate this:

(17) a. 'What now?' said the Woman. 'End of the world?' Doyle did not waste time smiling. 'We watch for visitors.' (BNC, AC4 3133)

b. 'Since you've made up your mind, we won't waste time discussing fact or fantasy. I'll take you home.' (COCA 1993, FIC)

Sense 1 examples of this pattern are also found, but are less common:

(18) Richie did not waste any time in responding to Patrick's appeal. (BNC, HTJ 553)

This is genuinely ambiguous, but in the wider context the Sense 1 meaning becomes clear: Richie quickly responds to Patrick's appeal.

It should be evident from the points made in this section that the semantics of *waste no time + (in) + V-ing* are not clear-cut. This ambiguity, or semantic opacity, is likely to be the main factor that increases the cognitive burden – perhaps with many English speakers on a subconscious level,

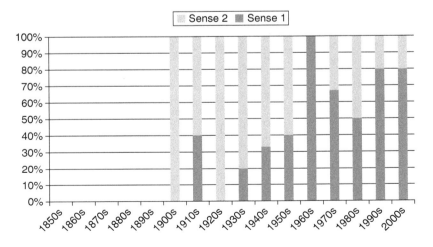

Figure 7.2 The semantic shift of *waste no time + V-ing* in AmE over 100 years

since there does appear to be a general lack of awareness of the alternate Sense 2 meaning – and triggers the use of the more grammatically explicit version.

7.4 Conclusion

In this chapter I have aimed, first of all, to provide some new information on the complementation features of the verb *waste* in the *waste no time* + (*in*) + *V-ing* pattern, by comparing it to the related verb *spend*, which has already had some attention. To this end it was confirmed that preposition use with this pattern is, in general, rapidly decreasing. The Complexity Principle has provided the theoretical framework against which the data are explained, and it was found to be a simple matter to relate the findings for *spend* to the principle, but the case of *waste* proved less straightforward. This chapter has argued that, with the majority of BrE fiction tokens of the more explicit version with *waste* being of the *waste no time* type, there may be issues relating to the semantics of the pattern that increase the level of cognitive complexity. Evidence from historical and present-day AmE and BrE suggests that, due to a semantic shift that is still underway but looks to be nearing completion, it may be that not all speakers are entirely sure of the meaning of the pattern, and the main source of cognitive complexity may indeed stem from its ambiguous and idiomatic nature. Several points raised in this regard suggest promising avenues for future research, not least the link between preposition use and semantic interpretation.

Notes

1. Corpus details: CLMETEV Part 1: 1710–1780, 3.0 million words; Part 2: 1780–1850, 5.7 million words; Part 3: 1850–1920, 6.3 million words (https://perswww.kuleuven.be/~u0044428/clmetev.htm); BNC prose fiction subsection: 1960–1993, 16.0 million words. Despite the CLMETEV containing a small amount of material that is not prose fiction, these two corpora may be seen as being comprised of sufficiently similar content to enable a valid comparison.
2. Two additional prepositions, *with* and *by*, are found with *waste* in earlier forms of English: *I left a restless couch, and came to waste the irksome hours with gazing on the fair approach of morning* (CLMETEV1); and ... *whether to go on ahead with Dick or remain to assist her mother, wasted vigour by running from one to the other* (CLMETEV2). Both have been set aside in this study; *with* due to its rarity (one token in CLMETEV1), and *by* (four tokens) because it is seen here as introducing an adjunct, rather than a complement.
3. An anonymous reader pointed out that, since *on* is frequently found introducing an NP complement in this type of pattern – e.g. *I won't waste my time on you* – this token appears to be ambiguous. The wider context, however, shows that *deceiving* is being used as a verb here.
4. It is not difficult to come up with examples of *spend* being used like *waste* to express a negative implication: *When a man spends every night staggering from bar to bar or from music-hall to music-hall...* (CLMETEV3).

5. The label PRO is used here to represent the understood subject of a sentential complement in control structures, as is common in the literature today.
6. The fact that, with *waste*, so few tokens that here have been judged as being cognitively complex (those featuring non-canonical word order, complex and lengthy NPs, inserted elements) are found (11 out of the total 143), may be seen as noteworthy. *Spend* appears less conspicuous in this regard, with 37 out of the total 163 deemed 'complex'.
7. Here the Complexity Principle is used in a somewhat extended sense, to cover cases of semantic complexity, in addition to clearer manifestations of cognitive complexity.
8. Corpus details: COHA 400 million words; COCA 450 million words.
9. Two COHA tokens were found to overlap with COCA tokens, which has been accounted for in these numbers.

References

Electronic corpora

BNC – The British National Corpus
COCA – The Corpus of Contemporary American English
COHA – The Corpus of Historical American English
CLMETEV – The Corpus of Late Modern English Texts, extended version

Dictionaries

COBUILD – *The Collins Cobuild Advanced Dictionary of English*, 7th edn (2014) J. Sinclair (ed.) (Glasgow: Harper Collins Publishers).
OED online – *The Oxford English Dictionary Online* (Oxford: Oxford University Press) (www.oed.com, accessed April 2014).
ODCIE – *The Oxford Dictionary of Current Idiomatic English* (1998) A. P. Cowie, R. Mackin and I. R. McCaig (eds) (Oxford: Oxford University Press).
OALD – *The Oxford Advanced Learner's Dictionary*, 8th edn (2010) J. Turnbull (ed. in chief) (Oxford: Oxford University Press).

Secondary sources

De Smet, H. (2013) *Spreading Patterns: Diffusional Change in the English System of Complementation* (Oxford: Oxford University Press).
Dixon, R. M. W. (2005) *A Semantic Approach to English Grammar* (Oxford: Oxford University Press).
Fillmore, C., P. Kay and M. C. O'Connor (1988) 'Regularity and Idiomaticity in Grammatical Constructions: the Case of Let Alone'. *Language*, 64 (3): 501–38.
Herbst, T., D. Heath, I. F. Roe and D. Götz (2004) *A Valency Dictionary of English* (Berlin: de Gruyter).
Huddleston R. and G. Pullum (2002) *The Cambridge Grammar of the English Language* (Cambridge: Cambridge University Press).
Kortmann, Bernd (1991) *Free Adjuncts and Absolutes in English. Problems of Control and Interpretation* (London: Routledge).
Leech, G., M. Hundt, C. Mair and N. Smith (2009) *Change in Contemporary English: a Grammatical Study* (Cambridge: Cambridge University Press).
Mair, C. (2006) *Twentieth Century English* (Cambridge: Cambridge University Press).
Makkai, A. (1972) *Idiom Structure in English* (The Hague: Mouton).

Rohdenburg, G. (1996) 'Cognitive Complexity and Increased Grammatical Explicitness in English'. *Cognitive Linguistics*, 7 (2): 149–82.

Rohdenburg, G. (2002) 'Processing Complexity and the Variable Use of Prepositions in English' in H. Cuyckens and G. Radden (eds) *Perspectives on Prepositions* (Tübingen: Niemeyer Verlag), pp. 79–100.

Rohdenburg, G. (2007) 'Functional Constraints in Syntactic Change: the Rise and Fall of Prepositional Constructions in Early and Late Modern English'. *English Studies*, 88 (2): 217–33.

Ross, J. R. (2004) 'Nouniness' in B. Aarts, D. Denison, E. Keizer and G. Popova (eds) *Fuzzy Grammar* (Oxford: Oxford University Press), pp. 351–422.

Rudanko, J. (1999) *Diachronic Studies of English Complementation Patterns: Eighteenth Century Evidence in Tracing the Development of Verbs and Adjectives Selecting Prepositions and Complement Clauses* (Albany, NY: State University of New York Press).

Sellgren, E. (2010) 'Prevent and the Battle of the -ing Clauses' in U. Lenker, J. Huber and R. Mailhammer (eds) *English Historical Linguistics 2008: Vol. 1: The History of English Verbal and Nominal Constructions* (Amsterdam: John Benjamins), pp. 45–62.

8
From Doubt to Supposition: the Construction-Specific Meaning Change of the Finnish Verb *Epäillä*

Jutta Salminen
University of Helsinki

8.1 Introduction

This chapter introduces an interesting meaning change phenomenon concerning the Finnish mental process verb *epäillä* 'doubt/suppose'. The chapter will also illustrate how different complementation patterns may affect the interpretation of the main clause verb. In Modern Finnish, the verb *epäillä* displays a peculiar polysemy: in certain contexts it is interpreted to convey *doubt*, and in certain other contexts *supposition*. Both meaning variants describe the epistemic stance of the conceptualizer,[1] but the directions of this stance are mutually contrary. This current polysemy is the result of diachronic changes (cf. Hansen 2012: 241).

The verb *epäillä* has its etymological roots in the negative auxiliary *e(i)*, which in Finnish stands for standard negation (see e.g. Miestamo 2007: 554). The form *epä* morphologically consists of the negative auxiliary stem *e-* and the present participle ending *-pA*. In all attested states of Finnish, *epä* serves as a negative prefix indicating a moderate contrary opposition, illustrated for example in the adjectives *epäsuora* ('indirect') and *epämukava* ('uncomfortable') (ISK 2004: section 1630).[2] Different etymological sources offer slightly distinctive suggestions for the development of the verb *epäillä*, but the explanations all share the view that the history goes back to the negative auxiliary.[3]

Given that the verb stems from the negative auxiliary, it is quite logical that an inherently negative 'doubt' meaning antedates the non-negative 'suppose' variant. Example (1) is from Early Modern Finnish (EMF, approx. nineteenth century), while (2) exemplifies Modern Finnish use (MF) (for data abbreviations, see endnote 8):

(1) Epäile-n=pä,   että usko-vat   tämä-n historia-n.
    doubt-1SG=CL that believe-3PL this-GEN story (history)-GEN
    'I (do) doubt that they believe this story.' (CEMF, EMF)
    The stance: **no**, *they probably do* **not** *believe the story.*

(2) Tutkija-t　　tule-vat　aina　kulke-ma-an vinti-lle porta-i-ta
　　 researcher-PL come-3PL always go-INF-ILL　　attic-ALL stair-PL-PART
　　 myöten ja　epäile-vät　vahvasti, että niin teke-vät muut=kin.
　　 along　and suppose-3PL strongly　that so　do-3PL　others=too
　　 'Researchers will always use stairs when going to the attic, and they
　　 strongly suppose that other people will, too.' (FTC, MF)
　　 The stance: yes, other people will probably act similarly.

Despite the schematically similar forms of (1) and (2), namely an affirmative form of *epäillä* and an affirmative *että* ('that') complement, the polar
interpretations of these examples display a contradiction. The first person
conceptualizer in (1) does not indicate belief in the truthfulness of the proposition of the complement 'they believe this story', while in (2) it is stated
that researchers do believe in the truthfulness of the proposition 'so will the
other people'. Since there is no explicit marking of this difference, the construction[4] *epäillä* + *että* clause carries two distinctive polar orientations. The
meaning variant exemplified in (1) will be called *negation-inclining* (⇨ –),
since the conceptualizer is inclined to regard the proposition of the complement as untrue. Following the same logic, the variant displayed in (2) will
be called *affirmation-inclining* (⇨ +).[5] (For the term *inclination* see Langacker
2008: 450.) In other words, the epistemic stance described by *epäillä* has a
polar value (+ or –) and a degree of uncertainty.

The variety of actual polar interpretations increases, as the verb *epäillä*
may, naturally, also appear in negative form (negative auxiliary + *epäillä*; for
example *en epäile* 'I do not doubt/suppose'). Such utterances basically represent a refutation of either one or the other polar interpretation of *epäillä*:
the conceptualizer either denies a doubtful stance or denies his commitment
to a supposition. Because of space limitations, the negative forms of *epäillä*
will remain untouched in this analysis.

In addition to the epistemic evaluation (semantic distinction between nega-
tion- and affirmation-inclination; untrue or true), a desirability evaluation is
quite often present in the contextual meaning of *epäillä*. To be more specific,
the assessment expressed by this verb often carries a tone of undesirability.
The undesirability evaluation always concerns the polar version which the
conceptualizer is inclined to: 'the expressed idea is not a desirable state of
affairs from my point of view'. In the analysis, this meaning aspect will
not be discussed, but an awareness of it will help to understand the different translation equivalent verbs of affirmation-inclining *epäillä* ('suppose',
'suspect').

Introducing the meaning change of *epäillä* via examples (1) and (2) creates an oversimplified picture of the case. The two polar meaning variants
of *epäillä* have existed side by side for a long time in Finnish. Thus, the
meaning change discussed neither presumes that the affirmation-inclining
variant is fundamentally new nor that the negation-inclining variant is a

relic. The actual *change* has occurred in the emphasis and the probability of the polar interpretation of the verb. In fact, the core of the verb's meaning could be expressed as the mental process of being unsure (cf. *higher-order-schema* in Iwata 2005; more in section 8.5). With respect to the two polar meaning variants, this mental process inherently contains both possible directions of inclination.[6]

In this chapter the following constructions will be analysed: (1) *epäillä* + finite *että* clause; (2) *epäillä* + non-finite complement; (3) *epäillä* + embedded question; and (4) *epäillä* with no overt complement.[7] I will concentrate on the contexts where the doubt or the supposition, expressed by the verb, has a clearly recognizable object; these contexts comprise most of the verb's use. Nevertheless, it must be remembered that this either/or picture is a deliberate simplification, and that usage patterns in which the verb *epäillä* denotes plain uncertainty also exist.

8.2 Data and tools of analysis

In this section I will introduce the data used in the chapter. The data derive from three periods of literary Finnish: Old Finnish (OF, sixteenth–eighteenth century), Early Modern Finnish (nineteenth century), and Modern Finnish (twentieth and twenty-first centuries). The data have been collected from several corpora comprising different written genres.[8] I have compiled all the uses of the verb *epäillä* in finite verb constructions, and the numbers of such occurrences in the above-mentioned constructions are shown in Table 8.1.[9]

All the examples were categorized according to the polar interpretation of the verb *epäillä* and the contextual factors supporting the reading. The contextual factors, the actual tools of the analysis, comprise the following: polarity items in the complement, mood of the complement (only in the finite complements), and the givenness of the information provided in the complement (see Shore 2008: 28–34, Prince 1981: 226, 228). The main treatment of these factors will be divided according to which complement types best exemplify the use of each factor: mood will be touched upon with

Table 8.1 Numbers of different constructions in the corpora

	Finite *että* complement	Non-finite complement	Embedded question complement	No overt complement (Ø)
Old Finnish (*n* = 132)	56	4	14	58
Early Modern Finnish (*n* = 619)	200	97	199	123
Modern Finnish (*n* = 288)	135	73	42	38

että clause complements, polarity items with non-finite complements and embedded questions, and givenness with *epäillä* and no overt complement. Since the analysis of givenness is not unequivocal or clear-cut, it has not been coded systematically in the data (Shore 2008: 32–4; more in section 8.4.2). The presence of polarity items and the choice of mood, on the other hand, have been systematically coded.

In addition to the three tools of analysis introduced above, other contextual clues, such as markings of contrast, or wider thematic background knowledge, may direct the polar interpretation. In the analysis I will compare the conventional readings of each construction in every subset of the data, and through this comparison present a wider picture of the construction-specific meaning change in question. In addition, by analysing individual examples, I will illustrate how different contextual features direct and support the disambiguation of the verb.

8.3 The reanalysis mechanism and the constructions affected

In this section I will present the mechanism for a reanalysis, which is required in order to get from the interpretation of (1) to the contrary interpretation of (2). In addition, I will present the data evidence, which reveals that the first two constructions have actually undergone this change. The reanalysis mechanism pertains to the finite *että* complement, which is why I begin with this construction. After that, the non-finite complement will be dealt with.

8.3.1 The clausal *että* complement

Table 8.2 introduces the polar interpretations of *epäillä* occurring with the finite *että* complement in all the subsets of the data.

The background colours link the affirmative and negative forms of the same polar reading of *epäillä* (e.g. the darkest colour: both negation-inclining 'doubt' and refuted negation-inclining 'not doubt' uses). The letter P refers to *paratactic negation*, that is, instances where the complement

Table 8.2 The polar interpretations of the construction *epäillä* + *että* clause in the data

	Old Finnish (*n* = 56)	Early Modern Finnish (*n* = 200)	Modern Finnish (*n* = 135)
⇨ –	1	18	2
– (⇨ –)	42	121	3
⇨ – P	1	10	45
– (⇨ –) P	10	44	11
⇨ +	2	6	70
– (⇨ +)	0	1	4

of *epäillä* is formally negative: *Epäilen, ettei hän tule* (doubt/suppose-1SG that=NEG he come-CNG). The underlying semantic structure of this construction is ambiguous (as the gloss reveals). Because of this underlying equivocalness, the very construction enables the reinterpretation (discussed in the next subsection).

An overview of Table 8.2 reveals that, with the *että* complement, the emphasis of a conventional polar interpretation of *epäillä* has moved from a negation-inclining reading to an affirmation-inclining one. This conclusion can be drawn by comparing the numbers on the dark grey (negation-inclining) and white (affirmation-inclining) backgrounds in chronological succession. In the Old Finnish and Early Modern Finnish data, affirmation-inclining readings are extremely rare (altogether nine examples), whereas, by contrast, in the Modern Finnish data negation-inclining instances are clearly in the minority (five examples). The numbers for the paratactic construction as a whole display no considerable change.

8.3.1.1 The mechanism of reanalysis

Since the Finnish standard negation marker is a person-inflected auxiliary, only finite constructions may contain it. The ability of the finite *että* complement to contain separate clausal negation is the key to the change under discussion. The schematic example series shown in Table 8.3 presents the potential succession of diachronic phases, and thus the mechanism for the reanalysis. The letters A and B code the similar forms of utterances in both phases.

In the first phase, which, generally speaking, comprises Old Finnish and extends into Early Modern Finnish, the construction with an affirmative *että* complement (form A) results in a doubtful stance. Thus the verb *epäillä* is clearly negation-inclining. With a complement clause of negative form the reading is paratactic: the doubtful stance is a function of both the verb *epäillä* and the negation in the complement. The construction with an overtly negative complement, however, also serves as a favourable context for the meaning change, which is indicated in phase 2 (cf. Fortson 2006: 651). The difference between the EITHER and OR options of (B) in phase 2 boils down to the question of whether the negation-inclining meaning is a function of both the verb *epäillä* and the overt marking of negation (*negation-inclining verb* + NEG; paratactic reading), or only a function of the clausal negation in the subordinate clause (*affirmation-inclining verb* + NEG; compositional reading). The overt coding of negation in the complement allows for the latter, compositional reading, in which the verb *epäillä* is reinterpreted as affirmation-inclining: *epäillä* only represents an uncertain epistemic stance, suggesting that what will be expressed by the complement probably will hold true (OR reading in phase 2). The reanalysis is further illustrated in Figure 8.1.

Since *epäillä* is no longer 'responsible' for coding a doubtful stance, a reading with a complete lack of marking or interpretation of negation becomes

Table 8.3   The two phases of the polar interpretation of the *epäillä + että* complement

	Form of an expression		Polar interpretation of *epäillä*	Stance described by the whole expression
PHASE 1	(A) Epäilen, että hän tulee. doubt-1SG that he come-3SG		negation-inclining (⇨ –)	'he probably won't come'
	(B) Epäilen, että hän **ei** tule. doubt-1SG that he NEG come-CNG		negation-inclining (⇨ –)	'he probably won't come' (by merging the two negative elements = paratactic negation)
PHASE 2	(B) Epäilen, että hän **ei** tule. doubt-1SG that he NEG come-CNG	either:	negation-inclining (⇨ –)	'he probably won't come' (by merging the two negative elements = paratactic negation)
	(B) Epäilen, että hän **ei** tule. suppose-1SG that he NEG come-CNG	or:	affirmation-inclining (⇨ +)	'he probably won't come' (deriving from the negation in the subordinate clause = compositional reading)
	(A) Epäilen, että hän tulee. suppose-1SG that he come-3SG		affirmation-inclining (⇨ +)	'he will probably come'

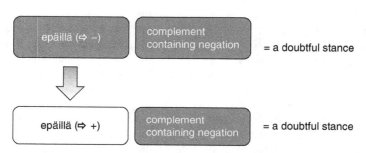

Figure 8.1   The reanalysis mechanism of *epäillä* (B example in phase 2 of Table 8.3)

possible (A in phase 2). This is how the two formally identical expressions (form A) produce contrary readings diachronically.

The reanalysis of the polarity of the verb *epäillä* displays *semantic bleaching*, a mechanism associated with grammaticalization: over the course of time certain semantic features bleach out from a linguistic unit, and as a result only the semantic core of the unit remains (see e.g. Heine 2006: 578–9). Even if the meaning change of *epäillä* does not count as grammaticalization, this part of the model accounts for the phenomenon:[10] the semantic core of *epäillä*, the meaning of an uncertain stance, is present in both polar interpretations of the verb, while the meaning of negation has bleached out from the affirmation-inclining reading.

The underlying difference between a paratactic and compositional reading of (B) is so subtle that it is not possible to make an accurate distinction between them in the data. For this reason, all the instances containing a negative complement clause have been categorized as paratactic, even if this is a simplification.

8.3.1.2 A tendency – not a rule

Examples (1) and (2), presented in the introduction, exemplified the tendency of the meaning change. Even if this change from a negation-inclining reading to an affirmation-inclining one is quite obviously visible with the *että* complement, Table 8.2 indicates that counterexamples also exist. In the Modern Finnish example (3), there is no overt marking of negation, but the stance is still doubtful:

(3) **Epäile-n**, että hän pysty-isi   lyhentä-mä-än ja
     doubt-1SG that she be.able.to-COND.3SG pay.off-INF-ILL and
     hoita-ma-an   koro-t   koska   o-n   työtön.
     take.care.of-INF-ILL interest-PL because be-3SG unemployed
     'I doubt that she could pay off [the loan] and take care of the interest, because she is unemployed.' (AD, MF)

The use of the conditional mood, utilized in the complement of (3), is multifunctional with the verb *epäillä*. The schematic meaning of non-factuality and intensionality combines unproblematically with both a negation- and affirmation-inclining reading, since the stance always contains uncertainty (see Kauppinen 1998: 161, 166).[11] Still, particularly in Modern Finnish, the use of the conditional strongly supports the otherwise rare negation-inclining reading of *epäillä*. In addition to the use of the conditional mood, the justification of the opinion, expressed in the adverbial clause, clarifies the reading. Since the person in question is described as having no job, it is quite logical that the proposition 'she is able to pay off...' is questioned.

Example (3) exemplifies how the mood of the complement may function as one disambiguation clue. The morphologically unmarked indicative mood dominates in the complement clauses in my data. However, the use of the conditional, seen in (3) – and (11) in section 8.4.1 – is fairly recurrent.

Table 8.4   The polar interpretations of the construction *epäillä* + non-finite complement in the data

	Old Finnish (*n* = 4)	Early Modern Finnish (*n* = 97)	Modern Finnish (*n* = 73)
⇨ −	1	34	1
− (⇨ −)	3	41	1
⇨ +	0	21	70
− (⇨ +)	0	1	1

Since the mood is multifunctional, it is impossible to summarize the basic meaning of it in the data.[12]

To sum up, the meaning change of the interpretation of the *epäillä* + *että* complement is not complete: despite the predominant change, exceptions exist. For this reason, the New Dictionary of Modern Finnish (KS s.v. *epäillä*) also contains a note on the use of the *epäillä* + *että* clause construction; in some contexts both of the polar meanings introduced above may be equally available to the reader, if the surrounding context does not disambiguate the intended meaning.

8.3.2   Non-finite complement

The non-finite structure, appearing in the complement position, is semantically close to the *että* clause, only with a more restricted domain of use (see ISK 2004: sections 473, 538). The lower number of occurrences in Table 8.4 (when compared to Table 8.2) reflects this restriction. The construction *epäillä* + non-finite complement has undergone a change of interpretation identical to that undergone by the *että* clause construction discussed above. Even if the constructions are not completely synonymous, the similarity in meaning prompts an analogical transfer of the meaning change (cf. Traugott and Trousdale 2010: 36).[13]

Table 8.4 lacks the markings of paratactic constructions (indicated with 'P' in Table 8.2), because the non-finite complement is incapable of containing clausal negation. The verb form in this complement construction consists of a present or past participle and a genitive suffix. In addition, the subject is in the genitive case. Since the morphology of the construction is not the issue at hand, I will refer to the verb of this construction simply with an 'NFC' (non-finite complement) in the glosses.

Examples (4) and (5) present the negation-inclining and affirmation-inclining uses of *epäillä* with a non-finite complement:

(4) Ennen pitkä-ä   alka-a   hän **epäil-lä**   raha-nsa
riittä-vän=**kään**
before long-PART begin-3SG he   doubt-INF money-GEN.PX
suffice-NFC=CL
häne-lle elatukse-ksi   kuolopäivä-ä-nsä   asti.
he-ALL   living-TRANS day.of.death-ILL-PX until
'Before long he begins to doubt if his money will suffice until the end
of his life.' (CEMF, EMF)

In (4), one linguistic element undisputedly directs the reading to a negation-inclination, namely a negative polarity item (NPI), the clitic *-kään*. The basic meaning of this NPI is 'also, too (not)', but in this context the clitic conveys a contrast: the insufficiency of the money counters the earlier assumptions.

While the NPIs disambiguate the negation-inclining reading, the positive polarity items (PPIs), naturally, direct the reading towards an affirmation-inclining one, as in the following example:

(5) Kirjoittaja **epäile-e**   ministeri-n=**kin**   hapuile-van häne-n
writer   suspect-3SG minister-GEN=too grope-NFC he-GEN
laiha-a   lompakko-a-an.
thin-PART wallet-PART-PX
'The writer suspects that the minister too is groping for his thin wallet.'
(FTC, MF)

The PPI in (5), the clitic *-kin*, is the positive variant of *-kaan/-kään*, seen in (4). In this context, the clitic conveys the prototypical additive meaning.

The use of polarity items (PIs) is relatively rare in Old Finnish. Therefore the following characterizations about the commonness of PIs concern the Early Modern Finnish and Modern Finnish data sets. Of the constructions discussed in this chapter, the PIs appear as often with *että* clauses as they do with non-finite constructions: approximately 20 per cent of the occurrences contain PIs. With embedded questions, the PIs appear even more regularly: in both the Early Modern Finnish and the Modern Finnish data approximately 40 per cent of question complement examples contain PIs. I will return to these examples in the next subsection.

To sum up, it can be said that the meaning change also concerns the non-finite complement constructions. However, as with the *että* complements, the same disclaimer must be added here: even if the prototypical meaning of *epäillä* + non-finite complement is affirmation-inclining in Modern Finnish, the negation-inclining variant is not impossible either (see Table 8.4). This is only natural, since the negation-inclining variant still flourishes in other constructions, which I will now move on to.

8.4 The persistence of the negation-inclining meaning

This section discusses the constructions in which the negation-inclining variant of *epäillä* has remained. The analysis of *että* clause and non-finite complements above revealed that, even though highly dominant with these constructions in Modern Finnish, the affirmation-inclining interpretation is not all-pervasive. The same tendency-like nature also characterizes the interpretations of the constructions discussed below: even if the typical polar meaning of *epäillä* has remained negation-inclining, the change, introduced above, occasionally leaks to these contexts as well.

8.4.1 Embedded questions

The verb *epäillä* combines with several embedded question types, of which the polar *yes–no* questions are the most common. In Modern Finnish, polar questions are marked regularly with a question clitic -*kO* (QC in glosses) attached to the element that is questioned, usually the finite verb (*Kuulet ~ Kuulet-ko?* 'You hear' ~ 'Do you hear?'). The Old Finnish and Early Modern Finnish data also include embedded *yes–no* questions initiated with the conjunction *jos* ('if'); the share of these variants is indicated in parentheses in Table 8.5. This form, which is avoided in present-day Standard Finnish, is likely to be a loan from Swedish, where *yes–no* questions begin with the conjunction *om* ('if') (SAOB: s.v. om; cf. also English *if/whether* clauses).

The dominance of *yes–no* questions in the complements of *epäillä* is natural, since the verb usually denotes a unidirectional polar inclination; a *yes–no* question offers a proposition to which a negation-inclining (or an affirmation-inclining) *epäillä* may be directed (cf. *closed type* in Iyeiri 2010: 140). However, some instances of alternative questions and *wh*-questions exist (*open type*; ibid.). Alternative questions explicate the twofold meaning of the verb *epäillä*: both contrary variants are visible (7); ⇨ – / ⇨ + in Table 8.5. With most *wh*-questions, an implication of a *yes–no* question is available (8). If this is not the case, it is impossible to define the polar orientation of *epäillä*, and the meaning comes close to one of open speculation or hesitation (cf. Iyeiri 2010: 141). In Table 8.5 I refer to such occurrences with a

Table 8.5 The polar interpretations of the construction *epäillä* + embedded question in the data

	Old Finnish (*n* = 14)	Early Modern Finnish (*n* = 199)	Modern Finnish (*n* = 42)
⇨ –	9 (6)	165 (62)	35
– (⇨ –)	1 (1)	10	0
⇨ +	0	3	2
– (⇨ +)	0	1	1
⇨ – / ⇨ +	1 (1)	8	4
?	3	12	0

question mark, but will leave these cases outside the current discussion as they do not clearly exhibit the polar meaning variation of *epäillä*.

(6) Hän **epäile-e,** o-n=ko häne-n olo-ssa-an Los Angelesi-ssa
he doubt-3SG be-3SG=QC he-GEN being-INES-PX L.A.-INES
mitään miel-tä.
any sense-PART
'He doubts whether there is any sense in his staying in L.A.' (FTC, MF)

(7) [O]-n=kin syy-tä **epäil-lä,** o-n=ko geen-i-en osuus
be-3SG=CL reason-PART doubt-INF be-3SG=QC gene-PL-GEN share
60 prosentti-a vai jotain muu-ta.
60 per cent-PART or something else-PART
'It is reasonable to doubt if the share of genes is 60 per cent – or something else.' (FTC, MF)

(8) [H]e **epäile-wät** cuinga he nij-den [hyv-i-en teko-j-en]
they doubt-3PL how they they-GEN [good-PL-GEN deed-PL-GEN]
cautta taita-wat pysy-ä Jumala-n edes.
via can-3PL stay-INF God-GEN in.front.of
'They doubt how they with the help of these [good deeds] can remain in God's favour.'
→ 'They doubt if they can remain in God's favour with the help of these [good deeds].' (COLF, OF)

In (6), the negation-inclining reading is supported by the NPI *mitään* 'any'. According to the conceptualizer of the sentence there might be no sense in him residing in L.A. As an example of a completely regular use of *epäillä* in Modern Finnish, (6) illustrates that the change, discussed in the previous section, does not cover constructions consisting of *epäillä* + embedded question complement. The reason for this will be suggested below.

The alternative question variant is exemplified in (7). Although Iyeiri (2010: 140) and Huddleston and Pullum (2002: 983) label this complement type as *open*, the openness of the reading is fairly superficial. At least with the verb *epäillä* in my data, alternative question complements seem to be merely extensions of *yes–no* questions. This is because the order of the alternatives is strictly fixed: the first alternative is the target of the doubt, and the second, a rhetorical device, explicates the view which the conceptualizer favours. Example (7) follows this logic: the proposition 'the share of genes is 60 per cent' comes under doubt, and the alternative '[the share is] something else' is presented as a more correct option. Thus by excluding the additional alternative (in (7) *jotain muuta* 'something else'), the alternative question complements of *epäillä* resemble simple *yes–no* question complements – from both the formal and interpretational points of view.

In (8), an example from Old Finnish, the *wh*-question complement beginning with the interrogative proadverb *cuinga* 'how' (in MF *kuinka*) functions as a complement of *epäillä*. As already mentioned, formally open *how* questions appearing in a complement position often imply *yes–no* questions, as does the complement in (8) (implication is indicated in the second idiomatic translation). The sentence seems to imply that the proposition 'they can remain in God's favour with the help of good deeds' is questioned; the concrete means for achieving this state of affairs is not actually asked for (cf. rhetorical questions). This implication relates to other findings concerning the functions of *kuinka* initial embedded clauses: Juvonen (2014) asserts that, in her matriculation essay data, some *kuinka* complements display a representation-oriented interpretation with a declarative rather than interrogative quality. This resembles the pragmatics of the embedded *cuinga* question in (8): the means or the manner is not searched for, but the content of the question is treated like a proposition whose truthfulness may be assessed.

In all of the examples above, the polar interpretation of *epäillä* is negation-inclining. Looking at the numbers in Table 8.5, one can conclude that whenever the polar orientation of *epäillä* is available for analysis with an embedded question complement, the prototypical reading is, and has always been, negation-inclining. The reason for the persistence of this meaning lies in the independent semantics of the embedded question complement. Remarks on the semantic closeness of questions and negation are fairly common in the literature; the connection is usually elaborated so that questions may imply negation (see e.g. Iyeiri 2010: 145, Jespersen 1924: 336–7, Jespersen 1917: 22; for a structural discussion, see Horn 1989: 472–3). Thus it is a short step from expressing a question to inclining to negation.

One piece of evidence underlining the fact that embedded *yes–no* questions support the interpretation of negation-inclination is the restrictions on the distribution of this complement type. Embedded *yes–no* questions avoid verbs conveying an undisputable affirmation-inclining stance (e.g. *luulla* 'think', *arvella* 'guess'). The reason for this avoidance may lie in semantic incompatibility. However, even if the form and meaning of embedded questions easily combine with a negation-inclining stance, the interpretation must also exist in the verb *epäillä* itself: a genuine question, naturally, also enables a positive response. The discussion on the role of the verb and the complement in meaning formation will continue in section 8.5.

As was already mentioned, PIs are very frequent with embedded question complements: close to 40 per cent of instances in the data contain one. The commonness of PIs may, of course, be explained by the fact that in addition to the scope of negation, the questions themselves also license NPIs. In the complements of *epäillä*, though, NPIs clearly support a negation-inclining reading of the verb construction. Example (6) above represents a prototypical instance of NPIs: *mitään*, 'any', steers one to negation-inclination. In the Early Modern Finnish data, PIs are exceptionally common with *jos* 'if' initial embedded *yes–no* questions (almost 68 per cent of *jos* complements contain one):

(9) **[E]päile-mme**, jos nii-stä   **milloinkaan** o-n   oikea-n
doubt-1PL   if   they-ELA ever   be-3SG real-GEN
siwistykse-n   edistäj-i-ksi.
education-GEN promoter-PL-TRANS
'We doubt whether they will ever contribute to real education.' (NL, EMF)

The number of PI occurrences, of course, relates to the question of the environments in which PIs naturally occur. For example, the use of certain pro-words or particles forces a choice of polarity (e.g. *milloinkaan* 'ever'), since they obligatorily mark this meaning dimension. However, the extensive number of NPIs with *jos* initial embedded *yes–no* questions might also indicate that a clarification of the polarity is often needed in this construction.

Although the connection between NPIs and PPIs, on the one hand, and negation- and affirmation-inclining interpretations of *epäillä*, on the other, is fairly obvious, there are a few deviations from this logic. All counterexamples appear with embedded question complements. In (10), the formally undisputed PPI *todellakin* ('really') (cf. *-kin* in (5)) appears in the complement of a clearly negation-inclining *epäillä*:

(10) Isku-j-en   tulokse-t o-vat   pan-neet   **epäile-mä-än**,
raid-PL-GEN result-PL be-3PL make-PTCP.PL doubt-INF-ILL
edusta-a=ko   harmaa talous **todellakin** vain 20 miljardi-a
embody-3SG=QC grey economy really   only 20 billion-PART
vuositaso-lla.
per.year-ADE
'The results of the raids have made one doubt if the black economy is really only 20 billion per year.' (FTC, MF)

The usage of the morphologically positive polar *todellakin* in a negation-inclining context like (10) is not a mystery, nor an error, since this lexeme has a challenging contextual meaning variant implying an inclination to negation ('Does this *really* hold true?').

I will conclude this section with an example which concretizes the fact that it is only a tendency that the negation-inclining meaning has maintained in the construction *epäillä* + embedded question complement throughout the history of literary Finnish. As Table 8.5 reveals, affirmation-inclining instances have occurred sporadically. Consider the following:

(11) [H]ajanaisuus – – anta-a   aihe-tta   **epäil-lä**,   vo-isi=ko[14]
heterogenity   give-3SG reason-PART suppose-INF can-COND=QC
kysee-ssä   ol-la   **jokin** vanha jäänne.
question-INES be-INF some old   relic
'The heterogeneity [of the case agreement system in the Uralic language family] offers a reason to suppose that it could be a question of an old relic.' (AD, MF)

The complement of *epäillä* in (11) contains the PPI *jokin* ('some'), which directs one to an affirmation-inclining reading of *epäillä* in spite of the embedded question form of the complement. In addition, the complement clause is in the conditional mood, which in this context carries the meaning of a suggestion (cf. example (3) and discussion in section 8.3.1.2).

8.4.2 Epäillä with no overt complement

The final construction to be discussed is defined by the omission of an overt syntactic complement. In a prototypical case of this use of *epäillä*, there is, in the preceding context, a linguistic unit which functions as a semantic complement of the verb. However, this relation is not indicated syntactically. In the data, the semantic complement is sometimes not obviously available, and thus the meaning of *epäillä* resembles hesitation and open speculation (cf. *wh*-question complements). As with the question complements, I will leave these instances untouched. The cases relegated to the row marked with a question mark in Table 8.6, however, remind us of the fact that the meaning of *epäillä* is not always clearly inclined to one or the other polar variant.

The overall picture of the use of *epäillä* with no overt complement remarkably resembles the picture presented in the previous section of the embedded questions: the prototypical interpretation of the verb is negation-inclining, and the occasional instances of affirmation-inclining readings are clearly in the minority. Example (12) illustrates the use of *epäillä* with no overt complement:

(12) Välistä   luul-i-n,   että hän=kin o-n   sama-an
     sometimes think-PST-1SG that she=too be-3SG same-ILL
     onnettomuute-en joutu-nut;   välista   taas **epäil-i-n.**
     misery-ILL   get.into-PTCP sometimes again doubt-PST-1SG
     'Sometimes I thought that she had fallen into the same misery; and
     sometimes I doubted.' (CFLC, MF)

The *että* clause, which functions as a complement of the verb *luulla* ('to think') in (12), may also be easily comprehended as a semantic complement of *epäillä*. The contrastive pattern *sometimes X and sometimes Y* occurring with the two verbs also supports the negation-inclining reading of *epäillä*;

Table 8.6 The polar interpretations of the construction *epäillä* + Ø in the data

	Old Finnish (*n* = 58)	Early Modern Finnish (*n* = 123)	Modern Finnish (*n* = 38)
⇨ –	29	53	20
– (⇨ –)	22	44	4
⇨ +	0	2	3
– (⇨ +)	0	1	0
?	7	23	11

there is no sense in producing the same epistemic stance in both parts of this structure. The whole expression therefore conveys that the conceptualizer has struggled, undecided between the two contrary views: 'perhaps she shares the same misery, or perhaps not'.

The semantic complement of *epäillä* may also appear in a question form:

(13) Tä-llä   tava-lla=ko   se saavute-taan? Rohkene-n **epäil-lä.**
     this-ADE mean-ADE=QC it achieve-PASS dare-1SG   doubt-INF
     'Is this the way to achieve it? I dare to doubt.' (FTC, MF)

In (13), the verb *epäillä* is used in the response to a question (in a letter to the editor). The question offers a suggestion, representing the view of someone else, and the writer expresses doubt regarding this view. In both (12) and (13) the previous linguistic context introduces a proposition, to which the negation-inclining stance, described by the verb *epäillä*, is directed. The nature of such utterances is profoundly reactive, and this is key to the persistence of negation-inclining meaning in this context. It is pragmatically more natural to negate something already contextually given or known, than something totally new to the discourse (Horn 1989: 203). This phenomenon (which I must now leave without deeper discussion) has been characterized as the inherent context-bound nature of negation (see e.g. Verhagen 2005: 72, 74, Givón 1978: 109). If not already present in the discourse, the use of negation tends to evoke the possibility of its affirmative counterpart – and thus reacts to it. Since a negation-inclining *epäillä* contains a semantic negation element, it also carries the reactive meaning potential. Consequently, when the verb *epäillä*, for example, is used to answer a question and has no overt complement of its own, the reactive nature of the phrase steers one to a negation-inclining reading of the verb.

In some discourse contexts the semantic complement of *epäillä* is not as clearly present in the linguistic surroundings as in (12) and (13). Still, the target of the doubt may be apparent through cultural knowledge and schemas (cf. Shore 2008: 34). One such context is religious discourse. The following example is from Old Finnish:

(14) O sine heicowskoinen / mixi sine epäl-i-t?
     O you of.little.faith   why you doubt-PST-2SG
     'O thou of little faith, wherefore didst thou doubt?' (translation: KJV[15]) (COLF, OF)

In religious discourse, the verb *epäillä* usually functions as a contradictive counterpart of the verb *uskoa* 'to believe'. Thus, depending on the context, the unexpressed complement of the verb is typically God's existence, love, promises, and so on. (14) is from the Gospel of Matthew, the narrative of how Jesus calms the storm and scolds the disciple who is frightened on the boat and does not believe that they would survive. The construction with no overt complement is no exception when it comes to the (in)variability of the polar readings of *epäillä*. Table 8.6 indicates that there are isolated instances of the affirmation-inclining reading with this construction also. Basically, in these cases the verb *epäillä* has, in the previous linguistic context, an affirmative-inclining meaning (for example with an *että* clause complement), and as a repetition, the elliptical *epäillä* carries the same meaning. Nevertheless, such affirmation-inclining uses of *epäillä* occurring with no overt complement are undeniably in the minority throughout the data.

8.5 Conclusion: construction-specific meaning change

In sections 8.3 and 8.4 I have shown that, based on the diachronic data of this study, the typical polar interpretation of *epäillä* has changed to affirmation-inclining in the constructions *epäillä* + *että* clause and *epäillä* + non-finite complement, while remaining negation-inclining in the constructions *epäillä* + embedded question and *epäillä* with no overt complement. Since the change does not concern all usage contexts of the verb, the phenomenon under scrutiny has to be perceived as a construction-specific change. The result of such a change is synchronic polysemy, which relates to the notion of *divergence*, whereby a lexical item may grammaticalize or change its meaning in some contexts and retain its original meaning in others (Hopper 1991: 24–5).

Most diachronic approaches to constructions concern schematic constructions under change: for example Hilpert (2012) has analysed how the meaning of the *keep V-ing* construction has developed due to the change in its collocations. The change discussed in this chapter concerns verb-specific constructions (cf. *mini constructions*, Boas 2005: 451–6), with a focus on how the syntactic constructions affect the meaning change of the verb. Such change is a specific type of constructional change – a construction-specific meaning change (cf. Fried 2013).

A synchronic perspective on the phenomenon is also available: the complement type affects the interpretation of the verb *epäillä*. Numerous observations have been made on this dynamic interrelation between a verb and its complement (see e.g. Goldberg 2013: 18–19, Rappaport Hovav and Levin 1998: 127–30). For example, Suzuki (2000: 42) characterizes the semantic relation between the verbs, denoting different levels of speakers' conviction, and their complements in the following way: 'the character of a verb alone does not reflect the strength of the speaker's conviction'. In addition, Iyeiri (2010: 140, 2009: 156–7) has stated that the degree of unlikeliness expressed by the verb *doubt*, a partial equivalent to *epäillä*, varies depending on the specific complement type used. Therefore the complement does not merely introduce the proposition to which a mental process verb, such as *epäillä*, directs its invariable meaning, but the inherent syntactic–semantic features of each complement type contribute in large part to the meaning formation. With *epäillä* the share of complements is exceptionally significant, since the verb has two contrary meaning variants.

In section 8.3.1.1 I maintained that the finite *että* complement, and its ability to contain clausal negation, had made the meaning change possible. In addition, in section 8.3.2 I stated that the non-finite complement construction had analogically followed this change. Without challenging these explanations, the configuration could also be turned around. Since the verb *epäillä* seems to have the potential to incline to both negative and affirmative polarity, why have certain constructions resisted this change? The answer has already been presented: the interrogative element in the embedded question complement, discussed in section 8.4.1, combines more naturally with a negation-inclining reading of *epäillä* than an affirmation-inclining variant. The verb with no overt complement, discussed in section 8.4.2, also prototypically carries a semantic–pragmatic property in its context, namely the reactive character, which steers one to a negation-inclining reading. When assessing the reasons for the synchronic polysemy of the verb *epäillä*, the semantic–pragmatic properties of these complement constructions, which resist the polar meaning change, have great significance.

In the end, one may ask whether the negation-inclining and affirmation-inclining meaning variants are properties of the plain verb *epäillä*, or whether it might be more accurate to view these directional interpretations as residing in the constructions consisting of the verb and the complement. I claim that instead of a simple choice between the two views, there is some truth in both of them. Iwata (2005: 104) separates two layers of verbal meaning: *L-meaning* (Lexical Head Level Meaning), and *P-meaning* (Phrasal Level Meaning), which denote the schematic core of a verb's semantics, and the constructional realization, respectively. If the polar meaning variants are regarded as the properties of the constructions, and not the verb *epäillä* itself, it is problematic to explain why there are deviations from the typical polar meanings in each of the constructions discussed. Thus I claim that the L-meaning of *epäillä* consists of both the higher-order schema (cf. Iwata 2005: 115–16) of an unsure assessment or mental processing, and the more specific inclined meaning variants, that is, the negation-inclining and affirmation-inclining readings. These meaning variants are, however, also substantially connected to the different complement constructions. Given the variation, the complement type only informs the actual contextual interpretation of the verb *epäillä*, and additional contextual factors may also participate in the final interpretation. I therefore conclude that the negation- and affirmation-inclining meaning variants are the properties of both the verb *epäillä* and the constructions consisting of the verb and its complement.

Notes

1. In this chapter the term *conceptualizer* systematically refers to the referent of the verb's subject argument, from whose point of view the proposition of the complement is assessed (see Langacker 2008: 445–6).
2. It is assumed that prior to Proto-Finnic (approx. 1000 BC) the form *epä* had functioned as a singular third person form of the negative auxiliary (Hakulinen 1979: sections 23.B, 32).
3. Some sources indicate that the verb *epäillä* is derived directly from the root *epä* (literally: *someone/-thing that not...*), while others suggest that there has been one derivation step between *epä* and *epäillä*, namely the verb *evätä* ('refuse, reject'). (SSA s.v. *epäillä*, SKES s.v. *epäillä*.)
4. The term *construction* refers here to verb-specific constructions (cf. Boas 2005).
5. The deviation from the traditional symbols for negation (¬ or ~) is intentional (cf. e.g. Horn 1989, Allwood et al. 1977). This is because no symmetrical affirmation pair exists for either of the traditional symbols of negation, since there is no such logical operator as an affirmation. However, for convenience, the affirmation-inclination needs its own symbol, too.
6. It is worth mentioning that in many languages the word denoting 'doubt' inherently consists of the idea of *two*fold thought: in Old English *tweogan* (from tweon 'two'; an antecedent of *doubt*); in German *zweifeln* 'doubt' (from *zwei* 'two'); and in Latin *dubitare* (from *duo* 'two'), to name a few. (OnED s.v. *doubt*.)
7. The verb *epäillä* also occurs with NP objects (e.g. *Poliisi epäilee häntä* 'The police suspect him' or *Epäilen hänen rehellisyyttään* 'I doubt her honesty') and as a reporting verb of direct quotes. These patterns are disregarded in the current chapter for the sake of brevity.
8. OF: Corpus of Old Literary Finnish (COLF): http://kaino.kotus.fi/korpus/vks/meta/vks_coll_rdf.xml; EMF: Corpus of Early Modern Finnish (CEMF): http://kotus.fi/korpus/1800/meta/1800_coll_rdf.xml, and a sample from the Newspaper and Journal Collections of the National Library (NL) http://www.nationallibrary.fi/services/digitaalisetkokoelmat/historiallinensanomalehtikirjasto17711890.html; http://www.nationallibrary.fi/services/digitaalisetkokoelmat/aikakauslehdet.html. MF: a sample from the Finnish Text Collection (FTC): http://www.csc.fi/english/research/software/ftc, a sample from the Corpus of Translated Finnish (CTF), Corpus of Finnish Literary Classics (CFLC): http://kaino.kotus.fi/korpus/klassikot/meta/klassikot_coll_rdf.xml, and additional data examples added by the author (AD).
9. The total number of data examples in each data set are: OF 257; EMF 1232; MF 492. The short history of written Finnish limits the amount of data one can obtain. In addition to this quantitative limitation, there is also a genre imbalance: almost all instances of the verb *epäillä* in Old Finnish – and the majority in Early Modern Finnish – occur in religious texts.
10. In fact, it is reasonable not to separate the principles of grammaticalization and other diachronic – for example semantic – changes (Hopper 1991: 19).
11. There is no space here for a thorough treatment of the functions of the Finnish conditional mood. In short, the uses of the conditional in my data comprise the implication of counterfactuality (example 3), suggestion (see example 14 in section 8.4.1), unspecific reference and future orientation.
12. In addition, there are some instances of potential mood complements, especially with embedded question complements in Early Modern Finnish. When occurring

in questions, the Finnish potential mood typically conveys hesitation and doubt-fulness (ISK 2004: section 1598). Thus, the use of potential in the question complements of the verb *epäillä* supports the negation-inclining reading.
13. The application of *analogy* in this context calls for a broad definition of the term: in addition to phonological changes, analogical change may also involve semantic and discourse-pragmatic properties (Givón 1991: 258).
14. The stem of the verb *voida* ('can') is *voi-*; the vowel *i* in the end of the stem is merged with the first *i* of the sign of conditional mood *isi*.
15. King James Version, 1611; http://www.kingjamesbibleonline.org/1611-Bible/.

Bibliography

Allwood, J., L-G. Andersson and Ö. Dahl (1977) *Logic in Linguistics* (Cambridge: Cambridge University Press).
Boas, H. (2005) 'Determining the Productivity of Resultatives. A Reply to Goldberg and Jackendoff'. *Language*, 81: 448–64.
Fortson IV, B. W. (2006) 'An Approach to Semantic Change' in B. D. Joseph and R. D. Janda (eds) *Handbook of Historical Linguistics*, 2nd edn (Oxford: Blackwell), pp. 648–66.
Fried, M. (2013) 'Principles of Constructional Change' in T. Hoffmann and G. Trousdale (eds) *The Oxford Handbook of Construction Grammar* (Oxford: Oxford University Press), pp. 419–37.
Givón, T. (1978) 'Negation in Language: Pragmatics, Function, Ontology' in P. Cole (ed.) *Syntax and Semantics*. Vol. 9: *Pragmatics* (New York: Academic Press), pp. 69–112.
Givón, T. (1991) 'The Evolution of Dependent Clause Morpho-Syntax in Biblical Hebrew' in E. C. Traugott and B. Heine (eds) *Approaches to Grammaticalization*, Vol. I (Amsterdam: John Benjamins), pp. 257–310.
Goldberg, A. (2013) 'Constructionist Approaches' in T. Hoffmann and G. Trousdale (eds) *The Oxford Handbook of Construction Grammar* (Oxford: Oxford University Press), pp. 15–31.
Hakulinen, L. (1979) *Suomen kielen rakenne ja kehitys* [The Structure and Development of Finnish Language] (Helsinki: Otava).
Hansen, M-B. M. (2012) 'A Pragmatic Approach to Historical Semantics' in K. Allan and J. A. Robinson (eds) *Current Methods in Historical Semantics* (Berlin: De Gruyter Mouton), pp. 233–58.
Hilpert, M. (2012) 'Diachronic Collostructional Analysis: How to Use It and How to Deal with Confounding Factors' in K. Allan and J. A. Robinson (eds) *Current Methods in Historical Semantics* (Berlin: De Gruyter Mouton), pp. 133–60.
Heine, B. (2006) 'Grammaticalization' in B. D. Joseph and R. D. Janda (eds) *Handbook of Historical Linguistics*, 2nd edn (Oxford: Blackwell), pp. 575–601.
Hopper, P. (1991) 'On Some Principles of Grammaticization' in E. C. Traugott and B. Heine (eds) *Approaches to Grammaticalization*, Vol. I (Amsterdam: John Benjamins), pp. 17–35.
Horn, L. R. (1989) *A Natural History of Negation* (Chicago: The University of Chicago Press).
Huddleston, R. and G. K. Pullum (2002) *The Cambridge Grammar of English Language* (Cambridge: Cambridge University Press).
ISK 2004 = Hakulinen, A., M. Vilkuna, R. Korhonen, V. Koivisto, T-R. Heinonen and I. Alho (2004) *Iso suomen kielioppi* [A Comprehensive Finnish Grammar] (Helsinki: SKS).

Iwata, S. (2005) 'The Role of Verb Meaning in Locative Alternations' in M. Fried and H. C. Boas (eds) *Grammatical Constructions. Back to the Roots* (Amsterdam: John Benjamins), pp. 101–18.

Iyeiri, Y. (2009) 'The Historical Development of the Verb *doubt* and Its Various Patterns of Complementation' in U. Römer and R. Schultze (eds) *Exploring the Lexis–Grammar Interface* (Amsterdam: John Benjamins), pp. 153–69.

Iyeiri, Y. (2010) *Verbs of Implicit Negation and their Complements in the History of English* (Amsterdam: John Benjamins).

Jespersen, O. (1917) *Negation in English and Other Languages*. Det Kgl. Danske Videnskabernes Selskab. Historisk-filologiske meddelelser I, 5. Copenhagen: Andr. Fred. Høst & søn.

Jespersen, O. (1924) *The Philosophy of Grammar* (London: George Allen & Unwin).

Juvonen, R. (2014) 'Näkökulma kirjoitelman dialogisuuteen. *Kuinka-* ja *miten-* yhdyslauseet ylioppilasaineessa [Kuinka* and *miten* 'how' Clause Constructions in Finnish Matriculation Essays]'. *Virittäjä*, 118: 72–106.

Kauppinen, A. (1998) *Puhekuviot, tilanteen ja rakenteen liitto. Tutkimus kielen omaksumisesta ja suomen konditionaalista* [A Study of Acquisition of Language and Finnish Conditional Mood] (Helsinki: SKS).

KS = *Kielitoimiston sanakirja* [The New Dictionary of Modern Finnish] (2006) Helsinki: Kotus.

Langacker, R. W. (2008) *Cognitive Grammar – a Basic Introduction* (Oxford: Oxford University Press).

Miestamo, M. (2007) 'Negation – an Overview of Typological Research'. *Language and Linguistic Compass*, 1/5 (2007): 552–70.

OnED = Online Etymology Dictionary. http://www.etymonline.com/

Prince, E. F. (1981) 'Towards a Taxonomy of Given–New Information' in P. Cole (ed.) *Radical Pragmatics* (New York: Academic Press), pp. 223–55.

Rappaport Hovav, M. and B. Levin (1998) 'Building Verb Meanings' in M. Butt and W. Geuder (eds) *The Projection of Arguments. Lexical and Compositional Factors.* (Stanford: CLSI), pp. 97–134.

SAOB = Svenska Akademiens Ordbok. g3.spraakdata.gu.se/saob/

Shore, S. (2008) 'Lauseiden tekstuaalisesta jäsennyksestä [On the Textual Organization of Clauses]'. *Virittäjä* 112(1): 24–65.

SKES = *Suomen kielen etymologinen sanakirja* [The Etymological Dictionary of Finnish] (1981) (Helsinki: Suomalais-ugrilainen seura [Finno-Ugrian Society]).

SSA = *Suomen sanojen alkuperä: etymologinen sanakirja 1: A–K* [The Origin of Finnish Words: Etymological Dictionary] (1992) (Helsinki: SKS).

Suzuki, S. (2000) 'De Dicto Complementation in Japanese' in K. Horie (eds) *Complementation* (Amsterdam: John Benjamins), pp. 33–57.

Traugott, E. C. and G. Trousdale (2010) 'Gradience, Gradualness and Grammaticalization. How Do They Intersect?' in E. C. Traugott and G. Trousdale (eds) *Gradience, Gradualness and Grammaticalization* (Amsterdam: John Benjamins), pp. 19–44.

Verhagen, A. (2005) *Constructions of Intersubjectivity. Discourse, Syntax, and Cognition* (Oxford: Oxford University Press).

Part III
Boundaries

9
Multiple Sources in Language Change: the Role of Free Adjuncts and Absolutes in the Formation of English ACC-*ing* Gerundives[1]

Teresa Fanego
University of Santiago de Compostela

9.1 Introduction

This chapter examines the rise of ACC-*ing* gerundives (ACC-*ing* for short), as in (1–2), in the light of recent proposals (see Van de Velde et al. 2013, and references therein) on the possible multiplicity of source constructions in language change, with change understood as often involving historically distinct 'lineages' merging into a new lineage.

> (1) COPC 1689 Stevens, *Journal*, 1Q17 0004/029-P0: **The man** *being an Irishman and a Catholic* made his ill carriage towards us appear the more strange, but his religion and country he thought would bear him out.[2]
> (2) COLMOBAENG 1861 Dickens, *Great Expectations*, 75: I not only prevented **him** *getting off the marshes*, but I dragged him here.

Like all other gerundives, ACC-*ing* gerundives have a characteristically nominal distribution, and hence can function as subject (1), object (2), predicative or prepositional complement. However, they differ from other subtypes of gerundives both in their chronology (their emergence in English being comparatively late) and their formal characteristics, in that they have a subject argument either in the 'common' case, if it is a full noun phrase (*the man* in (1)) or in the accusative case, if it is a personal pronoun (*him* in (2)); hence they contrast both with 'bare' gerundives (3), which lack an explicit subject, and with POSS-*ing* gerundives (4), whose subject argument is marked for the genitive:

> (3) HC 1550–52 *Diary of Edward VI*, 355: The duches, Crane and his wife [...] were sent to the Towr *for devising thies treasons*; Jaymes Wingfeld also, *for casting out of billes sediciouse*.

(4) HC 1599–1601 Hoby, *Diary,* 78: then I Came hom to dinner, neccltinge
my Costomarie manner of praier *by reason of my Lord Ewrie and my
lades being there*:

In this chapter, I will argue that ACC-*ing* gerundives, unlike other gerundives, do not emerge from former nominal gerunds through a gradual
process of accretion of verbal characteristics, but have developed, rather,
as an 'intersection' (see Trousdale 2013: 493) of a number of pre-existing
constructions, among them absolute participles.

The discussion is structured as follows. Section 9.2 gives an overview of the
corpus material used in this study. Sections 9.3 and 9.4 offer, respectively,
an outline of the development of English gerundives since Old English
times, and a brief discussion of some related structures. Section 9.5 focuses
specifically on the gerundive subtype (the ACC-*ing* gerundive), which is the
main concern of this chapter, discussing its origins and probable course of
development in light of the evidence drawn from the corpora described in
section 9.2. Section 9.6 considers this proposed course of development with
reference to the analytical framework in Van de Velde et al. (2013).

9.2   The corpus

My earlier research (Fanego 1998: 100–4, 2004: 41–5) on ACC-*ing* gerundives
relied primarily on a 392,110-word sample from the Early Modern English
section of the Helsinki Corpus. For the present analysis this sample has been
expanded to 945,413 words through the incorporation of material from other
corpora and periods, as indicated in Table 9.1. In all cases, the variety examined
is British English and the time span 1500–1750, since it is clear from my prior
findings that this is the crucial period for the formation of the construction.

With respect to the composition of the corpora used, the inventory of genres
represented does not remain constant across the three subperiods examined,
but it is unlikely that this has greatly influenced the findings: the specific
type of nominalization under analysis here is associated with expository and
academic writings in their various forms, and with narrative texts, whether
imaginative (fiction) or non-imaginative (diaries, letters, journals, travelogue).
Statutory writings (statutes) and texts written to be spoken (comedies) are thus
the only text categories not in principle welcoming of the ACC-*ing* construction, and that is why they have not been included in my corpora for subperiod III (1700–49). For widely accepted classifications of genres and forms of
discourse, see especially Werlich (1976: 39–41) and Biber (1988).

9.3   Origins and early history of the English verbal gerund

The precursor to the English verbal gerund was an abstract noun of action
formed through the addition of the suffixes -*ung* or -*ing* to a verb stem, as in
sceawung 'observation' (< *sceawian* 'observe') and *wending* 'turning' (< *wendan*

Table 9.1   Range of corpora and subperiods examined

Subperiod I: 1500–1640	Subperiod II: 1640–1700	Subperiod III: 1700–1749
– A Representative Corpus of Historical English Registers (ARCHER, version 3.2): 29,697 words from 1600 to 1640; genre: early prose[1]	– A Representative Corpus of Historical English Registers (ARCHER, version 3.2): 115,797 words from 1650 to 1699; 5 genres (diaries, fiction, journals, letters, sermons)	– A Representative Corpus of Historical English Registers (ARCHER, version 3.2): 118,809 words from 1700 to 1749; 5 genres (diaries, fiction, journals, letters, sermons)
– Helsinki Corpus of English Texts (HC): 261,630 words from subperiods EModE1 (1500–1570) and EModE2 (1570–1640); 11 genres (comedies, diaries, fiction, handbooks, letters (private), philosophy, science, sermons, statutes, travelogue, trials)	– Helsinki Corpus of English Texts (HC): 130,480 words from subperiod EModE3; 11 genres (comedies, diaries, fiction, handbooks, letters (private), philosophy, science, sermons, statutes, travelogue, trials) – Century of Prose Corpus (COPC): 89,000 words from decades 1680 to 1700[2]	– Corpus of Late Modern British and American English Prose (COLMOBAENG): 200,000 words from 1700 to 1726; genres: fiction and non-fiction[3]
Total: 291,327 words	**Total: 335,277 words**	**Total: 318,809 words**

Notes:
1. ARCHER is an ongoing project and continues to expand its diachronic coverage of genres. For the first half of the seventeenth century it still does not contain samples of diaries, fiction, journals, letters or sermons (the genres used in the two later subperiods of my study). ARCHER's early prose, however, proved very useful for my purposes, in that it includes both fiction and non-fiction texts and is thus largely comparable to the rest of the corpora examined.
2. COPC is organized in terms of decades and covers the span 1680–1780. It is intended to constitute 'an inventory of the daily language of the literate members of English society' in the eighteenth century (Milic 1995: 329) and comprises samples of the following ten genres: biography, periodicals, education, essays, fiction, history, letters and memoirs, polemics, science, travel.
3. Like COPC, COLMOBAENG is biased towards texts written by literate members of English and American society in the eighteenth and nineteenth centuries. The 200,000-word sample used for the present study contains 124,000 words of fictional prose and 76,000 words of non-fiction representing the same genres that make up COPC. For further details, see Fanegò (2012).

'turn'); see Kisbye (1971–72: 51–4) and Kastovsky (1985: 241–3) for details. These nouns behaved like any other noun in all relevant respects, and could therefore take nominal dependents of various kinds. The following Middle English examples illustrate their use with determiners (*the, his*) and with *of*-phrases serving as their notional objects:

(5) 1472–88 *Cely Letters*, 94/5 [Tajima 1985: 68]:
   at <u>the</u> makyng <u>of thys lettyr</u>
   'when writing this letter'

(6) *c.*1385 Chaucer, *Troilus and Criseyde*, V 1833 [Tajima 1985: 70]:
    And thus began *his* loving *of Criseyde*
(7) ?a1300 *Kyng Alisaunder*, 558 [Tajima 1985: 62]
    Wiþouten doyng of any harme
    'without doing any harm'

In Early Middle English, the suffix -*ung* rapidly died out and -*ing* became the regular form (*OED* s.v. -ing.1, Kisbye 1971–72: 54). Also over the course of Middle English, -*ing* nominals began to acquire verbal properties. According to Tajima's analysis (1985, 1996), which is based on a very large sample of Middle English writings covering the span 1100–1500, the verbalization of the gerund proceeded as follows. Around 1300 the first instances with direct objects appeared (8), and from the end of the Middle English period or in Early Modern English other verbal features were found, such as the ability to express distinctions of voice (1417 'without *being stolen*'; cf. Tajima 1985: 113–16) and tense/aspect (1580–81 'after *having failed*'; cf. Tajima 1985: 111–13, Fanego 1996: 127–32). Subject arguments in non-genitive form (9) occurred sporadically from Late Middle English onwards,[3] but remained very rare for a long time afterwards, as will be shown later in this chapter.

(8) *c.*1300 (MS a1400) *English Metrical Homilies*, 112/2–4 [Tajima 1985: 76]:
    Sain Jon was [...] bisi *In ordaining of priestes, and clerkes*, And *in casting kirc werkes*
    'Saint John was [...] busy ordaining priests and clerics, and in planning church works'
(9) *c.*1400 *Laud Troy Book*, 6317–18 [Tajima 1996: 574]:
    he was war *of hem comyng* and of here malice
    'he was informed of them coming and of their wickedness'

Two other aspects of the grammar and development of the gerund are relevant to the present research. One is that throughout its history the English gerund, whether nominal or verbal, appears to have been used preferably after prepositions. More work is still needed regarding the exact frequency of prepositional gerunds in Old English, but the association of the gerund with prepositional use since at least Middle English times seems clear in light of evidence adduced by Houston (1989), Expósito (1996) and De Smet (2008). Houston (1989: 176) examined 1464 -*ing* forms dating from the tenth to the seventeenth centuries and found that 'across time, there is a fairly constant trend for them to occur as the objects of prepositions'. Likewise, Expósito's research (1996: 173–80), which provides data only on nominal or partly nominal gerunds in Chancery English *c.*1400–50, found that 81.50 per cent of the 135 gerundial structures occurring in her 48,000-word corpus were found after a preposition, 12.60 per cent were objects and a further 5.90 per cent subjects. These figures are in agreement with my own findings for the Early Modern period: in a sample of 317,621 words in the Early Modern English section of the Helsinki Corpus of English Texts, I recorded 1286 gerunds (= 79.50 per cent) functioning as prepositional complements, compared to 332 (= 20.50 per cent) in other clause functions (Fanego 1996: 122–3).

Secondly, as made clear by Donner (1986), Koma (1980), Houston (1989: 181) and De Smet (2008: 61–2), the gerund's acquisition of direct objects started with those gerunds that were dependent on a preposition, as in (8) above. In other syntactic positions the use of direct objects and other verbal features was very slow to develop, as I have shown in previous research (1996, 1998, 2004).

With all this in mind, let us now briefly consider the much debated question of the interconnections between gerunds and various classes of participial constructions.

9.4 Gerunds and related constructions

The possible role of present participles in the first appearance of verbal gerunds is hard to verify, but has been discussed in the literature at various times. In Old English the ending of the present participle (*-ende*) was distinct from the suffix *-ing/-ung* of the abstract deverbal noun. However, during the Middle English period the two forms coalesced as *-ing* (see Mustanoja 1960: 547–8, Lass 1992: 145–6), first in the south of England and subsequently in other areas. This coalescence, according to Curme (1931: 484), Mustanoja (1960: 570) and Kisbye (1971–72: 55), among others, may have promoted the transfer of verbal properties from the present participle to the verbal noun (see Jack 1988: 24–7 for a useful summary of this view).

However, as Jack aptly notes (1988: 25–7), the coalescence of the verbal noun with the present participle was not a feature of all dialects of Middle English. In the north of England the two endings remained distinct, with *-and(e)* being used for the participle and *-ing* for the verbal noun. As it happens, some of the earliest instances of verbal gerunds, such as (8) quoted above, are found in texts of Northern provenance, and from this Jack argues that 'the development of the [verbal] gerund could take place quite independently of any merger between the verbal noun and the present participle' (ibid.: 27).

Shortly after the publication of Jack's influential paper, Houston (1989) again discussed the extent of the relationship between participles and (verbal) gerunds. More specifically, she argued that the functional similarity between what she terms 'appositive' participles and nominal gerunds preceded by a preposition led to the analogical transference of verbal properties from the former to the latter. Appositive participles ('free adjuncts', in the terminology employed later in this chapter; see section 9.5.2) do not have an overt subject NP and by default are interpreted as sharing the subject of the matrix clause:

(10) Old English, *ÆCHom*, ii.578.28 [Mitchell 1985: section 1434]:
   and þæt folc [...] ham gewende, ðancigende þam Ælmihtigan ealra his goda
   'and the people went home, thanking the Almighty for his goodness'

From a semantic point of view, the relation holding between appositive participles and their matrix clause is often an adverbial one, and in this, as noted by Houston (1989), they resemble prepositional gerunds, which are also very often employed to provide supportive commentary about the time, manner, cause, means or goal of foregrounded events, as in *On hearing a cry, she dashed into the garden* (see also (5) above). Houston therefore claimed that the similar discourse function of appositive participles and prepositional gerunds 'may have contributed to users' association of the two forms and to the consequent verbal qualities of the modern verbal gerund' (ibid.: 173).

The chief justification for Houston's position lies in the plausibility of such a development, and also in the fact that, as noted in section 9.3, prepositional gerunds were indeed the first to acquire direct objects. It must be acknowledged, however, that the fact that prepositional gerunds took the lead here might also be explained through a number of different factors which for reasons of space cannot be described here but which are discussed in detail in Fanego (2004: sections 2.2.4–5). At any rate, beyond the largely unsolvable issue of the role played by participles in the initial stages of the verbalization of the gerund, it becomes evident from Middle English onwards that the boundaries between certain uses of the gerund and the present participle were not always clear-cut, as briefly noted in Fanego (1996: 102–6) in relation to structures such as (11–13):

(11) HC 1608 Armin, *A Nest of Ninnies*, 14: Jack, my foole, *is* in my moate, up to the arme-pits, *eating of the pie*.
(12) 1605 Shakespeare, *King Lear*, II.i.39: Here *stood* he in the dark, his sharp sword out, *mumbling of wicked charms*, [Visser 1963–73: section 1121]
(13) HC 1553–59 Machyn, *Diary* 101: then *cam* the men rydyng, *carehyng of torchys* a lx bornyng, at bowt the corsse all the way;

(11) constitutes a variant of the progressive (BE + -*ing* participle) in which the object of the verb surfaces as an *of*-phrase, thus resembling the object of a nominal gerund. The construction has been on record since the late fourteenth century and becomes 'substandard about the beginning of the nineteenth' (Visser 1963–73: section 1869; see also Jespersen 1909–49: IV, section 12.3(4); Elsness 1994: 14–15); for some time, it coexisted with the

progressive proper (*he was eating the pie*). As regards (12–13), the use of participles with verbs of rest (*stand*) and movement (*come*) goes back to Old English times; witness sequences such as *starigende stodon* 'stood looking fixedly', *com fleogende* 'came flying'. However, a gerundial variant of such structures, with *of* preceding the object of the *-ing* form, 'first appears in the fourteenth century, remains rare until the end of the fifteenth century, but then becomes remarkably frequent in the sixteenth century and the first decades of the seventeenth century [...] nowadays it is only dialectal or substandard' (Visser 1963–73: section 1121).

Finally, the tendency for gerunds and participles to merge can also be observed in the case of the construction which is the concern of this chapter, namely, ACC-*ing* gerundives. In this case, as will be argued in section 9.5.2, the coalescence is with the subtype of absolute participle illustrated in (14); this precedes its superordinate clause and 'controls' its subject, to the extent that this is deleted under identity with the subject of the absolute (*Vaughan's Testimonie*):[4]

(14) HC 1554 *The Trial of Sir Nicholas Throckmorton*, PI, 69.C1: and so **Vaughan's Testimonie** *being credited*, ø may be the material Cause of my Condemnation, as the Jury may be induced by his Depositions to speak their Verdict,

9.5 Sources of the ACC-*ing* gerundive

As already noted (section 9.3), the use as subjects of the gerund of common case NPs (instead of PossPs) and objective case pronouns (instead of possessive determiners), was only in its inception in Early Modern English: in a 392,110-word sample from the Early Modern English section of the Helsinki Corpus I recorded only 11 instances of ACC-*ing*. In the same sample, by contrast, gerunds with an initial possessive totalled 261 (see Fanego 1998: 90–1). With respect to the way or ways in which the acquisition of that important verbal feature by the English gerund may have taken place, I have suggested elsewhere (Fanego 1998: 100–3, 2004: 41–5) that one likely source was that of gerundial constructions in which the subject of the gerund lacked an overt genitive inflection for one reason or other. Essentially, such uninflected NPs belonged to one of the following subtypes:

1. Nouns ending in the fricatives /s, z/ (e.g. *Moses, mistress, Highness*), with which the genitive form was often avoided in Early Modern English on phonotactic grounds, as Visser (1963–73: section 1101), Altenberg (1982: 45–8) and others have noted.

(15) ARCHER 1666 Allin, *The Journals of Sir Thomas Allin* (alli_j2b): I went aboard, where I received the news of **his Highness** *going to the Royal James to the westward*.

2. The majority of plural nouns. The use of the apostrophe as a case marker after the plural -(*e*)*s* morpheme did not develop in written English until the late eighteenth century (Altenberg 1982: 53), so that in gerundial structures such as (16–17) it was formerly impossible to ascertain whether the subject of the -*ing* form was intended as a possessive phrase in the 'genitive' plural or as a noun phrase in the common case:

(16) HC 1689–90 Evelyn, *Diary*, 900: [...] people began to talke *of the **Bishops** being cast out of the House*:[5]

(17) ARCHER 1677 Morrice, *The Entring Book of Roger Morrice* (morr_y2b): January the 14th (77). It's said the Highlanders are to Randesvouz at Sterling the 24th of this Instant, and soe to march into the west, where they say most dessenters live, There is a Proclamation prohibiting ***any subjects, Noblemen or others*** *coming out of that Kingdome (Tradesmen Excepted) upon any account whatsoever,*

3. The pronoun *her*, with which there is no formal distinction between the possessive and the accusative form, so that in (18), *her* could be interpreted either way.

(18) HC 1619 Deloney, *Jack of Newbury*, 81: Moreouer, ***her** prattling to Mistresse Winchcombes folks of their mistresse,* made her on the other side to fall out with her,

4. Various sorts of complex NPs with which a genitive form would prove awkward or simply impossible (for further discussion, see Visser 1963–73: section 1101); this accounts for the absence of the clitic -*'s* in an example like (19):

(19) HC 1665 Hooke, *Micrographia*, 13.5, 211: it [= a louse] is troubled at nothing so much as at a man that scratches his head [...] that makes it oftentime sculk into some meaner and lower place, and run behind a mans back, though it go very much against the hair; ***which ill conditions of it*** *having made it better known then trusted,* would exempt me from making any further description of it, did not my faithful [...] Microscope bring me other information of it.

It is evident that the existence of these various classes of uninflected NPs must have contributed greatly to strengthening the feeling that a common case NP might be used as the subject of the gerund, as already pointed out by Jespersen (1909–49: V section 9.4). Yet although they were no doubt partial sources of the ACC-*ing* construction, they cannot have been its only source, for they cannot explain some of its distinctive features during the early stages of its development, as will be discussed in what follows.

Table 9.2, which is based on a manual search of all the -*ing* forms occurring in the corpora examined, gives an overview of ACC-*ing* in terms of two variables, namely: (a) subperiod; (b) syntactic function in the superordinate structure. Table 9.3, in turn, provides information on the noun phrases and pronouns occurring as subject arguments of the -*ing* forms. Illustrative examples of the various syntactic functions distinguished in the tables are (20) = object function, (21–22) = prepositional complement, and (1) above = subject function.

(20) COLMOBAENG 1705 Manley, *The Secret History of Queen Zarah and the Zarazians*, 102: when Favourites Flourish, the State Languishes, for Persons of their Characters being Rivals to one another, generally go cunningly to work, and so interrupt[6] *all other Business going forward but their own.*

(21) HC 1554 *The Trial of Sir Nicholas Throckmorton*, P.I, 69.C1: touchyng *the Earl of Deuon parting hence, and my going with him*, and also concerning the matter of the Earle of Pembroke, I do aduow and say that Vaughan hath said untruely.

(22) ARCHER 1664 Lowe, *The Diary of Roger Lowe* (1664lowe_y2b): 8th. — This night I was in a troubled condition, for Sarah Hasleden spoke in a backe-biting way of me, and she would tell her brother of me, but all was in a causeles matter, *for me spendinge 2d.*

At its most obvious, Table 9.2 confirms what was already clear from my earlier research on the gerund, namely that the ACC-*ing* pattern becomes noticeable only from the second half of the seventeenth century. Secondly,

Table 9.2 ACC-*ing* gerundives, per subperiod and syntactic function

1500–1640 (291,327 words)	1640–1700 (335,277 words)	1700–1749 (318,809 words)
As subject: 1 ex. (date: 1615) + 1 ambiguous ex. (date: 1619; the gerund's subject is the possessive *her*)	As subject: 10 ex. + 1 ambiguous ex. (the gerund's subject is plural)	As subject: 19 ex. + 1 ambiguous ex. (the gerund's subject is the possessive *her*)
As object: 1 ambiguous ex. (date: 1554; the gerund's subject is plural)	As object: 1 ambiguous ex. (the gerund's subject is plural)	As object: 2 ex.
As prepositional complement: 2 ex. (dates: 1554)	As prepositional complement: 11 ex. + 6 ambiguous ex. (the gerund's subject is plural)	As prepositional complement: 17 ex. + 1 ambiguous ex. (the gerund's subject is the possessive *her*)
TOTAL: 3 ex. + 2 ambiguous ex.	TOTAL: 21 ex. + 8 ambiguous ex.	TOTAL: 38 ex. + 2 ambiguous ex.

Table 9.3   NPs and pronouns functioning as subject arguments of ACC-*ing* gerundives

1500–1640 (291,327 words)	1640–1700 (335,277 words)	1700–1749 (318,809 words)
With ACC-*ing* as subject: Pronouns: *her* NPs: *grass*	With ACC-*ing* as subject: Pronouns (2): *it, there* NPs (9): *these small pellets; which ill conditions of it; so much Company; Ostorius; the man; his sickness; prince Arthur, or his chief patron Sir Philip Sidney, whom he intended to make happy by the marriage of his Gloriana; Themira; God*	With ACC-*ing* as subject: Pronouns (5): *it, her, she, which* 'whose' (2 ex.) NPs (15): *the number; the weather; the frost; the force of the heart and pectoral muscles; my father... and all his family; Zarah; his brother; these morals; the wind; the laws of Ginksy; the dram; Oliver; the pork; this trifle; the ladies*
With ACC-*ing* as object: NPs: *the Spaniards* With ACC-*ing* as prepositional complement: NPs (2): *the attorney; the Earl of Devon*	With ACC-*ing* as object: NPs (1): *any subjects, noblemen or others;* With ACC-*ing* as prepositional complement: Pronouns (2): *anybody; me* NPs (15): *the seamen; the French fleet; your ship; such a boundless space; any solid matter; the Prince of Orange; his Highness; Mr Baxter; the water; the bishops; the evil spirits; four soldiers; the Moscovites; C. Elliott and his ships; Socrates, Anaxagoras, and others*	With ACC-*ing* as object: NPs (2): *the Queen; all other business* With ACC-*ing* as prepositional complement: Pronouns (2): *her; it* NPs (16): *the play; some powers at Court; Mulgarvius; the noise; the electors; the river of that name; a plot; the Irish; the English army; the Bavarians and French; the Spaniard ship; his brother; Mr. Brown's wife's sister; the Princess of Wales; a custom; the Spaniards*

the data also confirm the important contribution to the rise and expansion of the ACC-*ing* pattern of plurals and other kinds of phrases which are ambiguous between a reading as common case phrases or as genitive phrases (see (16)–(18) above).[7] The most noteworthy aspect, however, is the high proportion of ACC-*ing* gerundives functioning as clausal subjects, which is exceptional if one bears in mind that, as noted in section 9.3, there is a constant trend over time for all subtypes of gerunds to occur chiefly as prepositional complements (e.g. *by John's looking at me*), to the extent that in Fanego (1996: 116, 122), in a sample of 317,621 words from the Early Modern English section of the Helsinki Corpus, I found only 8.7 per cent (= 141 tokens) of gerunds used as subjects, out of a total of 1618. The skewed distribution of ACC-*ing* gerundives, at least in the early stages of their development, is also confirmed by data from Dryden's usage: Söderlind (1958: sections 514, 516), in his detailed analysis of Dryden's extensive collection of prose writings, found only 12 instances of ACC-*ing* gerundives, seven of which function as sentence subjects, as against only five used as prepositional complements.[8]

In light of this finding, the question emerges as to what exactly were the sources behind the rise of ACC-*ing*. We know that for all other subtypes of verbal gerunds, the sources were the corresponding nominal subtypes, which underwent a prolonged process of accretion of verbal features whose effects can best be seen by comparing the pairs of gerunds in (23)–(25):

(23a) HC 1550–52 *Diary of Edward VI*, 367: The lord admiral toke his leave to goe into Fraunce, *for christening of the French kinges soone.* [bare nominal gerund: *of*-phrase as notional object]

(23b) HC 1624 *Oxinden Letters*, 14: I thanke you for your Care and paines *abowt enquireing and provideing Sheepe for mee,* [bare verbal gerund: NP object]

(24a) HC 1554 *The Trial of Sir Nicholas Throckmorton*, P.I, 66.C1: Moreouer, to accompte *the taking of the Tower* is uery dangerous by the Law. [definite nominal gerund: determiner combined with *of*-phrase as notional object]

(24b) HC 1629 *Barrington Family Letters*, 92: [...] that all the distempers of our bodys, which must need be many while we live here, may be a means *of the cureing the great distempers of our soles,* [definite hybrid gerund: determiner combined with NP object][9]

(25a) HC 1567 Harman, *A Caveat or Warening for Commen Cursetors*, 70: As *your pacient bearinge of troubles*, your honest behauiour among vs your neyghbours [...] doth moue vs to lament your case, [nominal POSS-*ing* gerund: possessive determiner combined with *of*-phrase as notional object]

(25b) HC 1666–67 Pepys, *Diary*, VIII.319: and then heard from Sir R. Ford the good account which the boys had given *of their understanding the nature and consequence of an oath,* [hybrid POSS-*ing* gerund: possessive determiner combined with NP object]

In the case of the ACC-*ing* pattern, the greatest affinity is evidently with the POSS-*ing* subtype, since both share the feature of having an explicit subject argument (respectively, the common case NP and the possessive determiner). That POSS-*ing* indeed contributed to the formation of ACC-*ing* has already been mentioned; however, POSS-*ing* gerundives, like all other gerundives, were uncommon as subjects – there are only 18 instances used with this function in my data from subperiod I (1500–1640). But, more importantly, they differed markedly from the ACC-*ing* type in terms of their internal syntax. In other words, the majority of my examples of POSS-*ing* as sentence subjects in that first subperiod are purely nominal structures lacking an explicit patient argument or any other kind of post-head dependent (an adverbial, a prepositional phrase, etc.), and hence not providing a good model for the development of a typically clausal structure such as ACC-*ing*; witness the following examples, and see also (25a) above:

(26) HC 1534 More, *Letters*, 545: For Christen charitie and naturall loue and *your verie doughterly dealing (funiculo triplici, (vt ait scriptura) difficile rumpitur)* both binde me and straine me therto.

(27) HC 1608 Armin, *A Nest of Ninnies*, 10: he [the knight] loued the foole aboue all, and that the household knew, else Jack had paid for it, for *the common peoples dauncing* was spoiled

There are only a couple of examples (28)–(29) exhibiting a greater degree of internal complexity and thus resembling the more versatile and extended gerund structures that become common from subperiod II (1640–1700), coinciding with the widespread verbalization of -*ing* nominals. For, as I have shown in earlier research (Fanego 1996: 119–21), as gerunds moved away from noun phrases over the course of the Early Modern English period, a noticeable increase took place in the frequency of post-head dependents inside gerund phrases, which thus came to mirror VP structure much more closely. This trend, however, is chiefly observable from subperiod II onwards.[10] All things considered, then, it seems worthwhile to explore whether a source other than POSS-*ing* gerundives can be found to help us account satisfactorily for this hitherto unexplained aspect of the grammar of the ACC-*ing* pattern, namely, its high incidence as clausal subject.

(28) HC 1554 *The Trial of Sir Nicholas Throckmorton*, PI, 75.C2: *Your adhering to the Queenes Enimies within the Realme* is euidently proued:

(29) ARCHER 1617 Speght, *A Mouzell for Melastomus* (speg_p1b): [...] to make her husband partaker of that happinesse, which she thought by their eating they should both haue enioyed. *This her giuing Adam of that sawce*, wherewith Sathan had serued her, [...] was that, which made her sinne to exceede his:

9.5.1 Free adjuncts and absolute participles in Early and Late Modern English

Following the terminology in Kortmann (1991: 1–2), I will refer to the -*ing* clauses in (30)–(32) as, respectively, free adjuncts (30) and absolutes (31)–(32). Both are tenseless structures that function as adjuncts with respect to the matrix clause or 'anchor', being set apart from this by an intonational break which in present-day English is 'more often than not [...] indicated by commas in writing' (Kortmann 1991: 1). Comma punctuation, however, is often absent in earlier instances of both constructions, as Early Modern English punctuation differed from that of present-day English in many respects (Salmon 1999, Río-Rey 2002: 309–10, 321).

(30) HC 1608 Armin, *A Nest of Ninnies*, 48: This lusty jester, *ø forgetting himself*, in fury draws his dagger, and begins to protest.

(31) HC 1603 *The Trial of Sir Walter Raleigh*, I, 210.C1: *The Lord Cobham being requir'd to subscribe to an Examination*, there was shewed a Note under Sir Walter Raleigh's hand; the which when he had perus'd, he paus'd, and after brake forth into these Speeches:

(32) HC *c.*1535–43 Leland, *Itinerary*, Sample 2, PI, 140: Insomuch that *leade beyng made ther at hand* many houses yn the toune have pipes of leade to convey water from place to place.

In contemporary usage, there are essentially two defining differences between these two participial types. First, the presence of an overt subject NP in absolutes (*the Lord Cobham* and *leade* in the case of (31)–(32) respectively; henceforth: Sub$_A$) versus its absence in free adjuncts. Secondly, the fact that in canonical instances the covert subject of free adjuncts is 'controlled' by the subject of the matrix clause (*this lusty jester* in (30); henceforth: Sub$_M$), whereas in absolutes their explicit subject and the subject of the matrix clause are not coreferential. Thus, as Kortmann (1991: 103) notes, the default usage today is that 'given referential subject identity, free adjuncts are to be employed, whereas absolutes are appropriate whenever non-coreference holds between the subject of the [participial] construction and the matrix subject'.

There is evidence, however, that this neat distinction between free adjuncts and absolutes in terms of referential subject identity or lack of it did not apply in earlier stages of the language, so that the two constructions did not specialize in the fulfilment of complementary tasks until well into the Late Modern English period. Jespersen (1909–49: V section 6.2.2), Söderlind (1958: section 502), Visser (1963–73: section 1085) and, more recently, Río-Rey (2002: 318–21) adduce many examples of absolutes showing full coreference between the subject of the absolute and the matrix subject; (33) is an example from Río-Rey (2002: 319):[11]

(33) HC 1526 *A Hundred Mery Talys*, Sample 3, 39–40: **The wyfe of the house** *perceyuyng that he toke all suche fragmentys & vytayle with hym that was last & put it in hys male/* she brought vp that podege that was last in the pot

Absolutes of this kind are also very frequent in my material, where four subtypes exhibiting full coreference can be distinguished; all of them are obsolete in present-day English:[12]

1. Sub_A is a full NP; Sub_M is a coreferential personal pronoun. (33) above is an example; (34) is another:

> (34) ARCHER 1661 Flatman, *Don Juan Lamberto* (1661flat_f2b): Now it fell out that **Sir Baxtero** *having heard how that Sir Ludlow was departed out of Brittain,* **he** made great lamentation and moaning;

2. Sub_A and Sub_M are two coreferential pronouns identical in form:[13]

> (35) ARCHER 1673 Kirkman, *The Counterfeit Lady Unveiled* (1673kirk_f2b): [...] and **they** *designing to live in all freedom as man and wife,* **they** therefore left that lodging and went to another at a convenient distance.
>
> (36) ARCHER 1704 Dean, *The Journall of the Campaigne for the Yeare of Our Lord God - 1704* (1704dean_j3b): But no sooner did our Forlorne Hope appear but the enemy did throw in their volleys of canon balls and small shott among them and made a brave defence and a bold resistance against us as brave loyall hearted gentlemen souldiers ought to for there prince and country, and **they** *being strongly intrenched* **they** killed and mortyfyed abundance of our men both officers and souldiers.

3. Subject identity between Sub_A and Sub_M could go as far as Sub_M deletion, thus leading to a situation in which, as Kortmann notes (1991: 101), the subject of the absolute controls the matrix subject, rather than the other way round. In such cases, the line between absolutes and free adjuncts becomes blurred to an even greater extent than in the two previous subtypes:

> (37) HC 1554 *The Trial of Sir Nicholas Throckmorton,* P.I, 69.C1: [...] and so **Vaughan's Testimonie** *being credited,* ø may be the material Cause of my Condemnation, as the Jury may be induced by his Depositions to speak their Verdict, and so finally therevpon the Judge to giue Sentence.
>
> (38) ARCHER 1628 *The True History of the Tragicke Loves of HIPOLITO and ISABELLA* (1628anon_p1b): **The good and commendable proiect of this marriage** *being agreed on by these Parents,* and whereon they built the principall happinesse of their house and family, ø brought them much more ruine then it had promised them contentment; being the ordinary pleasure of fortune to build vpon the foundation of our designes, euents most contrary to our hopes.

(39) ARCHER 1628 *The True History of the Tragicke Loves of HIPOLITO and ISABELLA* (1628anon_p1b): A weake perswasion will carry a diuided and doubtfull minde, to that part whither it selfe inclines; so *these letters finding her leaning more to loue then dutie,* ø forced her through all the doubts that could oppose themselues, and after some discourse with her selfe, of such differing accidents in those occurrences as her able vnderstanding set before her; reason at length gaue place to loue, and respect to passion;

4. A subclass of the preceding subtype, also mentioned by Jespersen (1909–49: III section 10.1.4), Söderlind (1958: section 502), Visser (1963–73: section 1086) and Río-Rey (2002: 319), involves relative clauses, thus giving rise to a construction which, as Söderlind notes, 'is particularly bold':[14]

(40) HC 1526 *A Hundred Mery Talys*, Sample 2, 135: the frere and his felaw began Placebo and Dirige and so forth sayd the seruyse full deuowtly *which the wyues so heryng* / ø coude not refrayne them selfe from lawghynge and wente in to a lytyll parler to lawgh more at theyr plesure.

(41) HC 1619 Deloney, *Jack of Newbury*, 86–7: Whereupon hee willed him for two yeres space to take his diet and his Ladies at his house: *which the Knight accepting* ø rode straight with his wife to *Newbery*.

(42) ARCHER 1692 Congreve, *Incognita: or, Love and Duty Reconcil'd* (1692cong_f2b): [...] and Hippolito having made a Visit to his Governour, dispatch'd a Messenger with the Letter and Directions to Leonora. At the Signal agreed upon the Casement was opened and a String let down, *to which the Bearer having fastned the Letter,* ø saw it drawn up, and returned. It were a vain attempt to describe Leonora's Surprize, when she read the Superscription.

In Río-Rey's study (2002: 318–21), which is based on seven genres[15] and a 252,110-word sample from the Early Modern English section of the Helsinki Corpus, absolutes with full coreference represent about 30 per cent (101 tokens) of the 336 absolutes recorded in her material. The frequencies for subtypes 1 (24 tokens), 3 (65 tokens) and 4 (12 tokens) above[16] are carefully charted on the chronological dimension, and she shows that full coreference becomes particularly common during the second (1570–1640) of the three subperiods of Early Modern English distinguished in the Helsinki Corpus. This seems to be largely in keeping with the evidence from my own material: though I have not quantified all the absolutes precisely, as this would be an enormous task, examples showing full coreference are common in the seventeenth century and continue to be used into the eighteenth.

The relevance to the present research of Río-Rey's findings lies in the fact that, as will be argued in the next section, the subtypes with Sub_M deletion seem to have provided a model for the use of ACC-*ing* as sentence subject, a syntactic function whose great frequency with this type of gerundive needs to be adequately explained.

9.5.2　The role of absolutes in the historical development of ACC-*ing*

Following Naro (1981), work on morphosyntactic change has often pointed out that innovations are first used in contexts 'where surface differentiation between the old and new systems is zero (or nearly so)' (ibid.: 63). This view of linguistic change as 'sneaky', and as advancing 'most easily where it is least obtrusive, apparently thriving on structural ambiguities and [...] superficial resemblances to existing patterns' (De Smet 2012: 607), has been applied very explicitly to a number of changes described in the literature, including, for instance, the extension of the accusative with infinitive construction to verbs of knowing, thinking and declaring (e.g. *They know him to be wrong*) over the course of Middle English, under the influence of Latin analogues (Warner 1982: 134–57), the extension of bare verbal gerunds (e.g. *Slitting the bark is an excellent additional help*) to subject position in Late Modern English (Fanego 2007: 217–18), and the reanalysis of *all but* from a multi-word sequence meaning 'everything except' to a complex downtoner modifying adjectives with the meaning 'almost' (De Smet 2012: 611–13).

If we now turn to the ACC-*ing* construction and compare its examples as preverbal subject with the participial constructions in (37)–(42), which are also positioned sentence initially before their superordinate clauses, the surface resemblances between the two types become evident. In fact, the awkward, faulty syntax in five or six of my examples is halfway between a gerundial structure and a participial one. Note for instance that (43) starts with a pronoun (*she*) in the nominative case, as it corresponds to an absolute; but as one reads on, it becomes clear that the -*ing* clause has to be interpreted gerundially: '[the fact of] her being now a woman, and her father's age and some infirmities ... induced him to entertain her with discourse on marriage', and so on.[17] Thus also in (44), which is another hybrid, in this case between the subtype of absolute with continuative *which* discussed in section 9.5.1 and a gerundive: '[the fact of] Oliver knowing [which] and sending a messenger about it put the French into a great consternation', and so on. In (45), also appearing to originate in that subtype of absolute, the relative *which* has possessive value: '... the place she was to go, whose being so small a distance from Paris made him the more consoled at leaving her, because he could with ease make her a visit every day'.[18]

(43) COLMOBAENG 1725 Haywood, *The Fatal Secret: or, Constancy in Distress*, 209: she went a great way in the Mathematicks; understood several Languages perfectly well; and had she presever'd [*sic*] in Application, might have been as eminent for her Learning, as the celebrated Madam Dacier: But *she being now a Woman, and her*

Father's Age, and some Infirmities incident to it, making him believe he
had not long to live, and consequently desirous of seeing his beloved Child
dispos'd of before his Death, induced him to entertain her often with
Discourse of Marriage.[19]

(44) ARCHER 1717 Tomlinson, *The Diary of John Tomlinson* (1717toml_
y3b): 1717. Aug. 8th. Oliver Cromwell kept a correspondence
with the French king's secretary, thô they had promised to deliver
Mardyke to the English, yet they had formed secret counsels not to
do it—*which, Oliver knowing and sending a messenger about it*—putt
the French into a great consternation, it made them think he had
consulted the devil, for there were but two or three persons conscious to it.

(45) COLMOBAENG 1725 Haywood, *The Fatal Secret: or, Constancy*
in Distress, 230: The indulgent Parent heard the Proposal with
Satisfaction, and every Thing was ordered to be got ready for her
Removal with all Expedition. She was carried in a Litter for Ease, and
the assiduous Chevalier attended her on Horseback to the Place she
was to go, **which** *being so small a Distance from Paris*, made him the
more consoled at leaving her, because he could with Ease make her
a Visit every Day.

In a second group of examples in my data, the NPs coding the subject
arguments of the -*ing* forms (*grasse, so much Company, The weather* in the
examples below) are semantically compatible with the matrix predicates
(*occasion, makes ... scarce and dear, obliged*). An interpretation of these -*ing*
clauses as participial (rather than gerundial) is therefore not impossible, but
seems highly unlikely in view of the overall context, which makes it clear
that the focus is on the entire propositions functioning as subjects of the
higher verbs; in other words, in (46) it is not grass that 'will occasion the
greatest increase of milk', but rather the fact itself of grass being in 'its perfect goodness' in springtime. Hence also in (47), where it is the fact of there
being so many people living in the town that is said to be held responsible
for the scarcity of food or provisions, and so on.

(46) HC 1615 Markham, *Countrey Contentments*, 107: The best time for a
Cow to calue in for the Dairie, is in the later ende of March, and all
Aprill; for then **grasse** *beginning to spring to its perfect goodnesse* will
occasion the greatest increase of milke that may be:

(47) HC 1698 Fiennes, *Journeys*, 152: There are a great deale of Gentry
which lives in town tho' there are no good houses but what are old
rambling ones [SIX MORE LINES OF TEXT FOLLOW]; its a very dear
place **so much Company** *living in the town* makes provision scarce
and dear, however its a good excuse to raise the recknoning on
strangers.

(48) COLMOBAENG 1719 Bell, *St. Petersburgh to Pekin* 4Q10(1719)0008/
019-P0: We travelled to the city of Mosco in small parties, the more
easily to procure post horses. *The **weather** being very hot* obliged
us to make short stages, confining us mostly to the mornings and
evenings.

As frequently noted in the literature (see, among many others, Langacker
1977, Fanego 2004, Traugott and Trousdale 2013: 22–6, 35–6), such ambiguities in interpretation are characteristic of morphosyntactic changes involving the reanalysis of a construction or class of constructions in a given
language, so that a new form–meaning pairing is established, often without
language users actually being aware of the change having occurred (Keller
1994). The results of this are visible at the surface only when constructions
begin to be attested that 'could not have been fully sanctioned by [the] pre-
existing constructional type' (Traugott and Trousdale 2013: 22), as happens
in the following instances recorded in my data, along with several others.
In (49) the pronoun *there* is a dummy, and thus cannot be an argument of
the higher predicate *made it appear*; in (50)–(51) a reading of *God* and *The
man* as the subjects of, respectively, *was a daily miracle* and *made ... appear* is
semantically incoherent; and in (52) *the ladies* is in the plural, while *exposes*
is singular.

(49) HC 1698 Fiennes, *Journeys*, 151: a mile off by a little village
I descended a hill which made the prospect of the town still in view
and much to advantage; its but two parishes; the Market Cross has
a dyal and lanthorn on the top, and ***there** being another house pretty
close to it high built with such a tower and lanthorn also, with the two
churches towers and some other buildings pretty good* made it appear
nobly at a distance;

(50) ARCHER 1680 Long, *A Sermon against Murmuring* (1680long_h2b):
They acknowledged that God as well as his father designed him
for the Crown, and setled it on his head against all opposition, for
Adonijah usurped the kingdom, Abiathar, Joab and Shimei abetted
the Usurpation and were all defeated: ***God** appearing for Solomon not
once or twice for the preservation of him from such enemies*, was a daily
miracle:

(51) COPC 1689 Stevens, *Journal*, 1Q17(1689)0004/029-P0: Here first of
all we found difficulty in getting quarters, and, having got a billet
of the sovereign on an inn, were refused not only beds, but fire and
meat and drink for our money, [...] *The **man** being an Irishman and
a Catholic* made his ill carriage towards us appear the more strange,

(52) ARCHER 1716 *Lady Mary Wortley Montagu to Pope* (1716mmon_x3b):
The theatre is so large that 'tis hard to carry the eye to the end of
it, and the habits in the utmost magnificence to the number of one

hundred and eight. No house could hold such large decorations; but *the ladies all sitting in the open air*, exposes them to great inconveniences; for there is but one canopy for the imperial family;

Besides their surface affinities, important semantic affinities also exist between the ACC-*ing* construction as preverbal subject and the absolutes that served as its model. Referring first to the absolutes, these, as already mentioned, are tenseless structures that function as adjuncts with respect to the matrix clause; as adjuncts, they are able to code a variety of adverbial relations: time, place, cause, conditionality, concessivity, instrumentality and so on. With great frequency, both today (Kortmann 1991: 135–6, 230) and in earlier stages of the language (Visser 1963–73: sections 1063, 1080), they specify the causal motivation of the event or situation in the matrix clause; see in this regard examples (31)–(37), (39)–(41) cited earlier, plus note 14, among many others that could be adduced from my data.[20] In this respect, therefore, absolutes share the same discourse function as one important subset of the gerundives, namely, those introduced by causal *for*, as in (53)–(54) below. These, as shown by De Smet in a detailed study of the semantic relations expressed by prepositional gerundives over the period 1250–1640, are already recorded in Middle English, but, crucially, they increase sharply in frequency from 1500 onwards (De Smet 2008: 73, 80–1, and Appendix A1), that is, coinciding with the period when both ACC-*ing* gerundives and absolutes with full coreference between Sub_A and Sub_M were also becoming common.

(53) HC 1550–52 *Diary of Edward VI*, 355: The duches, Crane and his wife [...] were sent to the Towr *for devising thies treasons*; Jaymes Wingfeld also, *for casting out of billes sediciouse*.

(54) HC 1629 *Barrington Family Letters*, 78: He took noe unkindnes that I colde perceave *for your not seing him*, he did not speak a word of it tell I asked him.

It appears to me that a probable interpretation is that such a shared discourse function of *for*-gerundives and absolutes may have facilitated the expansion of ACC-*ing* as preverbal subject. Like those two constructional types, ACC-*ing* subjects are factive and, in the vast majority of cases, express the causal motivation for the situation or event in the superordinate clause; observe examples (18), (19), (43)–(49) and (51)–(52) cited earlier. It is precisely this semantic content that is responsible for the very high incidence of causative predicates in the sentences with ACC-*ing* subjects recorded in my data (see Table 9.4); that is, predicates such as *induce*, *make*, *oblige*, *occasion* and the like. Aside from causatives (25 tokens), commentatives[21] (8 tokens; see (50) for one of them) are the only other type of predicate taking ACC-*ing* subjects in my material. The presence of commentatives, however, was predictable,

Table 9.4 Matrix predicates with ACC-*ing* clauses functioning as preverbal subjects

---

Causatives (25): *cast (an impediment); deprive (sb. from sth.); draw (sb. to do sth.); exempt (sb. from V-ing); expose (sb. to sth.); give (sb. reason to do sth.); give (sth. a calm and continued impulse); give (apprehensions of sb.'s danger); give (content); induce (sb. to do sth.); introduce (a thought), i.e.* 'bring about, occasion (a thought)'; *make (sb./sth. do sth; 10 ex.); oblige (sb. to do sth.); occasion (sth.); put (sb. into consternation); stay (sb.'s flight), i.e.* 'check, hinder (sb.'s flight)'

Commentatives (8): *be a daily miracle; be the effect of duty; be a sufficient demonstration; be a continual snare; be a great article; be looked on as ...; be the better; prove the best means of ...*

---

as cross-linguistically subject clauses are often arguments to commentatives (see Noonan 1985: 116–18, Fanego 1990: II, 132, 1992: 81–2).[22]

9.6 Summing up: ACC-ing gerundives as multiple source constructions

The idea that '[t]hings in language are rarely simple, so that for any given linguistic phenomenon, a multiplicity of explanations need to be considered' (Joseph 2013: 675) has long been current in historical linguistics. Recently, however, work by Van de Velde et al. (2013) has tried to formalize this notion and provide a framework for the analysis of the widespread phenomenon of linguistic changes resulting not just from one, but from different source constructions simultaneously.

Based on Croft's conception (2000: 32–7) of constructions as forming diachronic lineages that are replicated in usage, with change viewed as typically occurring within a lineage through altered replication, Van de Velde et al. explore the interaction between lineages or between different branches of a lineage as leading to language innovation. The involvement of more than one lineage, or 'source construction', for a given change is examined with respect to developments at the levels of phonology, semantics and morphosyntax, such as the English *way*-construction, for example (Israel 1996, Traugott and Trousdale 2013: 76–91). This has the form of a sequence of a verb, a noun phrase consisting of a possessive pronoun and *way*, and an adverbial. It is used 'to mark movement' along a path accompanied or caused by the action denoted by the verb' (Van de Velde et al. 2013: 484). Remarkably, it accommodates both transitive and intransitive verbs, as in (55a) and (55b) respectively, quoted from Van de Velde et al.:

(55a) and we were actually kicking our way through rubbish on the stairs (BNC, FY8 633)

(55b) a lady who giggled her way through *Nightmare on Elm Street* (BNC, HGN 134)

The explanation proposed for this is that the present-day English *way*-construction stems, historically, from the combination of two distinct older constructions: one was the use of *way* as the object of a transitive verb denoting creation or acquisition of a path, as in (56); the other was the use of intransitive motion verbs with *way* functioning as an adverbial, as in (57):

(56) The ship [...] may make her way 2. or 3. pointes from her caping [i.e. 'course']. (1595, *OED*)

(57) Sir Beawmaynes [...] sawe where the blak knyght rode his way wyth the dwarff, and so he rode oute of his syght. (a1470, *OED*)

If we now turn to the specific construction discussed in this chapter and consider it once again in light of the evidence adduced in the preceding sections, we can hypothesize that, in producing it, a speaker or hearer in earlier English would have drawn on their knowledge or experience of a number of related constructions existing at the time. First here would have been a very frequent subtype of gerundive most commonly functioning as prepositional complement and coding a variety of adverbial relations with respect to its matrix clause;[23] its subject argument, if overt, was marked for the genitive case; semantically, it could have either an actional (58–59) or a factive (53–54) reading:

(58) HC 1534 M. Roper, *Letters*, 510: It is to me no litle comfort [...] to delite my self amonge in this bitter tyme of your absens, by such meanes as I maye, *by as often writinge to you, as shall be expedient* and *by readinge againe and againe your most fruteful and delectable letter,*

(59) HC 1599–1605 Hoby, *Diary*, Sample 2, 77: after, I walked a broad, and, *at my Comming home*, I tooke a Lector, and wrett a whill

Second, a variant of the preceding subtype which, largely as a result of the simplification and instability of the English inflectional system, lacked overt genitive marking (see also examples (15)–(18) earlier on):

(60) HC 1554 *The Trial of Sir Nicholas Throckmorton*, PI, 70.C1: the said Sir *Peter Caroe* sayd, the matter importing the *French* King as it did, he thought the *French* King would work to hinder *the Spanyards coming hither*, with whome the said *Sir Peter* dyd thinke good to practise for Armour, Municions and Money.

(61) COPC 1690 Locke, *Concerning Human Understanding*, 014/074–P05: It is a quite different consideration to examine whether the mind has the idea *of such a boundless space actually existing*, since our ideas are not always proofs of the existence of things;

Third, the type of absolute participle with full coreference between Sub_A and Sub_M discussed in section 9.5.1, which provided an analogical model for the expansion of the ACC-*ing* gerundive to the subject slot, one of its major functions in the early stages of its development. In this new use, ACC-*ing* incorporated the factive semantics of its participial source, and also a range of pronominal forms as subject arguments (see Table 9.3) that can likewise be traced back to that source; namely, the relative *which* (2 tokens), personal pronouns in the nominative case (1 token; see (43)), and expletives such as *it* (2 tokens) or *there* (1 token; see (49)), both of which occurred frequently with absolute participles (e.g. '*it* being Sunday, we had service on deck', '*there* being no survivors, the cause of the accident will never be known'; see Visser 1963–73: sections 1087–8, also Söderlind 1958: section 489).

In sum, the emergence and behaviour of the constructional type under discussion in this study illustrate that we can often come closer to a true understanding of innovation and developments in language by considering the possibility of not just one, but multiple causes and sources of change acting together.

Notes

1. This chapter has been made possible by the financial support of the European Regional Development Fund, the Spanish Ministry for Economy and Competitiveness (grants FFI2011-26693-C02-01 and FFI2014-52188-P) and the Autonomous Government of Galicia, Directorate General for Research, Development and Innovation (grant CN2014/004).
2. Henceforth gerund clauses will be in italics; subjects will be in bold.
3. Tajima (1996: 572–5) lists 28 Middle English examples of common case NPs or objective pronouns used as subjects of a gerund, as in (9), but as he himself acknowledges, many are doubtful and allow a different interpretation, so that only 12 of his examples (his nos. 10, 11, 12, 20, 21, 22, 23, 24, 25, 26, 27 and 28) might be accepted as possible instances of the ACC-*ing* construction. Out of these, eight function as prepositional complements and four as objects (three in the set expression *to pardon me so presuming*). In addition, Tajima adduces (i) as an example of ACC-*ing* functioning as the subject of its sentence:

   (i) *c.*1378 *Piers the Plowman* (B-text), VIII 31-2 [Tajima 1996: 573]:
   The wynde and the water and **the bote** *waggynge* Maketh the man many a tyme to falle
   'the wind and the water and the boat rocking often make a man fall'

   As will be seen later on (section 9.5), this example is particularly relevant to the present research. It is doubtful, however, that it can be accepted as a genuine instance of the construction: the noun *boat* is recorded already in Old English as the first element of nominal compounds such as *batswegen* 'boatswain' and *batweard* 'boat guard' (*DOE* s.v. *bat* n.), and was frequently used 'in compounds and combinations' throughout Middle English (*MED* s.v. *bot* n.[1] 3), some of them, such as *batespyking* 'spikes or nails for a boat', formed on -*ing* nouns (< *spiking*). *Bote waggynge* might therefore be interpreted as a compound noun, rather than a clause. Note too that the variant reading of this passage in the A-text of *Piers the Plowman* supports an analysis of the form *wagging* as purely nominal:

(ii) c1400(a1376) *PPl.A(1)* (Trin-C R.3.14) 9.26–8: Let bringe a man in a bot amydde a brood watir; Þe wynd & þe watir & þe waggyng of þe boot Makeþ þe man many tymes to falle & to stande, For stande he neuere so stif he stumbliþ in þe waggyng. [*MED* s.v. *wagging(e)* ger. (a)]

4. The use of the empty set (ø) in these and subsequent examples is to indicate that the covert subject of the superordinate clause is identical to the subject of the participle that precedes it.
5. The overall context shows that in this example *Bishops* is plural, not singular.
6. *OED* s.v. *interrupt* v. 4 'To hinder, stop, prevent, thwart'.
7. In Table 9.3 note also a few nouns ending in the fricatives /s, z/, such as *grass* (subperiod I) and *Ostorius, sickness, space* and *highness* (subperiod II); with these types of nouns, as mentioned earlier, zero genitive marking was frequent in Early Modern English.
8. In sections 515–16 and 518, where he gives the data for the gerunds used as objects and prepositional complements, Söderlind lists six further instances where the nominal is either in the plural (e.g. *of his homely Romans jesting at one another*) or is a classical proper noun ending in /s, z/ (e.g. *for Cleomenes not accepting the favours of Cassandra*). Since, as Söderlind points out (section 518), 'the apostrophe alone is never used as a sign of genitive' in Dryden, these six cases are ambiguous between a reading as PossPs with a 'zero' genitive (i.e. *of his homely Romans'*) or as common case NPs, and hence have been excluded from the count.
9. As I have shown in earlier research (Fanego 2006), definite hybrid gerunds were very common during the seventeenth and eighteenth centuries. From the end of the eighteenth century, however, normative pressures led to their disuse.
10. The tendency for more complex syntax to associate with the increasing verbalization of gerunds is also noted by De Smet (2008: 90–5) with reference to the period 1350–1640.
11. An anonymous reviewer points out that sequences such as (33–36) might be interpreted as instances of resumptive pronouns that were felt necessary by the complexity of the construction and the distance between the subordinate clause subject and the matrix clause, which led to the subject being 'evoked' again by a pronoun. In principle, there is nothing against this view, but this does not alter the fact that a pattern of Sub_A 'controlling' Sub_M, rather than the other way round, occurs with great frequency over the sixteenth, seventeenth and eighteenth centuries. In addition, not all instances of the pattern can be explained away on the basis of 'distance', as the two coreferential subjects could in fact occur in close proximity, as is the case in (36). Also, the most frequent cases of resumptive pronouns in the history of English involve a complement clause functioning as sentence subject which is resumed by *it*, as in Shakespeare's *The Winter's Tale* IV.iv.6: *To chide at your extremes **it** not becomes me.* For discussion, see further Visser (1963–73: sections 73, 901) and Fanego (1992: 77–8).
12. As Kortmann (1991: 99–101) notes, full coreference is marginally possible today in examples such as (iii), where the repetition of part of a noun phrase results in coreference between the subject of the absolute and the matrix subject:

(iii) In *one sense* all behavior 'has a genetic basis', *that sense* being that it also has an environmental basis.

13. For another example, see note 14 below.
14. Compare (40)–(42) with its variant with two coreferential pronouns: HC 1612 Coverte, *A Trve and Almost Incredible Report of an Englishman*, Sample 1, 16: The 21. day in the morning, wee espied three saile being small boats, slightly wrought together, called *Paugaias* which we made after and tooke, *which **they** on shore espying*, **they** sent out an Aduisor being also a *Paugaia*, which perceiued that wee had taken the other and returned to the shore.
15. Comedies, fiction, letters (private), science, sermons, statutes and travelogue.
16. Subtype 2 is not mentioned, so we can assume that no examples of this occurred in her data.
17. See further Jespersen (1909–49: V section 9.8.3) for a couple of similar examples.
18. On the possessive use of *which*, see *MED which* 2a, b and *OED which* 14.b. Compare also example (19) above (*which ill conditions of it* = 'whose ill conditions').
19. A closely related example, which I excluded from the count of ACC-*ing* as subjects, is (iv), where the -*ing* clause seems more participial than gerundial; note, though, that it is resumed later in the sentence by the pronoun *it*:

> (iv) HC 1619 Deloney, *Jack of Newbury*, 85: At length he watcht her so narrowly, that finding her going forth in an euening, hee followed her, *shee hauing one man before, and another behinde: carrying a verie stately gate in the street, **it** draue him into greater liking of her*, beeing the more vrged to vtter his minde.

20. The expression of a causal relation seems to have been especially common in the case of the absolutes with full coreference between Sub_A and Sub_M; note here Söderlind's important observation (1958: section 502) that Dryden's absolutes of this type all have 'temporal or causal connotations', time and cause of course being semantic relations that easily shade into each other.
21. That is, predicates providing 'a comment on the complement proposition that takes the form of an emotional reaction or evaluation [...] or a judgement' (Noonan 1985: 116–18).
22. The predominance of commentatives with subject clauses is a consequence of the preference for coding subjective reactions, evaluations and comments in the form of nominal or adjectival predicates – which usually operate, at the syntactic level, within copular sentences such as (50) above.
23. Note, of course, that not all prepositional gerunds function as adverbial adjuncts to the matrix clause, as one of their roles is merely satisfying the subcategorization requirements of their higher predicates (such as *cause* and *fear* in the sentences below):

> (v) HC 1502–03 *Plumpton Correspondence (William Plumpton)*, 234: Son Robart Plompton, I hertely recommend me to you [...]. The ***cause*** *of my writing to you now*; that I wold you should helpe this bearrer, yong Letham, in such buisenes as he hath in the Court of Augmentation,
>
> (vi) HC 1619 Deloney, *Jack of Newbury*, 74: his Wife [...] for ***feare*** *of hurting the set of her neckenger*, was glad to goe about and wash buckes at the Thames side,

Primary sources

ARCHER = A Representative Corpus of Historical English Registers (1990–1993/ 2002/2007/2010/2013). Originally compiled under the supervision of Douglas Biber and Edward Finegan at Northern Arizona University and the University of Southern California; modified and expanded by subsequent members of a consortium of universities. Current member universities are Northern Arizona, Southern California, Freiburg, Heidelberg, Helsinki, Uppsala, Michigan, Manchester, Lancaster, Bamberg, Zurich, Trier, Santiago de Compostela and Leicester.

COLMOBAENG = Corpus of Late Modern British and American English Prose. For details, see Fanego (2012).

COPC = Century of Prose Corpus 1680–1780. For details, see Milic (1995).

DOE = Healey, Antonette diPaolo (ed.) (2008) *The Dictionary of Old English: A–G on CD-ROM. Fascicle G and Fascicles A to F (with Revisions)* (Toronto: University of Toronto, Pontifical Institute of Mediaeval Studies).

HC = Helsinki Corpus of English Texts. For details, see Kytö (1996 [1991]).

MED = Kurath, Hans, Sherman M. Kuhn et al. (eds) (1952–2001). *Middle English Dictionary* (Ann Arbor: University of Michigan Press).

OED = *Oxford English Dictionary* (1884–1933). 10 vols. Murray, Sir James A. H., Henry Bradley, Sir William A. Craigie and Charles T. Onions (eds).

Supplement (1972–86), 4 vols. Robert Burchfield (ed.).

2nd edn (1989). Simpson, John A. and Edmund S. C. Weiner (eds).

Additions Series (1993–97). Simpson, John A., Edmund S. C. Weiner and Michael Proffitt (eds).

3rd edn in progress: *OED Online*, March (2000–). Simpson, John A. (ed.).

References

Altenberg, B. (1982) *The Genitive v. the of-Construction. A Study of Syntactic Variation in 17th Century English* (Lund: CWK Gleerup).

Biber, D. (1988) *Variation across Speech and Writing* (Cambridge: Cambridge University Press).

Croft, W. (2000) *Explaining Language Change. An Evolutionary Approach* (Harlow, Essex: Longman/Pearson).

Curme, G. O. (1931) *A Grammar of the English Language*, Vol. 3: *Syntax* (Boston: Heath).

De Smet, H. (2008) 'Functional Motivations in the Development of Nominal and Verbal Gerunds in Middle and Early Modern English'. *English Language and Linguistics*, 12: 55–102.

De Smet, H. (2012) 'The Course of Actualization'. *Language*, 88: 601–33.

Donner, M. (1986) 'The Gerund in Middle English'. *English Studies*, 67: 394–400.

Elsness, J. (1994) 'On the Progression of the Progressive in Early Modern English'. *ICAME Journal*, 18: 5–25.

Expósito González, M. C. (1996) *La estructura del sintagma nominal en el inglés de la Cancillería: 1400–1450* (Barcelona: Kadle Books).

Fanego, T. (1990) 'Finite Complement Clauses in Shakespeare's English, Part 2'. *Studia Neophilologica*, 62 (2): 129–49.

Fanego, T. (1992) *Infinitive Complements in Shakespeare's English. Synchronic and Diachronic Aspects* (Santiago de Compostela: Universidade de Santiago de Compostela).

Fanego, T. (1996) 'The Gerund in Early Modern English: Evidence from the Helsinki Corpus'. *Folia Linguistica Historica*, 17: 97–152.

Fanego, T. (1998) 'Developments in Argument Linking in Early Modern English Gerund Phrases'. *English Language and Linguistics*, 2: 87–119.

Fanego, T. (2004) 'On Reanalysis and Actualization in Syntactic Change: the Rise and Development of English Verbal Gerunds'. *Diachronica*, 21: 5–55.

Fanego, T. (2006) 'The Role of Language Standardization in the Loss of Hybrid Gerunds in Modern English' in L. E. Breivik, S. Halverson and K. Haugland (eds) *'These things write I vnto thee ...': Essays in Honour of Bjørg Bækken* (Oslo: Novus Press), pp. 93–110.

Fanego, T. (2007) 'Drift and the Development of Sentential Complements in British and American English from 1700 to the Present Day' in J. Pérez-Guerra, D. González-Álvarez, J. L. Bueno-Alonso and E. Rama-Martínez (eds) *'Of Varying Language and Opposing Creed': New Insights into Late Modern English* (Bern: Peter Lang), pp. 161–235.

Fanego, T. (2012) 'COLMOBAENG: a Corpus of Late Modern British and American English Prose' in N. Vázquez (ed.) *Creation and Use of Historical English Corpora in Spain* (Newcastle upon Tyne: Cambridge Scholars Publishing), pp. 101–17.

Houston, A. (1989) 'The English Gerund: Syntactic Change and Discourse Function' in R. W. Fasold and D. Schriffin (eds) *Language Change and Variation* (Amsterdam: John Benjamins), pp. 173–96.

Israel, M. (1996) 'The *Way* Constructions Grow' in A. E. Goldberg (ed.) *Conceptual Structure, Discourse and Language* (Stanford, Calif.: CSLI Publications), pp. 217–30.

Jack, G. B. (1988) 'The Origins of the English Gerund'. *NOWELE*, 12: 15–75.

Jespersen, O. (1909–49) *A Modern English Grammar on Historical Principles*. 7 vols (Copenhagen: Ejnar Munksgaard. Reprinted, London: George Allen and Unwin, 1961, 1965, 1970).

Joseph, B. D. (2013) 'Multiple Sources and Multiple Causes Multiply Explored'. Special issue of *Studies in Language*, 37 (3): 675–91.

Kastovsky, D. (1985) 'Deverbal Nouns in Old and Modern English: From Stem-Formation to Word-Formation' in J. Fisiak (ed.) *Historical Semantics–Historical Word-Formation* (Berlin: Mouton Publishers), pp. 221–61.

Keller, R. (1994) *On Language Change: the Invisible Hand in Language*. Translated by Brigitte Nerlich (London: Routledge. Originally published in 1990 in German).

Kisbye, T. (1971–72) *An Historical Outline of English Syntax. Parts I and II* (Aarhus: Akademisk Boghandel).

Koma, O. (1980) 'Diachronic Syntax of the Gerund in English and the X-Bar Theory'. *Studies in English Literature* (The English Literary Society of Japan): 59–76.

Kortmann, B. (1991) *Free Adjuncts and Absolutes in English. Problems of Control and Interpretation* (London and New York: Routledge).

Kytö, M. (1996 [1991]) *Manual to the Diachronic Part of the Helsinki Corpus of English Texts: Coding Conventions and Lists of Source Texts*, 3rd edn (Helsinki: Department of English, University of Helsinki).

Langacker, R. W. (1977) 'Syntactic Reanalysis' in C. N. Li (ed.) *Mechanisms of Syntactic Change* (Austin and London: University of Texas Press), pp. 57–139.

Lass, R. (1992) 'Phonology and Morphology' in Norman Blake (ed.) *The Cambridge History of the English Language*, Vol. 2: *1066–1476* (Cambridge: Cambridge University Press), pp. 23–155.

Milic, L. T. (1995) 'The Century of Prose Corpus: a Half-Million Word Historical Data Base'. *Computers and the Humanities*, 29: 327–37.

Mitchell, B. (1985) *Old English Syntax* (Oxford: Clarendon Press).

Mustanoja, T. F. (1960) *A Middle English Syntax. Part I: Parts of Speech* (Helsinki: Société Néophilologique).

Naro, A. J. (1981) 'The Social and Structural Dimensions of a Syntactic Change'. *Language*, 57: 63–98.

Noonan, M. (1985) 'Complementation' in T. Shopen (ed.) *Language Typology and Syntactic Description*, Vol. II: *Complex Constructions* (Cambridge: Cambridge University Press), pp. 42–140.

Río-Rey, C. (2002) 'Subject Control and Coreference in Early Modern English Free Adjuncts and Absolutes'. *English Language and Linguistics*, 6: 309–23.

Salmon, V. (1999) 'Orthography and Punctuation' in R. Lass (ed.) *The Cambridge History of the English Language*, Vol. 2: *1476–1776* (Cambridge: Cambridge University Press), pp. 13–55.

Söderlind, J. (1958) *Verb Syntax in John Dryden's Prose*, Vol. 2 (Uppsala: A.-B. Lundequist).

Tajima, M. (1985) *The Syntactic Development of the Gerund in Middle English* (Tokyo: Nan'un-do).

Tajima, M. (1996) 'The Common-/Objective-Case Subject of the Gerund in Middle English'. *NOWELE*, 28/29: 569–78.

Traugott, E. C. and G. Trousdale (2013) *Constructionalization and Constructional Changes* (Oxford: Oxford University Press).

Trousdale, G. (2013) 'Multiple Inheritance and Constructional Change'. Special issue of *Studies in Language*, 37 (3): 491–514.

Van de Velde, F., H. De Smet and L. Ghesquière (2013) 'Introduction: On Multiple Source Constructions in Language Change'. Special issue of *Studies in Language*, 37 (3): 473–89.

Visser, F. Th. (1963–1973) *An Historical Syntax of the English Language*. 3 parts in 4 vols (Leiden: E. J. Brill).

Warner, Anthony (1982) *Complementation in Middle English and the Methodology of Historical Syntax* (London: Croom Helm).

Werlich, E. (1976) *A Text Grammar of English* (Heidelberg: Quelle & Meyer).

10
The Relation between Hypotactic Integration and Complementation in Cognitive Grammar

Cristiano Broccias
University of Genoa

10.1 Introduction

Complementation figures prominently in the discussion of perceptual verbs such as *see* and *watch* in relation to the well-known alternation illustrated in (1):

(1) Tim watched Bill mend/mending the lamp. (Quirk *et al.* 1985: 1206)

The object of perception or 'percept' (see Gisborne 2010 on the latter term) can either be coded by means of an infinitival clause or an *-ing* clause and scholars have duly explored what criteria may bear on the selection of either (see for example Egan 2008). Seldom is it noticed (see Broccias 2010 and 2014 for an exception) that the competition among complementation patterns for perception verbs not only involves the alternation between infinitive and *-ing* clauses but also *as*-clauses, as is shown in (2):

(2) a. She watched Victor place two tall, white, tapered candles under delicate, hand-cut, antique glass hurricane covers, and carefully fold starched Irish linen napkins monogrammed with the initials C.S. (British National Corpus (BNC): FRS 2792)
   b. The rector leant against the dresser and watched her$_i$ as she$_i$ fetched a vase and arranged the freesias. (BNC: ASE 1937)
   c. She pulled her jumper off and handed it to him, then watched as he spread it out and laid the dead animal on it. (BNC: FRF 181)

All three sentences in (2) involve a 'preparation' or 'arrangement' scenario. In (2a), Victor is setting the table. The woman referred to by the pronoun *her* in (2b), the direct object of *watch*, which is coreferential with the subject *she* of the verbs *fetched* and *arranged*, is arranging freesias in the vase she fetched. In (2c), the man referred to by the pronoun *he*, the subject of the verbs *spread (out)* and *laid*, is similarly 'arranging' the animal on the jumper. Syntactically, (2a) instantiates the same pattern as (1), which I will refer to as the **non-finite pattern** or **VOv pattern**, where V stands for the matrix verb of perception (*watch*, here), O for the direct object (*Victor* in (2a)) and v for the embedded, non-finite verb(s) (*place* and *fold* in (2a)), which may either be an infinitive or an *-ing* form. (2b) and (2c) differ from (2a) in that they contain an *as*-clause, which seems to be recruited to either elaborate on or express the object of perception. In (2b), the verb *watch* takes a direct object, *her*, which could be regarded as the object of perception; the following *as*-clause specifies in some detail the process that the pronominal referent was engaged in. (2c) dispenses with a direct object altogether and expresses the percept solely by means of the *as*-clause. I will refer to the pattern in (2b) as the **VOas pattern** and to the objectless pattern in (2c) as the **Vas pattern**. In order to distinguish the VOv pattern, on the one hand, from VOas and Vas on the other, I will use the collective term *as*-**pattern** for the latter two.

It is worth stressing that the *as*-clause in the *as*-pattern in (2b) and (2c) is not (primarily) used to express the temporal frame with respect to which the event of watching takes place, but, whether in combination with a direct object or not, it is functionally equivalent to a non-finite clause, as in (2a). In other words, if non-finite clauses such as those in (1) and (2a) are analysed as complements, then it would be plausible to treat the *as*-clauses in (2b) and (2c), whether in conjunction with a direct object or not, as akin to complements rather than (temporal) adjuncts. Two examples will hopefully suffice to convince the sceptical reader of the plausibility of this proposal. Let us first consider the (almost) 'minimal pair' in (3):

(3) a. Next came two ladies, and after talking to the charwoman they also moved forward, and as Sue stood reaching upward, watched her hand tracing the letters, ... (Hardy, *Jude the Obscure*)
   b. Jude Fawley signed the form of notice, Sue looking over his shoulder and watching his hand as it traced the words. (Hardy, *Jude the Obscure*)

While (3a) instantiates the VOv pattern, (3b) makes use of the VOas pattern. Crucially, it is very difficult to say whether the difference in syntactic structure correlates with any difference in how the event of somebody's tracing letters or words (the percept) is construed. What seems to be unmistakably the case is that both the non-finite pattern and the string direct object plus *as*-clause are employed to express the object of perception.

Let us now consider the example in (4):

(4) As he made his final descent, I watched in terror as the plane hit the runway and sparks flew out. (*The Daily Mail*, 29 June 2012)

(4) contains two *as*-clauses. The first one, which is preposed to the main clause, obviously functions as a temporal adjunct. It depicts the event

(a plane approaching the runway) that frames the event of watching. Importantly, the second *as*-clause codes the percept, namely the plane hitting the runway and the ensuing sparks. It seems that the different positions of the two *as*-clauses correlate with their different functions, the preposed *as*-clause functioning as a temporal adjunct and the post-verbal *as*-clause functioning in a complement-like capacity.[1]

In sum, it seems more than plausible to suggest that *as*-clauses can be used with perception verbs to encode percepts. What I aim to do in this chapter is to investigate to what extent the characterization of the *as*-pattern as falling under the rubric of complementation is warranted not only empirically but also theoretically. Any syntactic theory needs to address the issue of how to capture the similarity between the VOv pattern and the *as*-pattern. In section 10.2, I will refer to two previous studies that discuss phenomena similar to the one under investigation. In particular, I will point out that the *as*-pattern is an instance of what Fischer (2007) calls **hypotactic integration** and that the notion of 'complement' depends on the analyst's theoretical orientation. In section 10.3, I will briefly summarize how complementation is handled in Langacker's Cognitive Grammar, which strives to offer a conceptual characterization of traditional linguistic labels such as complement. Section 10.4 will discuss the patterns presented here in Cognitive Grammar terms and conclude that the use of the term 'complement', as understood in Cognitive Grammar, is warranted for the *as*-pattern. Section 10.5 offers some conclusions.

10.2   Previous analyses

To the best of my knowledge, cases such as (2b) and (2c) have so far received little attention in the literature, an exception being Broccias (2010) and (2014). Fischer (2007) mentions an example similar to (2b) in her discussion of a possible continuum in clause combining from mere juxtaposition to embedding, as is summarized in (5), which is based on Fischer (2007: 214–29):

(5) a. *Mere juxtaposition (parataxis, no marking)*:
   I saw John at the garden centre – you know – John was buying flowers.
   b. *Juxtaposition with adverbial or deictic particles or resumptive (anaphoric) elements*:
   I saw John there. He was buying flowers.
   c. *Hypotactic integration*:
   I saw John when he was buying flowers.
   d. *Complete integration (embedding)*:
   I saw John buying flowers.

(5c), which is dubbed hypotactic integration by Fischer (2007), is akin to (2b), although the punctual perception verb *see* and the subordinator *when*, instead of *watch* and *as*, are used.[2] It need not concern us here whether the continuum illustrated in (5) is valid phylogenetically and/or ontogenetically (but see Broccias 2014 on the former possibility and Silva 1991 for some more general discussion of the acquisition of temporal clauses). What matters at present is the assumption that all the four options illustrated above are functionally equivalent. If this is the case, then the alternatives in (5c) and (5d), as was argued in section 10.1, can be related to the notion of complementation. In fact, few contemporary linguists would argue against the classification of *John buying flowers* as a complement in (5d), while the classification of *when he was buying flowers* in (5c) appears to be more problematic. Given the functional equivalence of (5c) and (5d), the *when*-clause should not be treated (only?) as a temporal adverbial framing the matrix process of seeing. It is intuitively clear that the *when*-clause describes primarily the event in which John (the direct object) was engaged. Consequently, it would make sense to analyse the complement of *saw* as being made up of the string *John when he was buying flowers*, thus effectively equating the *when*-clause to a modifier of *John*, although this analysis should be explored in more depth.

The need to distinguish between two senses of 'complementation', one formal and one functional, also emerges in another important work, namely Deutscher (2000).[3] He points out that 'there is no clearly marked borderline between finite complements (which are clausal arguments) and adverbial clauses (which are peripheral elements)' (Deutscher 2000: 9). In his view, this explains why for example the Akkadian word *kīma* developed from an adverbial subordinating conjunction into a marker of complementation (a complementizer; see below). Interestingly, Deutscher (2000) distinguishes complementation as structural embedding from the Functional Domain of Complementation (FDC). Using the examples from Fischer (2007) above, we could argue that (5a) and (5d) both belong to the FDC. In both cases, the second clause – whether it be an independent clause as in (5a) or an embedded clause as in (5d) – depicts a percept, which is of course an essential part of the semantic characterization of a perception verb. However, structurally, only the second clause in (5d) exhibits syntactic subordination and hence counts as an instance of complementation (with a lower case 'c') in Deutscher's sense. It would be more difficult to classify (5c) because, as Fischer (2007) points out, the degree of syntactic integration is lower than in (5d) and an intervening object is used. As was remarked above, the *when*-clause in (5c) and the *as*-clause (2b) may be analysed as modifiers of the object noun (at some level to be specified). By contrast, in (2c), where no intervening direct object is employed, the *as*-clause may more readily be identifiable as a complement in Deutscher's sense because it is syntactically dependent on the main clause and clearly expresses the percept argument of *watch*. To be sure, the issue cannot be settled unless a more precise definition of what counts as a complement is offered.

What is also of great importance for our purposes is Deutscher's observation that the early history of *kīma* is reminiscent of that of English *as* (see

Deutscher 2000: 61). He observes that both *kīma* and *as* started out as comparative particles and subsequently became temporal and causal adverbials. Further, both *kīma* and *as* (at least in some dialects of English) ultimately ended up as complementizers. As an illustration for *as*, Deutscher gives 'I don't know as [= if, CB] you'll like the appearance of our place' (*Oxford English Dictionary* (*OED*), s.v. '*as*, adv. and conj.' B.26). Another example, not mentioned by Deutscher but also offered in the *OED*, is 'That the Fop ... should say, as [= that, CB] he would rather have such-a-one without a Groat, than me with the Indies' (s.v. '*as, adv. and conj.*' B.26).[4]

What is remarkable is that the 'complementizer' use of *as*, that is, the use of *as* in the V*as* pattern, seems to emerge in a specific context (the perception verb *watch*) which is relatively low in transitivity; cf. *I saw *(her)* vs *I watched (her)*. Deutscher (2000) points out that this is precisely what happened with Akkadian *kīma*, which developed into a complementizer in low transitive contexts, involving, for example, perceptions verbs (see Deutscher 2000: 103, Table 3 for a summary).

In sum, although little has been written about the *as*-pattern specifically, references to similar phenomena in Fischer (2007) and Deutscher (2000), for example, show that the *as*-pattern should be treated at least functionally as belonging to (functional) complementation. In formal terms, the VO*as*-pattern, an instance of hypotactic integration in Fischer's analysis, is at the boundary of 'proper' syntactic complementation, that is, embedding. The V*as* pattern, in turn, is even closer to prototypical syntactic complementation by virtue of the lack of a nominal direct object. One could go as far as to say that, at least in the local context of perception verbs in the V*as* pattern, *as* has developed into a complementizer.[5]

10.3 Complements and all that in Cognitive Grammar

As Deutscher's (2000) work shows, it is of the utmost importance to have as clear a definition as possible of what one understands by the label 'complement'. Indeed, Croft (2001) has revealed the classificatory problems and conceptual circularity of much of modern linguistics, where Aristotelian definitions and classifications are (probably) impossible. Still, the nature of the *as*-pattern should be investigated and systematized in any linguistic theory one adheres to. One important approach that avoids the definitional conundrum typical of modern linguistics is Langacker's Cognitive Grammar (see Langacker 2008 for a recent and comprehensive review). Langacker not only proposes that syntax should not be regarded as an autonomous component of an autonomous language faculty, but also strives to provide conceptual characterizations of 'traditional' syntactic labels. He takes the following view:

> [T]raditional grammatical notions like head, adjunct, complement, and modifier are not themselves the basic units of [Cognitive Grammar]

description. They are more accurately thought of as convenient labels for certain kinds of configurations commonly observable at the semantic pole of symbolic assemblies. Thus it is not expected that every construction will have a head, or that every component structure combining with a head will be clearly and uniquely identifiable as a complement or a modifier. Like the factors defining them, these latter notions are matters of degree and are not mutually exclusive. (Langacker 2008: 205)

In more detail, Langacker suggests that what is traditionally called a **head** can be equated with a construction's profile determinant; this is the element that determines the entity that the construction describes or, in Cognitive Grammar terminology, profiles. For example, the nominal expression *the key on the desk* profiles a key, not a desk or a relation of contact between the key and the desk; hence, the profile determinant or head is *key*. A representation of a plausible compositional path illustrating how the various (sub)structures mesh together in the nominal *the key on the desk* is offered in Figure 10.1 where the substructures that determine the profile of an expression (so-called profile determinants) at various levels of conceptual organization are placed within boxes with a thicker perimeter. (For reasons of space, the semantic contribution of the definite article is ignored and hence the article is placed between brackets. The following description also omits various other features of the compositional path in Figure 10.1. The interested reader is referred to Langacker 2008 for details.) Within the nominal *the key on the desk*, the prepositional phrase *on the desk* is analysed as a **modifier**, that is, a structure that contains a salient substructure elaborated by the head. The preposition *on* profiles a relation of contact between two elements since one element, the trajector (*tr* in Figure 10.1), is located with reference to the other, the landmark (*lm* in Figure 10.1), by virtue of being on top of the latter. In our example, the trajector of *on* is obviously a salient substructure of the relational predicate *on* and, crucially, the trajector of *on* is elaborated by *key*, which is the head of the nominal. Hence, *on the desk* is regarded as a modifier. In Figure 10.1, the substructures that are elaborated (so-called e-sites) are hatched, and dashed curves connect entities that have identical reference. Within the prepositional phrase *on the desk*, *the desk* counts as a **complement** (of *on*) because a complement is defined as a structure that elaborates or specifies in more detail a salient substructure of the head. *The desk* elaborates the landmark of *on*, and *on* is the head of the phrase *on the desk*, as this expression profiles a relation of contact, rather than a location. It is thus apparent that Langacker's notion of complementation is a semantic/functional definition, which is by and large equivalent to Deutscher's notion of the 'Functional Domain of Complementation'.

Finally, Langacker uses the traditional label 'adjunct' for those cases where an element neither elaborates nor is elaborated by another structure. An example is *angry* in *He went away angry*, where *angry* is neither a complement

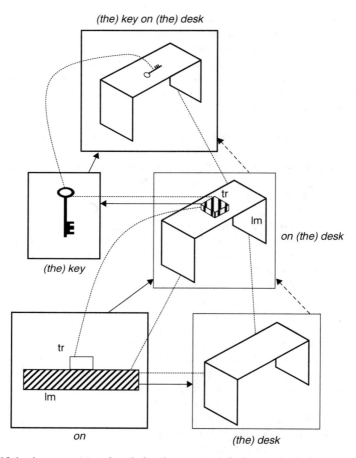

Figure 10.1 A compositional path for the nominal *the key on the desk*

nor a modifier of *go away* (see Langacker 2008: 204–5). The emotional state one leaves a place in is surely not a central feature of the event of leaving, so *angry* cannot be said to elaborate a salient substructure of that event and, hence, *angry* does not qualify as a complement. Further, *angry* does not contain any salient substructure that is elaborated by *go away*: a process is not a central feature for the conceptual characterization of *angry*; hence, *angry* does not qualify as a modifier either. On the basis of this analysis, an *as*-clause such as the preposed *as*-clause in (4), which has a temporal interpretation, cannot be described as an adjunct in Cognitive Grammar but rather as a temporal modifier. A temporal *as*-clause has a salient substructure, its trajector, which is elaborated by the main clause (see section 10.4 for more details). Hence, from now on, I will refer to the purely temporal interpretation of an *as*-clause as the temporal modifier interpretation rather than the temporal adjunct interpretation, in keeping with Langacker's terminology.

In the case of hypotactic integration investigated here, the *as*-clause clearly depicts a salient feature of the event of watching, namely the percept, and hence it would make sense to view it as a complement within a Cognitive Grammar framework. Still, it remains to be investigated how the various substructures in cases of hypotactic integration relate to one another. Although *as*-clauses may be prima facie described as complements, one should remember that in the VO*as* pattern a direct object is also present and, hence, the relation between the direct object and the *as*-clause must be investigated more thoroughly. However, from now on, for the sake of convenience, I will refer to an *as*-clause depicting an object of perception as an *as*-complement clause. Also, the relation between a 'complement' *as*-clause and the temporal 'modifier' interpretation, on the one hand, and the relation between the non-finite pattern and the *as*-pattern, on the other, should be studied in more detail. What conceptual operations underline the use of a 'complement' *as*-clause in comparison with a temporal 'modifier' *as*-clause? What are the differences, if any, between the non-finite pattern and the *as*-pattern in conceptual terms? These issues are addressed in the next section.

10.4   A Cognitive Grammar analysis of the non-finite and *as*-patterns

10.4.1   The infinitival pattern

Having pointed out that the *as*-pattern is semantically comparable with the non-finite pattern, we must now offer conceptual characterizations for both, which account for their similarity. Let us start with the infinitival pattern. First of all, it is helpful to consider how the verb *watch* is defined in dictionaries. The *Longman Dictionary of Contemporary English*, for example, paraphrases the sense of *watch* that we are dealing with as 'to look at someone or something for a period of time, paying attention to what is happening'.[6] Similarly, the *OED* defines *watch* as 'To keep (a person or thing) in view in order to observe any actions, movements, or changes that may occur' (s.v. *watch*, v.11). It is thus apparent that the object of perception or percept is not simply a person/thing but, rather, a participant (potentially) engaged in an event. The definitions given in the two dictionaries can thus be conveniently translated into Cognitive Grammar terms by saying that the percept of *watch*, at least as a first approximation, profiles a person/thing against a processual base, that is, a person/thing is profiled against the background (base) of an event (a process). The conceptual import of *watched* in a sentence such as *Harry watched Sally* can therefore be depicted diagrammatically as in Figure 10.2.

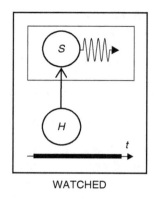

WATCHED

Figure 10.2 Diagrammatic representation of *Harry watched Sally*

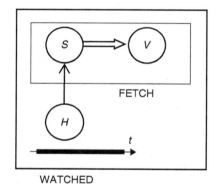

WATCHED

Figure 10.3 Diagrammatic representation of *Harry watched Sally fetch the vase*

Harry (*H*) makes visual contact with Sally (*S*), as is shown by means of the arrow connecting the two circles in Figure 10.2, for some time; see the time (*t*) arrow in the figure. The squiggly arrow departing from Sally is intended to depict the process Sally may be engaged in. The process is shown within a box for the sake of clarity.[7]

Building on this characterization, we can then depict the semantic pole of the VOv pattern, as in *Harry watched Sally fetch the vase*, as in Figure 10.3. Figure 10.3 is an instantiation of Figure 10.2. The processual base for the percept is elaborated as the event of fetching the vase (*V*) on Sally's part and its force-dynamic nature is shown by means of the thick arrow connecting *S* with *V*. In the case at hand, *Sally fetch the vase* can be analysed as a 'complement' because it elaborates a salient substructure of the verb *watch*, namely the percept (remember that the eventive percept includes both a person/thing and the process in which the person/thing is engaged). I would contend, however, that the 'head' or profile determinant of the complement is indeterminate in the sense that it may be identified with either the person/thing or the process. Although it was claimed above, on the basis of the dictionary entries, that the person/thing is what is profiled against the processual base, there is no reason why the alternative option where the overall process is the profile determinant should be excluded. The difference between the two cases amounts to where the spotlight of focal prominence is directed. In the sentence under discussion, it can be directed either onto Sally, the participant that corresponds to the trajector of the fetching process, or onto the whole fetching process. I will take the representation in Figure 10.3 as depicting the former option and that in Figure 10.4 the latter. Since the process is regarded as the profile determinant, the box containing it has been highlighted in bold in Figure 10.4.

It is important to point out that, even in the latter case, the arrow depicting visual contact is directed from *H* to *S* rather than stopping at the boundary of the box for the fetching event, as in the hypothetical conceptual representation in Figure 10.5.

A representation such as Figure 10.4 is to be preferred over that in Figure 10.5 because only Figure 10.4 conveys the intuition that the fetching event is accessed using Sally as a reference point (see Langacker 2008: 83–5 on the reference point ability). Indeed, the special status conferred upon Sally is reflected 'syntactically' by its nature as a direct object. Sally is thus given some degree of prominence even when the whole process of fetching is regarded as the head of the eventive percept.

Finally, there is another point which is worth remarking upon. The conceptual characterization offered in Figure 10.3 is in a sense similar to what traditional syntacticians would deem to be impossible in English, namely

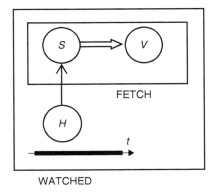

Figure 10.4 A processual profile determinant for the perceptual complement

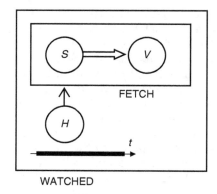

Figure 10.5   An alternative analysis of the perceptual complement

what they would call an infinitive relative clause. As was pointed out above, Figure 10.3 is intended to show that Sally is the head of the perceptual complement. In other words, the profile determinant in Figure 10.3 is nominal in nature rather than processual as in Figure 10.4. One may thus be tempted to consider the non-finite component *fetch the vase* a modifier since one of its salient substructures (the trajector) is elaborated by the head of the complement, *Sally*. It should be noticed, however, that the conceptual relations holding *Sally fetch the vase* together also involve the verb *watch* and are thus more complicated than an 'infinitive relative clause' would suggest. As was remarked above, *Sally* is understood against a processual base because of the nature of the perception verb used. Consequently, although the trajector of *fetch the vase* is elaborated by *Sally* (that is, the former would count as a modifier in traditional analyses and in Cognitive Grammar), *fetch the vase* also elaborates a structure associated with *Sally*, namely its processual base. The processual base is not intrinsic to the characterization of *Sally* as a participant since participants are conceptually relatively autonomous in contrast to processes (see for example Langacker 2008: 200). Therefore, *fetch the vase* is probably not to be regarded as a complement with respect to *Sally*, but the point remains that *fetch the vase* is not simply an 'infinitive relative clause' either.

In sum, the non-finite pattern can be analysed as involving a 'complement' whose head is either *fetch* or *Sally*; the latter option implies that to some extent, at least, the non-finite structure *fetch the vase* is a 'non-finite relative clause'.

10.4.2   The VO*as* pattern

In order to make sense of the first of the two *as*-patterns that need to be discussed, namely the VO*as* pattern, it is important to start off by considering the case where the *as*-clause merely depicts a temporal frame, that is, when the *as*-clause is used as a temporal adjunct (in traditional terminology) or temporal modifier (in Cognitive Grammar terminology). As was observed in section 10.1, in such cases the *as*-clause can be preposed, as in *As she$_i$ fetched the vase, Harry watched Sally$_i$*. A diagrammatic representation of a possible compositional path for this example is given in Figure 10.6.

As profiles a relationship between two events, one 'containing' the other. This has been shown as the two nesting squares at the lowest level of the compositional path in Figure 10.6. (For the sake of simplicity, the processual nature of the two events has been ignored and only two squares have been used.) The 'containing' event (the landmark) is the process elaborated by the verb in the *as*-clause, here the process of fetching, while the 'contained' event (the trajector) is the process elaborated by the main clause, here the process of watching. The overall profile determinant is the main clause, hence in Figure 10.6 the square for the landmark at the lowest level in the compositional path and the rectangle for the watching event at the highest level in the compositional path have been emboldened.

The conceptual representation in Figure 10.6 thus differs from that of Figure 10.3 in terms of containment. The complement interpretation of the fetching event implies that the fetching event is contained within the watching event. Although the fetching event may in fact have a temporal extension which is greater than that of the watching event, at least a sub-part of the former must be contained within the latter. By contrast, the *as*-temporal modifier interpretation requires the opposite arrangement in that the watching event should be contained within the fetching event. It is obvious that the *as*-complement interpretation stems from the fact that the *as*-event may be construed as both a temporal frame and an object of perception, which here is due to the correspondence between *Sally* and *she* (Harry watches Sally, who is involved in a temporal framing process, that of fetching the vase). This may trigger the reinterpretation of the *as*-clause as a complement, in particular if the *as*-clause follows the main clause. My contention is that such a reinterpretation is not 'pragmatic' in nature, that is, it is not a contextual interpretation but is part of our knowledge of English. In other words, I assume that the *as*-complement interpretation is stored as a construction (in the Construction Grammar sense, see Goldberg 2013) in our mind. Still, it is clear that a conceptual representation such as Figure 10.6 cannot depict the nature of the complement interpretation satisfactorily because it is too dissimilar from the representation for the non-finite pattern, of which the *as*-clause can be an equivalent.

I contend that the tension between the *as*-temporal interpretation and the *as*-complement interpretation can be solved if the relation of containment of the watching event within the fetching event becomes derivative; that is, in the *as*-complement interpretation, the percept, rather than the watching event itself, is what is contained within the fetching event (see Figure 10.7). This amounts to saying that the percept (symbolized by *Sally*) rather than

218

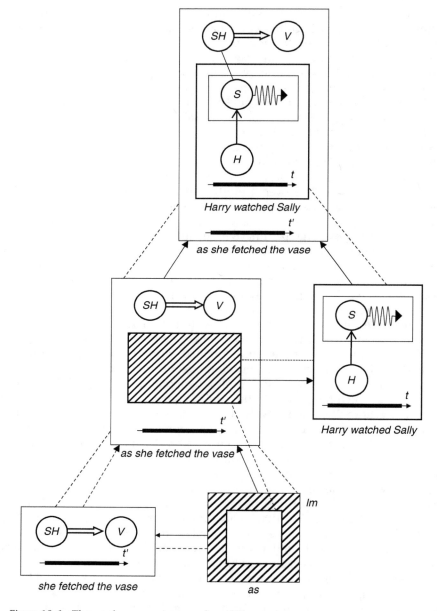

Figure 10.6 The *as*-clause as a temporal modifier

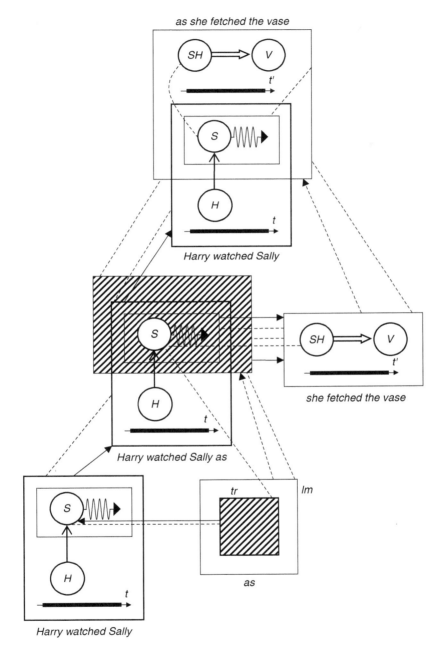

Figure 10.7 Diagrammatic representation of the VO*as* pattern

the watching event is the trajector of *as*. Further, redirecting the trajector of *as* from the watching event as a whole to one of its constitutive subparts can be regarded as an instance of Langacker's profile/active zone asymmetry (see Langacker 2008: 331–4). The person/thing being observed is of course a salient subpart of the watching event and is targeted as the trajector of *as* when the *as*-clause is used to depict an object of perception rather than a temporal frame. If one would like to stick to traditional labels, one could say that the complement of the verb is *Sally as she fetched the vase* since this string elaborates the percept of *watch*. The head of this complement may be identified with the nominal *Sally*, of which *as she fetched the vase* would then be a modifier. Still, as in the non-standard analysis of the infinitive as a 'relative' clause, it should be stressed that the situation is more complex than these traditional labels suggest. One very important aspect underlying the interpretation of the *as*-clause as a percept is that the *as*-clause must depict a process that is put in correspondence with the processual base of the person/thing being watched. Diagrammatically (see Figure 10.7), this is represented by means of the dashed straight line connecting the box that describes the percept of *watch* with the box for the force-dynamic process of fetching: the fetching event is categorized as an instance of the processual base of the percept of *watch*.

The configuration in Figure 10.7 is thus now similar to that in Figure 10.3, which is how it should be given that both configurations pertain to a complement interpretation. A difference seems to involve the fact that the box for the fetching event 'overspills' the boundaries of the box for *watch* in Figure 10.7 but not in Figure 10.3, where the whole of the box for the fetching event is depicted inside the box for the watching event. But, as was remarked above, the non-finite pattern is of course compatible with a scenario where the eventive percept of the watching event only corresponds to a subpart of the process profiled by the non-finite verb: one can watch somebody fetch a vase even if only a part of the fetching event is observed. As is pointed out by Egan (2008: 147–9), the use of an infinitive form over an *-ing* form with *watch* does not imply that the whole event profiled by the infinitive was witnessed. I have preferred not to represent this aspect explicitly in Figure 10.3, focusing instead on the dependency relation between watching and fetching. The fetching event is conceptually subordinate to the watching event, even if only a part of it may be observed, in the sense that it falls within the scope of the watcher's attention. In contrast, Figure 10.7 shows the potential 'overspilling' of the fetching event explicitly, so as to underline the origin of the *as*-complement interpretation from the *as*-temporal modifier interpretation. Intuitively, the 'overspilling' seems to be more salient in the case of the *as*-pattern than in the case of the non-finite pattern, although this point should be the subject of future research.

In sum, in this section I have argued that *as* does not always take a processual trajector (a clause) but can also take a nominal trajector (*Sally* in our example). In the VO*as* pattern, the string O*as* (*Sally as she fetched the vase*) is analysable as a 'complement' within which the *as*-clause functions similarly to what is traditionally regarded as a modifier. Independent evidence for this characterization of *as* is offered by examples such as (6), where the *as*-clause is akin to a relative clause (cf. '... drawing a picture of Sally, who was trying to teach Haysley to roll over'):

(6) Later in the evening I sat outside, drawing a picture of Sally **as** she tried to teach Haysley to roll over. It didn't come out right, so I crumpled up the page. (Tracey Baptiste, *Angel's Grace*, p. 22)

Needless to say, it is important not to confuse the traditional labels with the conceptualist position adopted in Cognitive Grammar. For the sake of convenience, however, I will say that in the VO*as* pattern the *as*-clause functions as a modifier, whose conceptual nature is explored in some detail by means of Figure 10.7.

10.4.3 The V*as* pattern

We now need to examine the V*as*-pattern, which, unlike the VO*as* pattern, lacks a nominal direct object. One possible analysis would be consonant with that adopted for the VO*as* pattern. This possibility is explored in abbreviated fashion in Figure 10.8, which only shows the final result of the compositional path.

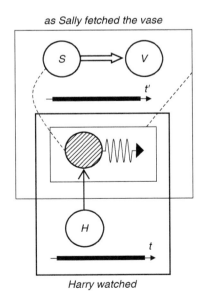

Figure 10.8 The V*as* pattern as involving a 'null' direct object

On this analysis, it is assumed that *watch* makes reference to a covert entity, represented as the hatched region in Figure 10.8, which is equated with the trajector of *fetched* in the *as*-clause. As before, the integration of the process of watching with the *as*-clause would require the fetching event to be construed as an instantiation of the processual base of the percept of *watch*. Still, this analysis is not completely satisfactory in Cognitive Grammar because it would be similar to recognizing the existence of a null element (a null direct object) which is coreferential with the trajector of *fetched*, symbolically *Harry watched $\emptyset_i$ as Sally$_i$ fetched the vase*. Given Cognitive Grammar's Content Requirement (see Langacker 2008: 24–6), which bans empty elements such as null objects in the sense of generative grammar, it is worth asking whether alternatives exist. My answer is affirmative and is summarized in Figure 10.9.

In Figure 10.9, the trajector of *as* is analysed not as the person/thing that is part of the percept of *watch* but as the whole percept. Further, unlike the analysis in Figure 10.8, there is no 'null' direct object, in that *Sally* is equated with the trajector of the processual percept of the verb *watch*. In other words, the event of fetching is projected onto the percept of *watch*. However, it should be observed that only a portion of the event of fetching is in fact equated with the percept of *watch*, which is what the middle tier in Figure 10.9 is intended to show. Watching implies the tracking through time of a person/thing; *as* here restricts the temporal scope of the fetching event to a subpart and it is this subpart that corresponds to the percept of *watch* or, to put it differently, it is this subpart that is tracked through time by the watcher (*Harry*). Hence, t, the amount of time that the event of watching occupies, is a subpart of t', the temporal profile of the whole event of fetching. Crucially, the relation of temporal containment is derivative because containment stems from the fact that the percept of *watch* is a subpart of the fetching event. If this were not so, we would end up with the temporal modifier interpretation illustrated in Figure 10.3. Instead, in the case depicted in Figure 10.9, *as* is in effect functioning as an imperfectivizer (see also Broccias 2011), that is, in a similar capacity to an *-ing* form. *As*, like *-ing*, restricts the scope of attention to a subpart of the process profiled by the verb appearing in the *as*-clause in the sense that the beginning and end points of this process are not in focus.

Indirect support for an analysis along the lines of Figure 10.9 may come from considering the contrast in (7):

(7) a. Harry saw Sally as she fetched the vase.
    b. *Harry saw as Sally fetched the vase.

See differs from *watch* in that a processual base for the person/thing which is coded as a direct object is much less salient than with *watch*. While one watches someone/something because one is interested in the course of

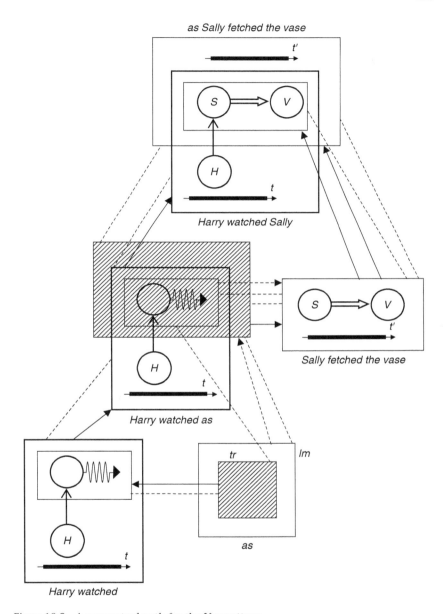

Figure 10.9 A conceptual path for the V*as* pattern

action in which that person/thing is involved or may be involved, *see* highlights the perception of a person/thing rather than the tracking through time of an entity. If the analysis offered in Figure 10.8 were on the right track, we should expect (7b) to be possible. *Sally* would correspond to the 'null' object of *saw*. Instead, if we opt for the analysis in Figure 10.9, we could argue that the percept of *saw* cannot instantiate the process profiled in the *as*-clause because the processual character of the former is not sufficiently strong. In other words, there appears to be a clash between the extended nature of the *as*-event and the nature of the percept of the verb *see*, which does not necessarily involve temporal extension. This may ultimately be related to the punctual nature of the verb *see* itself. It seems that the temporal extension implied by the *as*-clause must be mirrored by the matrix event, but this mirroring of temporality (or lack thereof) is only compatible with a conceptual representation along the lines of Figure 10.9.

10.5   Conclusion

In this chapter I have studied hypotactic integration within a Cognitive Grammar framework. One of the advantages of Cognitive Grammar is that it goes beyond traditional labels such as 'head', 'complement' and 'modifier' by investigating the conceptual operations that account for their emergence in linguistic analysis. Also, Cognitive Grammar makes extensive use of diagrams, which are employed as a heuristic tool for exploring meaning. These two aspects have played a crucial role in the present investigation. I have first pointed out that the interpretation of *as*-clauses as depicting eventive percepts should not be dismissed as a 'pragmatic' reading, but rather should be treated as an instance of a construction in its own right which competes with the non-finite pattern. The analysis of the non-finite pattern has led me to the conclusion that the head of the non-finite complement is indeterminate: it can be equated with either the verbal process or the person/thing engaged in it. The latter analysis, in particular, implies that an infinitive verb could, in some sense, be regarded as a relative, using traditional terminology. In the case of the *as*-pattern, I have underlined that a paradox seems to exist between the relation of containment demanded by the *as*-clause as a temporal modifier and its use as a means of depicting an eventive percept, which requires the watching event to have scope over the perceived event. I have argued that this paradox can be resolved by restricting the relation of containment to a subpart of the perceiving process, namely that including the percept. This conceptual representation amounts to viewing (in part) the *as*-clause in the VO*as* pattern as a noun modifier. Turning to the V*as* pattern, I have proposed that the *as*-clause functions as a complement. In particular, the temporal subordinator can be viewed as an imperfectivizer, allowing the percept to be equated with at least a subpart of the event expressed by the temporal clause.

The present study thus shows that a detailed investigation of hypotactic integration demands reference to the complexities of conceptual integration and highlights the need to go beyond traditional syntactic labels by exploring their conceptual underpinnings. It also makes us aware of the changing nature of the subordinator *as*, which at least in conjunction with perceptions verbs, seems to have developed, in a sense, into a complementizer.

Notes

1. Correlation, of course, is not the same as causation in the sense that a post-verbal position does not necessarily force a percept interpretation upon an *as*-clause, as the following example shows:

   (i) White House 'watching' as state of emergency called (http://www.theguardian. com/world/egypt, 15 August 2013)

   (i), which refers to the social unrest that occurred in Egypt in the summer of 2013 resulting in President Morsi's deposition, contains an *as*-clause which functions as a temporal adjunct. The United States is 'on the watch', that is, it is keeping an eye on events unfolding in Egypt after the ousting of President Morsi. It may be worth pointing out, however, that so far I have not come across any examples of a preposed *as*-clause which functions as a percept rather than as a temporal adjunct.
2. Corpus data show that the most common pattern of hypotactic integration for visual perception verbs involves the verb *watch* and the subordinator *as* (see Broccias 2010).
3. Traditionally, one of the tests used to distinguish between 'complement' and 'adjunct' is the *do so* test (see, for example, Huddleston and Pullum 2002: 222–3) but, as my focus is on functional equivalence and I do not regard 'complement' and 'adjunct' as primitive syntactic concepts (see section 10.3), I will omit any discussion of this test here.
4. It is unlikely, however, that the V*as* pattern under discussion is related to such dialectal uses. Broccias (2014) shows that V*as* is a relatively recent pattern. Until the end of the nineteenth century the preferred pattern for hypotactic integration was VO*as* rather than V*as* (see also example (3) above from the late nineteenth-century writer Hardy).
5. The *as*-pattern is of course not limited to the verb *watch*. The prepositional verb *listen*, which like *watch* has a durative nature (vs the punctual nature of *hear* and *see*, respectively), can also be used in the VO*as* and V*as* patterns, as is shown in (ii) below. Here, the label 'O' must be understood as also covering prepositional objects such as *to Sally* in (iia).

   (ii) a. Harry listened to Sally as she spoke about climate change. (VO*as* pattern)
       b. Harry listened as Sally spoke about climate change. (V*as* pattern)

6. See http://www.ldoceonline.com/dictionary/watch_1.
7. I have also omitted the temporal arrow in the box depicting the event Sally may be engaged in because this would lead to a discussion of the difference between the notions of summary and sequential scanning, which I do not subscribe to (see Broccias and Hollmann 2007), at least in cases such as those analysed here.

References

Broccias, C. (2010) 'As-Simultaneity Clauses as Complements of Perception Verbs: the Case of Watch'. *Textus*, XXIII (3): 583–602.

Broccias, C. (2011) 'A Puzzle for the Present: a Cognitive Grammar Analysis of Present Tense Simultaneity As-Clauses' in B. Bierwiaczonek, B. Cetnarowska and A. Turula (eds) *Syntax in Cognitive Grammar* (Częstochowa: Wyższa Szkoła Lingwistyczna), pp. 259–72.

Broccias, C. (2014) 'Watching As-Clauses in Late Modern English' in S. Pfenninger, O. Timofeeva, A.-C. Gardner, A. Honkapohja, M. Hundt and D. Schreier (eds) *Contact, Variation, and Change in the History of English* (Amsterdam: Benjamins), pp. 137–61.

Broccias, C. and W. Hollmann (2007) 'Do We Need Scanning in (Cognitive) Grammar?' *Cognitive Linguistics*, 18 (4): 487–522.

Croft, W. (2001) *Radical Construction Grammar: Syntactic Theory in Typological Perspective* (Oxford: Oxford University Press).

Deutscher, G. (2000) *Syntactic Change in Akkadian. The Evolution of Sentential Complementation* (Oxford: Oxford University Press).

Egan T. (2008) *Non-Finite Complementation. A Usage-Based Study of Infinitive and -ing Clauses in English* (Amsterdam: Rodopi).

Fischer, O. (2007) *Morphosyntactic Change: Functional and Formal Perspectives* (Oxford: Oxford University Press).

Gisborne, N. (2010) *The Event Structure of Perception Verbs* (Oxford: Oxford University Press).

Goldberg, A. (2013) 'Constructionist Approaches' in T. Hoffmann and G. Trousdale (eds) *The Oxford Handbook of Construction Grammar* (Oxford: Oxford University Press), pp. 15–31.

Huddleston R. and G. Pullum (2002) *The Cambridge Grammar of the English Language* (Cambridge: Cambridge University Press).

Langacker, R. (2008) *Cognitive Grammar: a Basic Introduction* (Oxford: Oxford University Press).

OED = *Oxford English Dictionary* Online (http://www.oed.com/).

Quirk, R., S. Greenbaum, G. Leech and J. Svartvik (1985) *A Comprehensive Grammar of the English Language* (London: Longman).

Silva, M. (1991) 'Simultaneity in Children's Narratives: the Case of *When, While* and *As*'. *Journal of Child Language*, 18: 641–62.

11

Control in Free Adjuncts in English and French: a Corpus-Based Semantico-Pragmatic Account

Patrick J. Duffley and Samuel Dion-Girardeau
Université Laval

11.1 Introduction

Three main sorts of approaches to control can be found in the linguistic literature: syntactic, semantic and pragmatic. The syntactic approach can be exemplified by Boeckx et al. (2010), who treat obligatory control as syntactic movement rather than binding, making PRO 'simply a residue of movement – the product of the copy-and-deletion operations that relate two theta-positions' (Hornstein 1999: 78). Thus in the derivation of *John hopes to leave*, *John* starts out in the subordinate VP *[John leave]* and raises to the sentential level, checking two theta-roles on its way and ending up with two cases, one corresponding to the 'hoper' and the other to the 'leaver' role. This purportedly explains the subject control reading (henceforth SC). In a purely conceptual approach such as that of Culicover and Jackendoff (2005), it is the semantic content of the matrix verb rather than syntactic movement which is the key factor. They argue that since control remains constant with a given lexical notion over a wide variety of constructions it cannot be a syntactic phenomenon – thus in (1a–d) below with the notion 'order', the NP *Fred* is understood to control *leave* in all cases even though its syntactic position varies considerably:

(1a) Bill ordered Fred to leave immediately.
(1b) Fred's order from Bill to leave immediately.
(1c) The order from Bill to Fred to leave immediately.
(1d) Fred received Bill's order to leave immediately.

Culicover and Jackendoff propose that with non-finite action complements only one controller is possible – 'the character to which the head assigns the role of actor for that action – whatever its syntactic position' (Culicover and Jackendoff 2003: 524): with *promise* the complement's subject is controlled by 'the giver/maker of the promise, wherever that character may be located in syntax' (Culicover and Jackendoff 2003: 529); with *persuade* the controller is always the person persuaded. An example of a pragmatic approach is Levinson (1987), who argues that 'the grammatical patterns follow the patterns predicted by our pragmatic apparatus: minimal forms prefer co-referential readings, less minimal forms prefer disjoint readings' (Levinson 1987: 420). Thus *Zelda₁ asked Mary₂ [PRO₂ to leave]*, being a non-minimal form with a direct object, favours a disjoint reading, that is, non-subject control (henceforth NSC); in contrast, *Zelda asked [PRO₁ to leave]*, a minimal form with no object, triggers a coreferential interpretation, ergo SC. These inferences are based on Levinson's I-principle according to which a speaker will say as little as necessary to convey his intended message.

Each of these approaches has its shortcomings. Without recourse to meaning, a strictly syntactic approach has no way to distinguish between *John managed to leave* and *John motioned to leave*, which leaves one with no explanation for why *John* is not assigned two thematic roles in the latter but is exclusively cast as the 'motioner'. By tying control to thematic roles determined by the matrix and defined independently of any particular configuration of sign–meaning units, Culicover and Jackendoff's approach abstracts away from the linguistically signified content of the utterance. Careful consideration of the evidence shows however that this is not feasible. On the lexical level, the content of the subject of *promise* and its pragmatic relation to the infinitive's event can in some cases have a determining impact on control, as can be seen from (2):

(2) There are dozens of programmes that promise you to have the body you always wanted to have in a very short period of time.[1]

On the grammatical level, the meaning of the complement form itself is also pertinent – with the very same matrix verb *choose*, the *to*-infinitive is exclusively attested with SC, whereas the gerund-participle also allows NSC, as shown in Duffley and Abida (2009):

(3) The federal government chose to make unemployment insurance harder to get, and changed the name of the programme to Employment Insurance.

(4) I've been teaching a course on Game Culture and Design […] and am in the midst of conducting some hands-on workshops with the students. We're building game mechanics and rules systems playable on the table-top. […] I deliberately chose going to the movies as a concept because it's a broad topic and doesn't immediately evoke game play ideas.

With regard to Levinson's pragmatic approach, his I-principle is unable to account for the difference in control between objectless infinitival and gerund-participial constructions such as:

(5a) John wanted to read *Brideshead Revisited*.

(5b) John suggested reading *Brideshead Revisited*.

Here the *to*-infinitive construction is more complex, being composed of *to* plus the bare stem; nevertheless, it is the *to*-infinitive that exhibits constant SC readings in such objectless structures, while the gerund-participle shows variability in control: SC with verbs like *enjoy, try* and *remember*, NSC with *suggest, advise* and *justify* (cf. Duffley 2006: 47–52).

In view of such facts, one can only agree with Kortmann (1991: 77) that 'any attempt to develop a theory able to predict the selection of a particular controller in a uniform way, especially when choosing a monocausal (for instance, solely semantics- or syntax-based) approach is bound to fail' and with Landau (2013: 254) who argues that non-obligatory control, of which adjunct control is a subcategory, 'falls outside the purview of core grammar and is best analyzed as a complex outcome of pragmatic factors'. The study of control in free adjuncts presented here will provide further evidence in favour of the need for a semantico-pragmatic explanation of adjunct control based on a complex interaction between such factors as the lexical meanings of the matrix subject and predicate, the lexical and grammatical meanings in the free adjunct, the position in the sentence occupied by the adjunct, and shared world knowledge of stereotypical scenarios.

Besides the generative studies by Williams (1992) and Kawasaki (1993), based on author-fabricated examples, a certain number of corpus-based explorations of free adjuncts have been carried out. Kortmann (1991) examines 1680 occurrences of free adjuncts and absolute constructions in a 450,000-word corpus and brings to light a number of significant generalizations. One is the fact that 91.5 per cent of his free adjuncts showed SC. Kortmann also investigates the contextual factors associated with NSC, two of which are relevant to our study. The most important of these is the presence of 'dummy subjects' (for example, *Driving at a speed of 100 m.p.h., it is not easy to read the road signs*); the other factor concerns 'speech-act qualifiers' (as in **To consider the real cases first,** *how narrow indeed is the distinction*), which do not modify the main clause but rather characterize an act performed by the speaker. However, whereas Kortmann lumps together all of the various types of item found in these constructions (infinitives, gerund-participles, past participles, nouns, adjectives, prepositional and adverbial phrases), the approach adopted here will aim at building up from the linguistic–semantic to the pragmatic level, and consequently will only examine two forms whose semantics we believe we have a sufficient grasp of – the infinitive and the gerund-participle. We have also excluded absolute constructions because they do not pose any problem for determining control assignment since the controller is always the nominal preceding the non-finite verbal (as in *I stood there alone, **my friends eating at another table**,* for instance). Moreover, the infinitive and the gerund-participle will be studied separately in order to ascertain the possible effects of their semantic content on their behaviour with respect to control.

Another corpus study of adjuncts was carried out on Early Modern English by Río-Rey (2002), who analysed 1183 free adjuncts and absolute constructions in a corpus of 252,000 words from texts published between 1500 and 1710. She found an even higher percentage of free adjuncts with NSC – 12.1 per cent. The focus of Río-Rey's study was the diachronic evolution of free adjuncts as opposed to absolute constructions, and so it does not identify factors favouring NSC or show how they contribute to producing this effect.

A third corpus-based study is Hayase (2011), who examined 956 examples from the British National Corpus of dangling modifiers involving gerund-participles in sentence-initial position with 96 specific lexemes, namely verbs of cognition (*supposing*), physical motion (*walking*), perception (*looking*), physical states (*standing*) and physical activities (*opening*). This study has a much more limited scope than ours in that it only examined the -*ing* form and only with certain types of lexeme. Hayase treats the structure as a ground-before-figure construction in which the participial clause 'describes an (atemporal) unbounded background situation (the ground), while the main clause describes a bounded (temporal) situation of Cognition or Perception (the figure), and the semantic link between them is inferred' (Hayase 2011: 99). While the tenseless nature of the gerund-participle and its placement in initial position do lend themselves to setting up a ground with respect to the main-clause predication, this is not the only effect this configuration can produce. Hayase's account runs into difficulty with cases where the participle denotes a punctual action such as:

(6) **Opening the exit to the fifth and top floor**, out came wafts of grey choking smoke.

The prior position of the gerund-participle is exploited iconically here to symbolize the chronological sequence holding between two actions and to suggest a cause–effect relationship, not to institute a ground–figure relation.

The fourth and final corpus-based study of which we are aware is Lyngfelt's (2002) investigation of Swedish, presented as extendable to English in Lyngfelt (2009). In the Swedish data he found three properties favouring NSC in adverbial adjuncts:

(a) sentence-initial position
(b) passive matrix verb
(c) expletive matrix subject

The first and third factors have already been evoked above; the second can be illustrated by:

(7) The study was done **using a well-tested methodology**.

As the English examples show, all three of Lyngfelt's factors are at work in NSC readings with free adjuncts in English.

A review of the literature on French shows that the only corpus analysis of free adjuncts is Combettes' (1998) book on detached constructions, which is based both on examples from grammars and previous studies, and on literary sources and the press. Like Kortmann, he includes among detached constructions absolute constructions containing their own linguistically expressed controller. Combettes proposes that such constructions obey 'grammaticalization', whereby a text-structuring device whose nature is essentially pragmatic/informational is integrated into syntactic structure. Detached constructions are divided into two types according to their degree of syntactic integration: (i) those equivalent to subordinate circumstantial clauses, which are only loosely integrated and allow syntactic dislocation; (ii) those equivalent to subordinate explicative clauses, which are strongly integrated and often accompanied by thematic breaks, being attached to a new rhematic element. This approach is similar in spirit to our own, although it is concerned with the textual function of detached structures rather than the problem of pinpointing what accounts for control.

There is thus a need for a corpus-based approach to control in infinitival and participial free adjuncts both in English and in French. The lone French study deals with this topic in the context of a broader investigation into the textual function of all detached constructions. In English, no large-scale corpus analysis of control in free adjuncts focusing on the English gerund-participle and infinitive has been carried out in order to verify the relative importance of the factors identified in previous studies or to investigate whether other factors such as the meanings of the forms themselves are at work in determining control. In order to remedy this situation, the 1 million-word International Corpus of English-Great Britain (ICE-GB) and a 300,000-word subsection of the French Treebank Corpus[2] (FTB) were examined for occurrences of the participle and infinitive in adverbial function. These corpora were chosen because they are both tagged and parsed, and allowed systematic extraction of all of the structures under study, thus providing a basis for statistical generalizations.

11.2   The English data

A total of 4133 occurrences of the two forms in adverbial function were analysed in English (1748 of the gerund-participle and 2385 of the infinitive). These had to be treated manually in order to separate out the free adjuncts: 1250 gerund-participles and 1911 infinitives.[3] One general observation based on the data is that the proportion of unattached or dangling gerund-participial and infinitival adjuncts was significantly higher than that found in previous studies. The gerund-participle showed 29 per cent and the infinitive 24 per cent NSC in free adjunct function. Nevertheless, SC still remains the norm for adjuncts, a datum which Combettes (1998: 40–1) argues is a reflection of the fact that the subject usually corresponds to the theme in information structure, it being natural for a secondary predication to apply to the utterance theme.

11.2.1 The gerund-participle

All three factors identified by Lyngfelt for Swedish were found to be relevant for NSC with the gerund-participle in English as well. Of the 1250 occurrences of -*ing* in free adjuncts, 141 fell into his three categories: NSC was observed in all 38 sequences with expletive matrix subjects (see Table 11.1), 66 of the 71 cases with passive matrix verbs (see Table 11.2), and 66 of the 238 sequences with initial position of the gerund-participle.[4]

The NSC ratio was both statistically significant and very high with the latter two categories: 93 per cent of passive matrix verb structures (vs 25 per cent for active voice) and 100 per cent of expletive matrix subject (vs 26 per cent in other cases) examples exhibited NSC. However, a number of divergences from Lyngfelt's findings also surfaced. Firstly, although sentence-initial gerund-participles represented a significant percentage of NSC (18 per cent of the 361 total), there were almost three times as many sentence-initial gerund-participles with SC as with NSC (172 vs 66). Overall therefore, initial position of the gerund-participle favours SC, which only makes sense due to the adjective-like nature of the -*ing*, its syntactic contiguity to the main-clause subject when it is in initial position, and the tendency noted by Combettes for a secondary predication to be applied to the overall utterance theme. More

Table 11.1 Contingency table: control type by matrix subject type for adjuncts with gerund-participle (English)

| | Matrix subject type | |
	Non-expletive subject	Expletive subject
Subject control	889 (74%)	0 (0%)
Non-subject control	323 (26%)	38 (100%)
Total	1,212 (100%)	38 (100%)

$\chi^2 \approx 93$; *p*-value < 0.01.[5]

Table 11.2 Contingency table: control type by matrix verb voice for adjuncts with gerund-participle (English)

| | Matrix subject voice | |
	Active	Passive
Subject control	884 (75%)	5 (7%)
Non-subject control	295 (25%)	66 (93%)
Total	1,179 (100%)	71 (100%)

$\chi^2 \approx 147$; *p*-value < 0.01.

importantly, over half of the 361 cases of NSC (53 per cent) did not exhibit any of the three properties identified by Lyngfelt. Among these, one type of construction even outranked all three of Lyngfelt's properties by a significant margin: structures with a sentence-final gerund-participle clause controlled by the whole proposition expressed by the matrix clause – what Williams (1985) describes as 'event control'. These accounted for 111 occurrences of NSC. This type is illustrated by the two examples below where the adjunct is paraphrasable by 'and **that** would leave/cause', with the demonstrative corresponding to the entire content of the preceding main clause:

(8) In order to reach orbit a V-2 would have to be filled with propellant up to as much as 98% of its take-off weight, **leaving only 2% for everything else.** (ICE-GB W2B-035)
(9) Consequently this layer will undergo starvation and ultimately death, **causing the entire biofilm to detach from its support.** (ICE-GB W2A-021)

The final position of the gerund-participle clause is an important factor contributing to the event control interpretation here, which was often associated with an impression of logical consequence as in (8) and (9) above; an impression that can be explained as a pragmatic effect deriving from the word order being exploited iconically. Another relevant factor was the lexical meaning of the gerund-participle: resultative notions such as *leave* in (8) above accounted for over 50 cases, causatives as in (9) for over 20 and lexemes denoting permission like *allow* for 15.

Another frequent case of NSC occurred with metalinguistic expressions as in:

(10) That's obviously not the reaction, well **judging from the way she behaved.** (ICE-GB S1A-080)

This type of structure, of which 46 instances were found in the corpus, can be paraphrased by a conditional clause and functions as a way of hedging the assertion made in the main clause by specifying the point of view from which this assertion is made or the conditions under which it is valid. Seventy per cent of the 46 occurrences of this structure manifested NSC (see Table 11.3).

The next most frequent type has also escaped notice in previous studies. Eight cases were found in which the controller of a gerund-participle adjunct was the implicit subject of another gerund-participle or infinitive, as in:

(11) To take Beckett's earlier works as being important for what they tell us about Beckett's better known later writings is *to grant* these early texts secondary status, **while still claiming that they contain more**

Table 11.3 Contingency table: control type by function type for adjuncts with gerund-participle (English)

	Adjunct function	
	Metadiscursive	Other
Subject control	14 (30%)	875 (73%)
Non-subject control	32 (70%)	329 (27%)
Total	46 (100%)	1,204 (100%)

$\chi^2 \approx 36$; p-value < 0.01.

> **transparent evidence of the author's underlying intentions.** (ICE-GB W2A-004)

Related to these, one case was found in which the controller was the implied agent of the action denoted by a deverbal noun:

> (12) However, lack of telial material on leeks in the UK has prevented *classification* **using this system.** (ICE-GB W2A-028)

This is clear evidence of the essentially pragmatic character of control assignment: in (12) the noun *classification* logically implies an agent performing the action of classifying, and due to the natural relation between a classifier and the use of a classificatory system, it is this agent who is interpreted as the person using the system in order to classify leeks.

Two cases were also found that did not fit into any of the above categories. In (13) below, the controller corresponds to an entity, the new form of Thames barge, whose existence is implied by the overall content of the matrix clause:

> (13) The form of the Thames barge evolved in the early nineteenth century, **replacing an earlier more primitive kind of sailing vessel.** (ICE-GB S2B-022)

Example (14) illustrates an intratextual use of a gerund-participle adjunct, whose controller corresponds to the content of the matrix clause that it introduces:

> (14) The Sigma makes sensible use of its technology, it cruises very well and it comes with a three-year warranty. **Countering that**, it has a bland appearance. (ICE-GB S2A-055)

Here the non-specificity of the gerund-participle's implicit subject is exploited as an anticipatory device signalling the forthcoming introduction of something countering the positive qualities of the Sigma.

11.2.2 The infinitive

As with the gerund-participle, the data showed that both passive matrix verbs and expletive matrix subjects favour NSC with infinitives. Regarding the first factor, 82 per cent of the 324 examples with passive matrix predicates exhibited NSC, as can be seen in Table 11.4; regarding the second, all 13 cases of expletive subjects showed NSC as well, as shown in Table 11.5.

Within the 18 per cent of SC readings with passives, two factors were found which facilitated the SC interpretation: (i) animate matrix subjects (42 per cent of the 58 cases of SC, cf. (15) below); and (ii) expressions of the type: *X is/was made/designed/created/prepared/produced to do Y* (30 per cent of SC, cf. (16) below):

(15) Patients entered in this study would be randomised **to receive a standard three-weekly regimen or the weekly intensive regimen.** (ICE-GB S2A-035)

(16) The copy was made at an earlier stage, uh maybe in the 7th century, **to go with the first basilica on the site.** (ICE-GB S2A-060)

However, the representation of the matrix subject as passive was over-whelmingly associated with NSC. The reason for this is pragmatic: since the matrix subject is represented as passive, it cannot easily be construed

Table 11.4 Contingency table: control type by matrix verb voice for adjuncts with gerund-participle (English)

	Matrix subject voice	
	Active	Passive
Subject control	1,397 (88%)	58 (18%)
Non-subject control	190 (12%)	266 (82%)
Total	1,587 (100%)	324 (100%)

$\chi^2 \approx 724$; p-value < 0.01.

Table 11.5 Contingency table: control type by matrix subject type for adjuncts with infinitive (English)

	Matrix subject type	
	Non-expletive subject	Expletive subject
Subject control	1,455 (77%)	0 (0%)
Non-subject control	443 (23%)	13 (100%)
Total	1,898 (100%)	13 (100%)

$\chi^2 \approx 38$; p-value < 0.01.

as acting for a purpose. Confirmation of this was found with stative matrix predicates, all five of which also exhibited NSC, as in:

(17) **To enable backtracking up the menu structure**, each menu object contains a pointer back up to its parent menu. (ICE-GB W1A-005)

Here the matrix subject is not acting at all, and so, as with passives, does not lend itself to being construed as acting for a purpose.

Lyngfelt's third factor favouring NSC, sentence-initial position, was indeed found to be slightly more frequent with this reading with the infinitive (54 per cent of the 81 occurrences of sentence-initial *to*-infinitive adjuncts), as opposed to the gerund-participle which exhibited only 18 per cent NSC in this position. In all cases, however, NSC was associated with some other contributing factor:

(a) metalinguistic function (cf. (18) and Table 11.6), 48 per cent of the 44 NSC contexts;
(b) passive matrix predicates (cf. (19) below), 36 per cent of NSC contexts;
(c) impersonal matrix predicates expressing deontic necessity (cf. (20) below), 9 per cent of NSC;
(d) inanimate matrix subjects (cf. (21) below), 7 per cent of NSC.

(18) But **to be candid**, she felt some doubt on the matter. (ICE-GB W2F-011)
(19) **To make the system more flexible**, a new function was written at the request of the survey. (ICE-GB W1A-005)
(20) **To build a vehicle that could achieve the speed required to put a satellite in orbit**, it therefore became necessary to build a series of vehicles mounted on top of each other. (ICE-GB W2B-035)
(21) However, **in order to maintain a near normal rhythm of speech**, the monitoring of the feedback is not so thorough. (ICE-GB W1A-016)

Table 11.6 Contingency table: control type by function type for adjuncts with infinitive (English)

	Adjunct function	
	Metadiscursive	Other
Subject control	34 (62%)	1,411 (76%)
Non-subject control	21 (38%)	435 (24%)
Total	55 (100%)	1,846 (100%)

$\chi^2 \approx 36$; p-value < 0.02.

The significantly higher proportion of SC with fronted *-ing* forms is due to the adjective-like character of the gerund-participle which leads it to be associated more readily with the most salient NP in the sentence – the matrix subject representing the utterance topic. The significant difference observed between the two forms of adjunct in initial position justifies our methodological decision to look at them separately so as to ascertain the possible effects of their particular semantic content on their behaviour with respect to control.

As with the gerund-participle, a considerable number of cases were found in which sentence-initial or sentence-final position was associated with event control (all of the 111 cases of event control occurring with the infinitive were in one of these two positions, 89 per cent final, 11 per cent initial). The most frequent structure (sentence-final) is illustrated in (22), the less frequent one in (23):

(22) Both fuel and oxidant were pumped together into the rocket motor, where they burned together **to produce hot gas at high pressure.** (ICE-GB W2B-035)

(23) **To prevent confusion between Occam channels and Mascot channels**, all text referring to Mascot channels will use a capital C. (ICE-GB W2A-038)

The position after the matrix is most often associated with an impression of temporal subsequence, the first event being felt to be the cause bringing the infinitive's event into existence, an impression which is not so clearly felt when the infinitive is in initial position. Thus, as with the gerund-participle, word order plays an iconic role guiding the pragmatic interpretation of the relation between the two events with the infinitive as well. The types of lexeme found with the infinitive and the gerund-participle are roughly similar: the top three with the infinitive included verbs of allowing (21 cases), helping (21 cases) and producing (15 cases).[6]

As with the gerund-participle, the controller of an infinitival adjunct can be pragmatically implied by another infinitive, as in (24), a gerund-participle (25), or even a deverbal noun (26):

(24) Both Marx and Lenin formulated theories on how *to increase* development in the 'Third World' **in order to decrease the 'gap' between the industrialized countries of the North and the agrarian/subsistence states mainly situated in the South.** (ICE-GB W1A-015)

(25) The training process consists of inputting the desired patterns in sequence, and *using* the delta (or Wedrow-Hoff) rule **to alter the connection weights.** (ICE-GB W2A-032)

(26) The vast majority of electronic enthusiasts will certainly own a sizable conglomeration of the most wonderful odds and ends tucked carefully away in every conceivable corner of the home. [...] Every

now and then, *a tidy up* is in order, if only **to muse for a while over the priceless cache.** (ICE-GB W2B-032)

The *to*-infinitive does not require its implicit subject to be any more precise than the unspecified agent implied by the non-finite verbal or deverbal noun preceding it. It is not surprising therefore to find infinitival adjuncts in contexts involving dilution of responsibility. Thus in the sentence below no one in particular is represented as responsible for doing something to improve the course referred to:

(27) What do the students think of the course in general and the B.A. and what could be done **to improve it?** (ICE-GB S1A-008)

Like the gerund-participle, the *to*-infinitive is used in a wide variety of style disjuncts, the two most frequent types involving reference to the speaker's sincerity and introduction of an example:

(28) Well, his recent work's shit, actually, **to be blunt.** (ICE-GB S1A-045)
(29) I mean, just **to give you a sort of swift example,** supposing uhm you've got a chain of gas stations [...] and they have one independent competitor. (ICE-GB S1B-005)

To-infinitive phrases can thus act as a device for the speaker to let the hearer know how he intends some portion of the discourse to be construed. This is consonant with the purposive meaning of the preposition *to* introducing the infinitive.

In some cases, there is a very large dose of pragmatics in the mix. Thus in the context below our encyclopedic knowledge of cooking and the reason why people put things in fridges guides the interpretation:

(30) When finished, shape into rolls, about 4–5 inches long and 1 inch thick and put these, if there is time, in the fridge **to chill for 1/4 hour.** (ICE-GB W2D-020)

If *chill* were replaced by *keep from thawing out*, SC would be induced due to the incompatibility of food with the agentive role in keeping something from thawing out. The external situation can also play a crucial role in control, a case in point being:

(31) Where are the vegetarians, **to give them the vegetarian dinner?** (ICE-GB S1A-011)

Here the *to*-infinitive expresses the purpose of the speaker's question about the place where the vegetarians are seated, and world knowledge about what someone asking such a question will do with the information guides the interpretation, which could be either that the speaker is going to give the vegetarians their dinner or the waiters working under his orders.

11.3 The French data

A roughly 300,000-word subsection of the French Treebank Corpus has been morphosyntactically and functionally annotated, which allowed us to extract all the infinitival and participial verb phrases marked as modifiers.[7] After automatically pruning away the past participle and absolute constructions, 1663 free adjunct candidates were left. Of these, 350 verb phrases wrongly tagged as modifiers were discarded,[8] bringing the total number of relevant free adjuncts to 1313: 809 infinitives and 504 present participles. As expected, the majority of adjuncts were SC. However, 29 per cent of infinitivals and 17 per cent of participials displayed NSC; compared to the results of previous studies, these proportions are significantly higher. Comparing these statistics with those derived from the English data is neither the purpose of this chapter nor methodologically sound procedure, as the French and English corpora used in this study are not comparable. Any difference one might attribute to the specific character of one of the two languages could actually be a matter of genre or medium, the FTB consisting of only written newspaper articles often related to economic matters, while the ICE-GB includes both spoken and written texts on a variety of topics from a wide assortment of genres.

11.3.1 The present participle

As was the case for English, several factors concerning the matrix clause were found to favour the appearance of NSC in participial adjuncts. For instance, as Table 11.7 shows, all eight cases with expletive *il* as matrix subject were NSC, for obvious semantic reasons. We found this type of constructions with *il* + *être* + ADJ + *de* (*il est nécessaire de* [*it is necessary to*], *il est possible de* [*it is possible to*]), and with *il* + VERB (*il* + *convenir* [*it is good to*], *il* + *falloir* [*it is necessary to*]). The logical subject of the participle is understood to be either generic human as in (32), or a more specific agent,

Table 11.7 Contingency table: control type by matrix subject type for adjuncts with present participle (French)

	Matrix subject type	
	Non-expletive subject	Expletive subject
Subject control	419 (84%)	0 (0%)
Non-subject control	77 (16%)	8 (100%)
Total	496 (100%)	8 (100%)

p-value < 0.01.[9]

either implicit or explicit, as in (33) where the controller is identified by the pronoun *nous*.

(32) l'inflation sous-jacente, qu'il est possible de mesurer **en suivant l'évolution de l'indice des prix hors énergie et produits alimentaires**, était fin 1992 un peu supérieure à 3% l'an. (FTB, 271190)
[Underlying inflation, which it is possible to measure **by following the evolution of the consumer price index excluding energy and food**, was over 3% per year at the end of 1992.]

(33) Alors, **en attendant** « **que les choses changent**, il nous faut [...] montrer que nous [...] sommes capables de faire fonctionner nos centrales nucléaires sans incident ». (FTB, 249061)
[So, **while waiting for** 'things to change', it is necessary for us to show that we are able to operate our nuclear power plants without incident'.]

Passive voice in the matrix also seems to increase the likelihood of an NSC interpretation, which occurred in 55 per cent of the 11 cases, as Table 11.8 shows.

Here is a typical case:

(34) Les pays industrialisés ont aussi toutes sortes de problèmes spécifiques qui doivent être surmontés **en instituant une économie plus efficace et ouverte**. (FTB, 249057)
[Industrialized countries also have many specific problems that must be solved **by instituting a more efficient and open economy**.]

This example shows the relevance, for control assignment, of understanding the participants implied by the matrix verb: in almost all cases, the controller is the overt or covert agent of the passive. In the latter case, the context is especially decisive.

When we looked at possible NSC scenarios, we found event control to be particularly salient with the present participle (35 of 39 cases of event

Table 11.8 Contingency table: control type by matrix verb voice for adjuncts with present participle (French)

	Matrix verb voice	
	Active	Passive
Subject control	414 (84%)	5 (45%)
Non-subject control	79 (16%)	6 (55%)
Total	493 (100%)	11 (100%)

p-value < 0.01.[10]

control are with participial adjuncts). It is also noteworthy that all 35 adjuncts were in final position, as in (35) below, similarly to what was found in the English data; French too thus exploits the iconic placement of the adjunct to denote a cause–effect relation. This type of construction also appears to select certain kinds of verbs, notably those that denote a change-of-state or a cause–effect relationship.

(35) La liste des pays qui demandent à participer à cette nouvelle donne ne cesse de s'allonger, **ouvrant ainsi de nouvelles possibilités d'investissements et de commercialisation.** (FTB, 224968) [The list of countries asking to participate in this new opportunity keeps expanding, **opening up new investment and commercialization opportunities.**]

Another type of use was represented by cases like (36) below, where the adjunct is metadiscursive and thus does not modify an element in the sentence but refers to the speech or thought act underlying the sentence's utterance. Other forms found in the corpus were *en tenant compte de* [*taking into account*] and *en se référant à* [*referring to*]. Since these metadiscursive adjuncts have no formal marking, pragmatic inferences must necessarily be made in order to assign control with them. There were only five occurrences of this type of predication with present participle adjuncts, but all of them were NSC as shown in Table 11.9.

(36) **En excluant le profit exceptionnel enregistré en 1990,** [...] la hausse du bénéfice 1991 est de 21%. (FTB, 249489) [**Excluding the exceptional profit recorded in 1990,** profit growth in 1991 is 21%.]

Interestingly, the controller can also be an NP embedded in the subject of the matrix, as in (37) below, where it is obviously not the unemployment rate that affects 11 per cent of the active population but unemployment itself. The controller can also corefer with the possessor in a possessive determiner

Table 11.9 Contingency table: control type by function type for adjuncts with present participle (French)

	Adjunct function	
	Metadiscursive	Other
Subject control	0 (0%)	419 (84%)
Non-subject control	5 (100%)	80 (16%)
Total	5 (100%)	499 (100%)

p-value < 0.01.[11]

in another NP, as noted by Kortmann (1991: 66). In (38), one does not understand that the strategy is waiting, but rather the man employing it.

(37) **Touchant 11% de la population active,** le taux de chômage atteint actuellement son niveau le plus haut depuis 1985 [...]. (FTB, 249322)
[**Affecting 11% of the active population,** the unemployment rate is now at its highest point since 1985.]

(38) **En attendant que la justice se soit prononcée dans le sens qu'il espère,** sa tactique est, apparemment, d'entretenir le doute. (FTB, 249819)
[**While waiting for court to rule in his favour,** his strategy is, apparently, to sow doubt.]

11.3.2 The infinitive

Most of the factors relevant for control in participial adjuncts are also pertinent to infinitives. Thus, an expletive subject in the matrix always corresponds to NSC, as shown in Table 11.10. One particularly prominent pattern had an expression of deontic modality both in the adjunct and in the matrix clause; an overwhelming majority of the 63 cases of expletive subjects had *pour/afin de* (both meaning 'in order to') + INFINITIVE as the adjunct and *falloir* as the matrix verb, as in (39):

(39) il faudra d'autres réunions [...] **pour essayer d'avancer vers un accord.** (FTB, 249103)
[other meetings will be necessary **to try to move towards an agreement.**]

Similarly, passive voice in the matrix also shows a higher NSC ratio with infinitival adjuncts (66 per cent) than does active voice (25 per cent), as Table 11.11 shows.

In sentences like (40) below, a wide variety of factors come into play in assigning control, namely the presence of the reflexive pronoun *se*, which

Table 11.10 Contingency table: control type by matrix subject type for adjuncts with infinitive (French)

	Subject type	
	Non-expletive subject	Expletive subject
Subject control	578 (77%)	0 (0%)
Non-subject control	168 (23%)	63 (100%)
Total	746 (100%)	63 (100%)

$\chi^2 \approx 167$; p-value < 0.01.

Table 11.11 Contingency table: control type by matrix verb voice for adjuncts with infinitive (French)

	Matrix verb voice	
	Active	Passive
Subject control	557 (75%)	21 (34%)
Non-subject control	190 (25%)	41 (66%)
Total	747 (100%)	62 (100%)

$\chi^2 \approx 44$; p-value < 0.01.

must corefer with the implicit subject, the meaning of the verb *imposer* [*to impose*], which implies a patient, and the knowledge of typical scenarios regarding driving tests and law enforcement.

> (40) un délai de six mois est imposé par la loi [...] **avant de pouvoir se représenter au permis de conduire** [...]. (FTB, 249710)
> [A six-month waiting period is imposed by the law **before being able to take the driving test again.**]

A similar case to (40), which did not occur with participial adjuncts in our corpus although nothing would seem to exclude it, is when the matrix verb is in the reflexive. In French, transitive reflexive verbs can be pragmatically equivalent to passives in which the semantic patient becomes the subject and the reflexive pronoun *se* the object, as in *Ce livre se lit facilement* [*This book reads easily*] and *La grève se poursuivra* [*The strike will continue*]. The count of reflexive verbs in the matrix was too low for statistical significance, but example (41) below will serve to illustrate the phenomenon. This type of construction has no exact equivalent in English, where this type of effect can only be created by using the passive voice:

> (41) Le magistrat a ajouté que des discussions se poursuivraient avec Abou-Dhabi **pour tenter de maximiser l'indemnisation offerte aux déposants.** (FTB, 226479)
> [The magistrate added that discussions would continue with Abu Dhabi **to try to maximize the indemnities offered to depositors.**]

As with participial adjuncts, several metadiscursive infinitival adjuncts like the one in (42) below were found in the corpus, including: *pour ne citer que* [*to cite only*], *sans oublier* [*not to omit*], *à en juger par* [*judging by*], *pour le dire autrement* [*to put it in other words*], *sans parler de* [*not to speak of*], *à en croire* [*if one is to believe*] and *à supposer que* [*supposing that*]. In all examples, the implicit subject was either the generic human *on* or the speaker himself. The only two

Table 11.12 Contingency table: control type by function type for adjuncts with infinitive (French)

	Adjunct function	
	Metadiscursive	Other
Subject control	2 (7%)	576 (74%)
Non-subject control	26 (93%)	205 (26%)
Total	28 (100%)	781 (100%)

$\chi^2 \approx 56$; p-value < 0.01.

sentences where such an adjunct was SC occurred when the matrix subject was expressed by the generic pronoun *on* itself, as in (43). Table 11.12 shows that the ratio of NSC is significantly higher for metadiscursive adjuncts.

(42) **à y regarder de plus près**, le bilan n'est peut-être pas aussi sombre. (FTB, 248982)
[**looking more closely**, the bottom line perhaps is not so bad.]

(43) **À considérer les dégâts infligés aux bilans des banques et des compagnies d'assurances parisiennes** [...], on commence à en être moins sûr. (FTB, 270449)
[**Considering the damage inflicted on the balance sheets of Parisian banks and insurance companies**, people are beginning to have doubts.]

Event control is also possible for infinitival adjuncts, although it occurs much more frequently with participials. Sentence (44) below is one of the four cases of event control with an infinitive in the FTB. Adjunct position seems to be freer for infinitival adjuncts, as two out of the four cases were sentence-initial, whereas all 35 event-controlled participial adjuncts were sentence-final.

(44) Et **pour noircir encore le tableau**, le passage du cyclone Andrew sur les côtes de Floride devrait coûter près de 45 milliards de francs aux assureurs. (FTB, 271201)
[And **to make matters worse**, the aftermath of Hurricane Andrew on the coast of Florida will probably cost insurers nearly 45 billion francs.]

As with present participles, the controller can also be embedded in the matrix clause's NP subject, as in (45) below, or be coreferential with the possessor of a possessive determiner, as in (46). In these cases, semantic and pragmatic incompatibilities between the subject of the matrix and the adjunct require a search for other potential controllers than the subject: thus one understands in (45) that the operation has to be what highlights the presence of deposit sites, not the operation's profitability, and in (46) that the position cannot be construed as negotiating agreements, but rather those who hold it.

(45) La rentabilité de l'opération est jugée aléatoire, **sauf à mettre en évidence d'autres gisements dans la région.** (FTB, 249630) [The profitability of the operation is judged to be doubtful, **except for highlighting other deposit sites in the area.**]

(46) Notre position est de prendre les devants **pour négocier des accords qui n'entraînent qu'une baisse minime des salaires** [...]. (FTB, 249694) [Our position is to take the lead **to negotiate agreements that result only in a very slight decrease in wages.**]

Finally, another possibility is for the controller to be the agent of a noun. In (47), the infinitive *conseiller* is controlled by *M. Mllemann*, which is the explicit agent of the deverbal noun *intervention*.

(47) Stern avait déjà révélé une autre intervention de M. Mllemann auprès de supermarchés **afin de conseiller l'achat d'un produit fabriqué par un cousin de son épouse.** (FTB, 271314) [Stern had already revealed another manoeuvre by Mr Mllemann **to recommend to supermarkets the purchase of a product manufactured by his wife's cousin.**]

The French data thus show more or less the same possibilities for the identification of the implicit subject of the infinitive as the English data. This subject can be the implicit agent of a passive or reflexive, a generic human agent, the speaker, the event of the matrix, another NP in the matrix, the possessor in a possessive determiner, or the agent implied by a deverbal noun.

11.4 Conclusions

One general conclusion that can be made regarding frequency is that the proportion of NSC in our corpus was significantly higher than that found in previous studies: 29 per cent of infinitivals and 17 per cent of participials in French, 24 per cent of infinitivals and 29 per cent of gerund-participials in English. This seems to indicate considerable semantico-pragmatic flexibility with infinitival and participial free adjuncts in contemporary English and French, allowing the speaker to use adjuncts for various kinds of predications, including reference to many elements that are not explicitly represented linguistically. Moreover, somewhat unexpectedly this seems to occur predominantly in written texts: the ICE-GB is only 40 per cent written and yet 71 per cent of NSC with the gerund-participle and 57 per cent with the infinitive came from the written portion of the corpus, and all of the FTB is made up of written texts. One conclusion regarding English that can be drawn from our study is that the difference observed between the two forms in initial position justifies the methodological decision to look at them separately so as to ascertain the effect of their semantic content on their behaviour with respect to control: the significantly higher proportion of SC with fronted participles is due to the adjective-like character of this form which leads it to be associated more readily with the most salient NP in the sentence, the matrix subject representing the utterance topic. In both languages, final position of the participle is exploited iconically with event control to imply a cause–effect relation between the actions expressed by the matrix and the adjunct. It is also worth noting that both languages make frequent use of metadiscursive adjuncts. These constructions seem to have undergone various degrees of lexicalization and can often be translated in the other language by a similar structure with a non-finite verbal that is also likely to display NSC.

On an even more general level, a comparison between free adjunct and complement functions with the English infinitive shows that, as regards control, free adjuncts are much less semantically integrated into the matrix than complements are: a survey of the 2676 infinitives in complement function in the ICE-GB turned up only 7 cases of NSC, that is, only 0.003 per cent of infinitival complements vs 24 per cent NSC with infinitival free adjuncts. As argued in Duffley (2006: 51) regarding complement function, in a construction such as *She tried to open the door*, the infinitive is represented as the terminus of a movement implied by the matrix verb's event, which entails that the matrix verb's subject aims to move to the realization of the infinitive's event, a construal that invariably implies SC. Infinitival and participial free adjuncts being less bound to the matrix's semantic content, they both allow NSC more frequently and require substantial pragmatic work to be interpreted. Bach (1982: 54) describes the chain of inferences determining control in *I bought 'Bambi' to give to Mary to pass on to John to take along on the camping trip to read to the children* as follows:

I buy *Bambi*; I have *Bambi*; I'm going to give it to Mary; then Mary will have it; she's supposed to pass it on to John; then he'll have it and will be able to take it along on the camping trip and it will be on hand (for John or anyone else on the trip) to read to the children. I have just worked out the most likely controllers of the purpose clauses in (75) [= the sentence above]. How did I do it? By understanding what it means to give, to pass on, to take along, and so on. How much of this can we or should we put into our theories of linguistic competence, into our theories of syntactic and semantic representations? I don't think we'll have a satisfying answer to this question until we've done a lot more work.

Based on our analysis of the data, our answer to Bach's question concerning how much knowledge needs to be incorporated into the explanation of control would be: all of it! As Landau (2013: 258) says, 'problems in control are challenging in that they bear no obvious mark as to which part of the grammar they belong to; lexicon, syntax, semantics or pragmatics – the proper analysis is always up for grabs'. As we have shown in this study, the controller can correspond to the matrix verb's subject, but also to another NP in the matrix clause, the event expressed by the whole matrix clause, the speaker himself, an implied generic human, the possessor denoted by a possessive determiner, the implicit or explicit agent of a deverbal noun or of a passive or reflexive verbal construction. The possibilities are legion, so much so that there is no way one can infer the intended message correctly without a considerable amount of knowledge, both semantic and pragmatic.

Notes

1. www.sixpacksmadeeasy.com
2. The FTB was provided to us courtesy of the Laboratoire de Linguistique Formelle at the Université de Paris 7.
3. Typical examples that had to be weeded out were:

   (i) he goes **shooting** off in the car up the road
   (ii) you may have local issues which you would like **to raise**.

   In these two sequences neither form is deletable or syntactically mobile.
4. These numbers do not add up to 170 because 29 cases involved both initial position and expletive matrix subjects, all of which showed NSC.
5. Unless otherwise indicated, Pearson's chi-squared test with Yates' continuity correction has been used to measure ratio independence between SC and NSC.
6. There are also differences: the verb *help* occurred nine times with the infinitive, but only once with the gerund-participle; the purely resultative lexeme *leave* was not attested at all with the infinitive, but occurred over 50 times with the -*ing* form. These differences seem to reflect the goal/result-directed orientation implied by infinitival *to*. Space does not permit us to pursue this matter further here, however.
7. In the function tagset, 'MOD' stands for *modifier* and is the tag given to mobile and optional phrases. Modifiers can be adverbial phrases ('AP'), prepositional phrases ('PP'), infinitival or participial phrases ('VPinf' or 'VPpart'), subordinate clauses ('Ssub') or noun/pronoun phrases ('NP').
8. An example of a frequent wrongly tagged phrase is the compound future with *aller*: 'il se demande où il va **loger sa famille de trois enfants**' (FTB, 248937) [he's wondering where he will **house his three-child family**] where the verbal phrase is neither mobile nor optional and thus should not have been considered an adjunct.
9. Since the count number is low and one of the cells in the contingency table has a value smaller than or equal to 5, Fisher's exact test was used to calculate ratio independence.
10. *Idem.*
11. *Idem.*

References

Bach, E. (1982) 'Purpose Clauses and Control' in P. Jacobson and G. K. Pullum (eds) *The Nature of Syntactic Representation* (Dordrecht: D. Reidel), pp. 35–57.

Boeckx, C., N. Hornstein and J. Nunes (2010) *Control as Movement* (Cambridge: Cambridge University Press).

Combettes, B. (1998) *Les constructions détachées en français* (Gap: Ophrys).

Culicover, P. W. and R. Jackendoff (2003) 'The Semantic Basis of Control in English'. *Language*, 79 (3): 517–56.

Culicover, P. W. and R. Jackendoff (2005) *Simpler Syntax* (Oxford: Oxford University Press).

Duffley, P. J. (2006) *The English Gerund-Participle. A Comparison with the Infinitive* (Frankfurt: Peter Lang).

Duffley, P. J. and R. Abida (2009) 'Complementation with Verbs of Choice in English'. *Canadian Journal of Linguistics*, 54: 1–26.

Hayase, N. (2011) 'The Cognitive Motivation for the Use of Dangling Participles in English' in K.-U. Panther and G. Radden (eds) *Motivation in Grammar and the Lexicon* (Amsterdam: John Benjamins), pp. 89–106.

Hornstein, N. (1999) 'Movement and Control'. *Linguistic Inquiry*, 30(1): 69–99.

Kawasaki, N. (1993) 'Control and Arbitrary Interpretation in English' (PhD diss., University of Massachusetts at Amherst).

Kortmann, B. (1991) *Free Adjuncts and Absolutes in English. Problems of Control and Interpretation* (London: Routledge).

Landau, I. (2013) *Control in Generative Grammar. A Research Companion* (Cambridge: Cambridge University Press).

Levinson, S. C. (1987) 'Pragmatics and the Grammar of Anaphora: a Partial Pragmatic Reduction of Binding and Control Phenomena'. *Journal of Linguistics*, 23: 379–434.

Lyngfelt, B. (2002) *Kontroll i svenskan. Den optimala tolkningen av infinitivers tankesubjekt* (Gothenburg: Acta Universitatis Gothoburgensia).

Lyngfelt, B. (2009) 'Control Phenomena' in F. Brisard, J.-O. Östman and J. Verschueren (eds) *Grammar, Meaning and Pragmatics* (Amsterdam: John Benjamins), pp. 33–49.

Río-Rey, C. (2002) 'SC and Coreference in Early Modern English Free Adjuncts and Absolutes'. *English Language and Linguistics*, 6: 309–23.

Williams, E. (1985) 'PRO and Subject of NP'. *Natural Language and Linguistic Theory*, 3: 297–315.

Williams, E. (1992) 'Adjunct Control' in R. Larson, S. Iatridou, U. Lahiri and J. Higginbotham (eds) *Control and Grammar* (Dordrecht: Kluwer), pp. 297–322.

Index

GPSR Compliance
The European Union's (EU) General Product Safety Regulation (GPSR) is a set
of rules that requires consumer products to be safe and our obligations to
ensure this.

If you have any concerns about our products, you can contact us on

ProductSafety@springernature.com

In case Publisher is established outside the EU, the EU authorized
representative is:

Springer Nature Customer Service Center GmbH
Europaplatz 3
69115 Heidelberg, Germany